The Compulsive
Spike Milligan

The Compulsive
Spike Milligan

edited by

NORMA FARNES

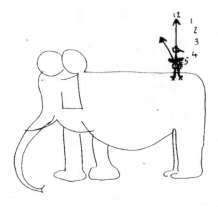

FOURTH ESTATE • *London*

First published in Great Britain in 2004 by
Fourth Estate
An Imprint of HarperCollins*Publishers*
77–85 Fulham Palace Road,
London w6 8jb
www.4thestate.com

Copyright © Spike Milligan Productions Ltd 2004

1

The right of Spike Milligan to be identified as the author of this work has been asserted
by him in accordance with the Copyright, Designs and Patents Act 1988

A catalogue record for this book is available from the British Library

ISBN 0-00-719333-5

Designed in Monotype Columbus and typeset by Geoff Green Book Design
Printed in Great Britain by Clays Ltd, St Ives plc

Contents

Acknowledgements

I would like to thank all those who allowed me to use their letters and extracts, particularly my dear friend Sir George Martin, who couldn't remember his 'kaze' letter.

Mike Hames for all his support.

Janet Spearman for her continued encouragement.

And a special thank you to Jack Clarke for his enduring patience and the help he gave me in compiling this volume.

Foreword

As I started to compile this book it was brought home to me yet again how prolific Spike was as a writer. Over eighty books, nearly all of them written during my time with him. In fact, I believe that he'd only written two before I arrived at Orme Court – *Puckoon* and *Silly Verse For Kids*. The walls of my office are lined with everything he wrote and I can easily pick out my favourites. But in making this compilation I really did make a conscious effort to be dispassionate in my selection. To start with, I sat down with all his poetry books. I have my own personal copies of these and his novels that are kept in my briefcase. Everyone who knows me is aware that they are not to be removed. There is a very good reason for this. When Spike did his own one-man show, which he varied and honed over the years, one section was devoted to readings from his books. This selection was his personal choice, his favourites, in fact. Originally he would only read from the actual books. I suggested we had the poems and extracts typed and put into script form so all he had to do was turn over the page. He wouldn't hear of it. How could he possibly get the same inspiration from a typed script? Later, of course, this became his idea and he had Janet do just that.

He was about to, as he would say, 'bin these', but I grabbed them, knowing that one day they might be needed. Sure enough they were.

He was due to perform his one-man show at the New Theatre at Hull. I arrived at the theatre an hour before 'curtain up' to check that everything was in order, lighting and sound. But, unusually, he was already in his dressing room – having a tantrum. His driver had totally misjudged the time it would take to travel to the theatre. Now he had an hour to kill. But it was worse than that.

'There isn't going to be a bloody show. I've forgotten my script.' Of course, he went on to say that it was all my fault because he couldn't possibly have forgotten all his books but he could forget just one script. But I knew Spike and also knew that a lie meant nothing to him. Abracadabra! I opened my briefcase and produced all his books exactly in the order he needed for the show, each extract with his paper marker. My partner, Jack Clarke, was with me in the dressing room and remembers I said, 'Make yourself scarce. Leave me alone with him.'

Later, he told me he fully expected I would have to go on the stage to announce that there wasn't going to be a show. He hadn't witnessed this sort of blackmail before. Jack had only encountered: 'Nice to see you, Jack. Have a glass of wine. Dinner after the show?'

Of course I managed to calm Spike and he did the show, incidentally with the script version he miraculously found – now, as I sit working from those very books and markings, it all comes back to me. He was such a prolific writer that in *The Essential Milligan* and now *The Compulsive Milligan* we have really only selected a fraction of the gems he penned. But in this book the old sod is once more having the last word, because what you are about to read is almost all Spike's choice.

How many times did I hear 'When I die they'll say, Spike Milligan wrote the Goon Shows and died'? It haunted him. When his novel *Puckoon* had reached sales of a million copies, I told him the good news and had hoped for a semblance of delight. His reply was: 'When I die they'll say, Spike Milligan wrote the Goon Shows and died.' So, to please him, there is not a *Goon Show* script in this volume. Here, in this book, is the proof that he wrote more than the Goon Shows. Just for him, I'll subtitle it The No Goon Show Book.

NORMA FARNES

I

Milligan Emerges

A Show Called Fred: 1956

Spike's first television show. Interestingly, everyone has been given a credit except the writer. Eric Sykes fought for years for credits and payment for writers, which he later achieved. Spike was awarded Best TV Show of the Year.

RUNNING ORDER

1.	Gong film
2.	Stills of cast
3.	Cartoon film
4.	Peter at Desk - B.P.
5.	Val at Desk
6.	Power Station still
7.	Power Station film (T/C)
8.	Val mending boot
9.	Shepherd film (4 shots) with captions over.
10.	Peter - periscope
11.	Max Geldray
11a.	1st 8 - cartoon film
11b.	2nd 8 - Mouth
12.	Finish - torpedoed
13.	Graham - wood worm
14.	Katie - wood worm
15.	Film - barrage
16.	Bed - B.P. of Atom bomb explosion
17.	Val and Katie
18.	Idiot Quartette
19.	Katie -Val dance...'FOOTO'

C O M M E R C I A L

20.	Rifle range
21	Employment Agency
22.	Banquet table
23.	Patti Lewis
24.	End of number - launched
25.	Jekyll and Hyde
26.	Drive me Home
27.	Cartoon marching film.

```
STUDIO   TWO
   WEMBLEY
```

9.30   to   10.0 p.m.

CAST:

Peter Sellers
Spike Milligan
Kenneth Connor
Valentine Dyall
Graham Stark
Patti Lewis
Catherine Boyle
Max Geldray
The Alberts
JohnVyvyan
Reg Owen Ork (10)

```
DIRECTOR......................DICK LESTER
Production Asst..............Marjorie Sullivan
Crew 1.......................Geoff Rimmer
Lighting.....................Ted Shankster
Sound........................John Hamilton
Grams........................David Law
Floor Manager................Len Swainston
Stage Manager................Ron Walsby
Vision Mixer.................Jenny Simpson
Designer.....................Tim O'Brien
```

- 1 -

CAMERA: VISION: SOUND:

                                            RECORDED MUSIC OF PETER AND SPIKE

ROLL FILM   J. ARTHUR RANK GONG

                 SEQUENCE

                 CAPTIONS: PETER SELLERS IN

                 A SHOW CALLED FRED WRITTEN
                                    + JOHN ANTROBUS
                 BY SPIKE MILLIGAN WITH THE

                 THESPIANS ... GRAHAM STARK..

CUT TO CAM: PHOTO OF GRAHAM.

                 KENNETH CONNOR...

CUT TO CAM: PHOTO OF KENNETH

                 VAN DYALL...

CUT TO CAM: PHOTO OF VAL

                 AND STARRING THE BAND OF THE

                 HOUSEHOLD CAVALRY.

                 BIOGRAPHIC CARTOON OF HYDE

                 PARK BAND

CAMERA:	VISION:	SOUND:
CUT TO B.P.	PETER AT DESK. ROAD FLASHING BY HORIZONTALLY	
		PETER: Hello, well now, first good news for house wives. Here's something you'll find an invaluable aid when out shopping.
CLOSE UP	HOLDS UP A PO ND NOTE .	PETER: Yes, its money, the new wonder currency, buy some today. Ask your local bank manager for details.
CUT BACK TO CAMERA	VAL CAUGHT DRINKING A HALF OF BEER. HE QUICKLY HIDES IT. ON EMPTY DESK AND CHAIR. VAL WALKS INTO SHOT. SITS DOWN.	VAL: Thank you Peter. First, here is a special news item by someone we all love and cherish. VAL: Good evening, here is a special news item. This week a new Power Station was opened in Scotland.
	PHOTO OF GIANT POWER STATION	(VOICE ONLY) Here you see it on completion. It was built to provide electricity.
CUT TO CAM:	PICTURE OF ADMIRAL CROSS EYES LITHOGRAPH FACING CAMERA. BIT ADMIRAL'S HAT ON WITH SEAGULL NESTING ON TOP. HORIZON IN BACK.	PETER: Here we have the brilliant Ex Admiral MacIdiot now in charge of the power station.
CUT TO CAM:	PICTURES OF ADMIRAL ON HORSE BACK ON BRIDGE OF BATTLE SHIP BRANISHING SWORD FOR THE CHARGE.	PETER: During the war the Admiral was noted for his revolutionary techniques.
CUT TO CAM:	LITHOGRAPH OF SAILORS IN THE SEA ON HORSE BACK. CHARGING A SUBMARINE LED BY THE ADMIRAL	

AUS TV show to p.6

CAMERA:	VISION:	SOUND:
	ON AN ELEPHANT ALSO IN THE SEA:	PETER: He never failed to surprise the enemy.
FILM: (UNDERCRANKED)	MOTOR CAR ADORNED WITH A LIFE BELT ON THE SIDE DRIVES UP TO SIDE OF TWO OR THREE STORIED BUILDING. A SAILOR IN OILSKINS AND A SAILOR HAT STANDS ON THE BONNET WITH A LINE AND A BOAT HOOK. CAR PULLS ALONG SIDE BUILDING. DOOR OF CAR OPENS. ADMIRAL (PETER) WEARING OILSKINS AND ADMIRAL'S HAT CAREFULLY WALKS ALONG RUNNING BOARD. OVER THE BONNET. A ROPE LADDER IS LOWERED FROM WINDOW. HE STARTS TO CLIMB UP.	PETER: Here you see Admiral MacIdiot arriving at the Power Station the day he took charge... this was also the day he was asked to resign.
		PETER: He was played aboard by the Band of the Hyde Park Marines.
ROLL FILM:	CARTOON FILM OF BAND (BIOGRAPHIC) PHOTO OF POWER STATION.	PETER: This power station then is bringing prosperity to England.
CUT TO	VAL MENDING HIS BOOT ON A BOOT ANVIL.	VAL: Yes, prosperity. Electricity had come to the Isle of Scront. As these films will show.
ROLL FILM:	SHEPHERD ON LONELY HILLSIDE SHAVING WITH ELECTRIC RAZOR. SMILES AT CAMERA. SAME SHEPHERD IN WOOD IRONING TROUSERS ON IRONING BOARD WITH ELECTRIC IRON. HE SMILES AT CAMERA. SAME	

CAMERA:	VISION:	SOUND:
	SHEPHERD LAYING UNDER A TREE	
	FROM A BRANCH HANGS A LIGHT.	
	HE READS A BOOK. PULLS SWITCH	
	TURNS OFF LIGHT. BLACKOUT.	PETER: (VOICE) Here we see the full bene-
CUT TO	SHEPHERD IN MIDDLE OF	fits that electricity brings to the island
	PLOUGHED FIELD WITH ARMCHAIR	and its people.
	WATCHING TELEVISION ON CON-	
	SOLE TYPE TV SET. THE SHEP-	
	HERD IS DRESSED IN ANCIENT	
	BRITON'S SHAGGY BEARSKIN WITH	
	SAXON CROSS OVER LEG BINDINGS.	
	HE CARRIES A SHEPHERD'S CROOK.	
	VAL ENTERS SHOT IN EVENING	
	DRESS CARRYING HAND MIKE AND	
	WEARING A TOPEE.	VAL: (MUTE) Good evening. Mind if I sit
		down?
	ALL IN MUTE. TRANSPARENT	
	CAPTIONS OVER. AS PER DIALOGUE	
	VAL SITS IN ARM CHAIR. HOLDS	
	MIKE TO SPIKE. SPIKE HOLDS	
	SHEPHERD CROOK TO VAL	VAL: Now - are you enjoying the benefits
		of the new electric power station?
		SPIKE: (NODS HEAD)
		VAL: (PUZZLED) By the way - haven't you
		got a house?
		SPIKE: I did have but they took all the
		bricks to build the power station.
		VAL: Ahem. Ah, but it must have been worth
		it. All the people on this island all have
		electricity. Oh, how many people are there
		on this island.

CAMERA:	VISION:	SOUND:
		SPIKE: Only me.
		VAL: Oh.
CUT TO B.P.	PETER....	PETER: Well there you have it. All this..
	HUGE POWER STATION MOVE CAMERA ALONG PHOTO OF POWER STATION TO SHOW FACE OF IDIOT SHEPHERD.	PETER: (VOICE ONLY) For this
	BACK TO PETER:	PETER: Well is it fair?
	GRAHAM CLUBS KEN'S HEAD.	KEN: (LEAPING) Noooo!
	PERISCOPE COMES DOWN IN FRONT OF PETER:	GRAHAM: (CLUBS HIM)
		PETER: (LOOKING THROUGH) Gad it's the Flying Dutchman.
	PERISCOPE INLAY OF MAX	PETER: Max Geldray!
ROLL FILM:	Max Plays finger MARCHING CARTOON (MIDDLE EIGHT)	MAX: 1st PART OF NUMBER
CUT TO CAM:	C.U. OF MOUTH. Nose.	2nd PART OF NUMBER
		LAST PART OF NUMBER
		PETER: Fire one!
	AS MAX FINISHES HIS NUMBER HE IS TORPEDOED - SMOKE FROM GROUND.	

	GRAHAM IN BALLET SKIRT BRACES AND MAGIC WAND. AND BLONDE FAIRY WIG.	GRAH: Naughty little wood worm Eating thru the wood. Surely all that sawdust can't

CAMERA:	VISION:	SOUND:
		Do you any good (FEW STEPS FORWARD) Naughty little woodworn eating all the chairs. Are you responsible for all my family sitting on the stairs?
CUT TO:	CLUB ON GRAHAM'S HEAD KATIE BOYLE, WEARING FALSE BEARD HELD ON BY EAR HOOKS	KATIE: Yes woodworms, have you got them? Aren't they a niusance, well, good news, here's a simple way of exterminating them
CUT TO FILM\$	EL ALEMAIN GUN BARRAGE BATTLESHIPS FIRING IN STORMY SEA. TANKS FIRING ON THE MOVE.	
CUT TO KATIE		KATIE: And it's only one and six a packet Get a packet today.
CUT TO KEN	IN NIGHT CAP. (AS WILLUM) AND GRAHAM HAIR IN CURLERS (WOMAN'S WIG) IN IRON BED, PETER HAS CAP ON.	GRAH: Have you got a packet Bert? KEN: No Glad, I gave it to young Fred to sprinkle in the garden
	KEN RAISES BLIND REVEALING OPEN WINDOW.	
B.P. BEHIND WINDOW SHOWS ATOM BOMB EXPLOSION	ON HORIZON.	KEN: Fred? Stop that, it's Sunday.
	CUT BACK TO KATIE	KATIE: Don't forget, it's a packet of MUC 1/6d.
	VAL SPRINGS ONTO HER. STRUGGLE	VAL: You're new here aren't you? KATIE: Unhand me - I have a duck pond to catch. VAL: Don't be silly - you're just ripe for the picking.
	VAL REMOVES HER BEARD.	VAL: Mother.

- 7 -

CAMERA	VISION	SOUND

KATIE: Jin!

SUPERIMPOSE
  CAMERA: Captions - "The End etc.,"   (OFF) Idiot Quartette start playing.

VAL AND KATIE DANCE ACROSS

TO THE IDIOT QUARTETTE

_____

CUT TO
CAMERA: Idiot Quartette in front of

B.P. of road flashing past

horizontally. Peter standing

in dustbin at piano, Spike in

dustbin too. The Alberts in a

gilded frame in background wearing

Westminster City dustmen's hats (fibre mute in their instruments)

PETER SPEAKS INTO ANCIENT HORN TYPE

  MICROPHONE.

Both dustbins have buttons on to

which are affixed braces over the

occupants shoulders.   PETER: Hello ...hello - modern rhythm

type record, modern rhythm type record -

English Fred.

SPIKE: (SINGS) When you're blue and low down

Don't get into a trance

Just jump into a dustbin and dance.....

PETER AND SPIKE JUMP ROUND

IN DUSTBINS   SPIKE: (SINGS) When your pals forsake you

And you can't find romance

Just get into that dustbin...and dance

PETER AND SPIKE JUMP ROUND.

- 7 -

- 8 -

CAMERA	VISION	SOUND

CUT TO: C.U. of PETER

PETER: (SINGS) Throw out all the rubbish
Show them you don't care
When they come to empty it (BREAK) it won't
be there.

CUT TO: IDIOT QUARTETTE

SPIKE: (SINGS) When you got no trousers
And lost your underpants
Just jump into a dustbin and dance.

PETER AND SPIKE START MAD
DUSTBIN DANCE

CUT TO
CAMERA: VAL STILL DANCING WITH

KATIE(SHE WEARS BALD WIG,
VAL WEARS WIG AND BEARD)

VAL: I could dance with you forever.

FX: Explosion

Pan down to Katie's and
Val's 'FOOTO' boots.

Graham is pushed sideways
into picture.

GRAHAM: Yes...dance _forever_ with 'FOOTO'.

C O M M E R C I A L

CAMERA	VISION	SOUND

PART TWO

C.U. of KEN - side view,
crouched over rifle. He is
adjusting the sights and wind
gauge at the side. Behind him
is his observer(Doug Gray) with
telescope. They are both lying and
squatting respectively, wearing Bisley
type head gear.

KEN takes careful aim and shoots.   FX: Rifle shot

DOUGLAS: Good shot, sir - a bull!

Pan along gun barrel to show
target tied to end of rifle
barrel.
Hand comes into picture turns
target round holds it into camera,
shows on reverse/ 'Employment Agency"

Scene.   EMPL

**X TO
CAMERA:**

Graham at desk, Patti sitting
opposite.

GRAHAM: Well, I'm sorry we haven't any

gamekeepers on our books just yet, Lady

Chatterly, but I'll let you know when we do.

PATTI: I've got to get another one.....

GRAHAM: Next please

PETER ENTERS AS A COPPER.
HE SITS IN CHAIR BACK TO
GRAHAM-   GRAHAM: Now sir....sit down.

PETER: This chair is facing the wrong way

mate.

GRAHAM: Miss Krint - bring in a chair fac-

ing me.

MAN BRINGS IN CHAIR   GRAHAM: Now, sir, name?

PETER: Constable Prunk.

GRAHAM: Oh, you're a policeman then....

now, what can we do for you?

CAMERA	VISION	SOUND

PETER: Well, I'm worried, you see I aint made an arrest for over 3 years now – and the Inspector's been on ter me. So I wondered if you had any unemployed criminals on your books.

GRAHAM: What kind of criminal had you in mind?

PETER: Well, one with good references – and a bit of clarst.....

GRAHAM BUZZES INTERCOM.

a bit of clarst –

GRAHAM: Miss Plinn? Send in the 'Duke'.

ENTER VAL IN TOP HAT AND EVENING DRESS, WHITE SCARF AND GLOVES.

GRAHAM: Constable – meet 'THE DUKE'.

PETER: How do you do, sir? – *can I touch 'im –*

not till he's paid for

GRAHAM: Just step up, 'Duke'

ORK: X   Plays "A Pretty Girl is Like a Melody"

Katie –

~~GRAHAM~~: 'Duke is wearing the ideal criminal outfit, difnified....unnoticed in the small hours and concealing all the tools of his trade.

PETER: Oh, I'll have him – just what I wanted – oh yus – 'e'll look lovely in the dock. I can see the sweat breaking aht on that noble *nut* ~~brow~~ when the Judge puts the black cap on.

VAL LEAPS UP

VAL: Black cap? Black cap? Look here, I'm not a murderer – I'm a forger!

CAMERA	VISION	- 11 -	SOUND

PETER: Ohh....well I wants a murderer -
forgers are easy ter get - No - I'm afraid -

VAL: Wait - I'm ..I'm not just a forger A
I once ran naked round a vicarage.

PETER: *oh mate* No...no...I'm ─

VAL: Look I need a break - I haven't been
nicked for a year and I can't afford to
live out much longer.

PETER: No, you ll 'ave to do a murder if
you wants to go in again

GRAHAM: Come one 'Duke' - hurry up - the
Waiting Room's full

VAL (with look of inspiration)
EXITS.

VAL: So there is *pardon me* - .

FX: Pistol shot followed by scream.

VAL RETURNS WITH PISTOL
SMOKING.

VAL: Well ?

PETER: Well done mate...oh my here -

GRAHAM: Will you both sign here (THEY
SIGN REGISTER) Now, have you the er...

PETER: Oh yers! (PRODUCES HAND CUFFS)

GRAHAM PUTS HAND CUFFS
ON VAL AND PETER.

GRAHAM: I pronounce you Constable and
Criminal.

VAL AND PETER EXIT.

FX: Wedding march on grand organ.
and
bells pealing.

ROLL
FILM: Car driving away with boots
tied to rear and card "Just Arrested"
- 11 -

CAMERA	VISION	SOUND

CUT TO: Neutral background.

Part of banquet table in front.

KEN IS SEATED BEHIND TABLE WEARING

DILAPIDATED SPECTACLES WITH THICK

LENSES. THE ALBERTS ON EITHER SIDE.

THEY ARE ALL TALKING AND LAUGHING. *Ken Good luck to the happy pair!*

FX: Sounds of banquet.

ALBERT ONE STANDS UP   ALBERT: (TO CAMERA)

My Lords, ladies and Gentleman

Will you take wine with the optician Royal

KEN HALF BLIND - GROPES FOR

HIS GLASS -   KEN: Here's to the nations eye-sight.

THEY ALL PUT THE SHERRY GLASSES

 TO THEIR EYES AND BATHE THEM -

BLINK THEIR EYES

MIX TO   *out of focus*
CAMERA: PATTI LEWIS   PATTI:
            AGAINST B.P. SCREEN,   "I LOVE YOU"
            ON A SMALL RAMP.

AT THE END OF THE NUMBER
CHAMPAGNE BOTTLE SWINGS INTO   VAL: (VOICE ONLY) I name you the PATTI
SHOTS AND HITS HER IN FACE   LEWIS!

-        KEN: (VOICE ONLY) And so do I!
SECOND BOTTLE LANDS IN.

BACK PROJECTION: runs to show SHIPYARD
            LAUNCHING SITE.   FX: Crowds cheering.

CAMERA	VISION	SOUND

PATTI SLIDES SLOWLY DOWN THE RAMP.

VAL LEAPS INTO SHOT.

VAL: You fools, that ship was my wife (DIVES AFTER HER)

MIX TO
CAMERA   C.U. of book "Dr. Jekyll and Mr. Hyde by Robert L. Stephenson.

CUT TO: Apothecary's laboratory table with shelf across it holding
lots of chemistry paraphanelia.
A light from underneath lights Peter's face as he leans over
the table., (To give effect of bunson burner spirit lamp
reflection, flickering) Peter is mixing a compound(liquid) in
medicine cup. Around him various glass cauldron's bubble.

SUPERIMPOSE
    CAMERA: Caption - "The Laboratory of
Dr. Jekyl - London 1887"

PETER: (pre-recorded) (VERY QUIET AND CLOSE
                          TO MIKE)

I was on the verge of a great discovery....
I had long been interested in the divis-
ion of good and evil in man...if only it
were possible to obliviate the evil in him
we would have the perfect spec-homo-
Sapiens - a man who was morally 100 per
cent good. After three years work, I
believed this potion would do just this -
remove the evil and leave only the good.

FX: Door opens

PETER HIDES GLASS OF LIQUID.

- 14 -

CAMERA	VISION	SOUND

SPIKE: Dinner is served, sir.

PETER: Harcourt, I don't want to be disturbed, I'll - I'll be spending the night in the laboratory.

SPIKE: I see, sir, I'll put your tea in the oven.

PETER: And Harcourt....

SPIKE: Yes, sir

PETER: This letter - is to be opened in the event of my death (HANDS SEALED ENVELOPE TO SPIKE)

SPIKE: (LOOKING AT LETTER) I don't understand, sir.

PETER: Do as I say

SPIKE: Good night, sir.

FX: Door closing

PETER PUTS GLASS ON TABLE.

CUT TO
CAMERA:

C.U. of PETER as he goes
to drink.   PETER: Now........

HE PAUSES AS THO REFLECTING
WHAT MIGHT HAPPEN AS THE RESULT
OF THE EXPERIMENT - THEN
SUDDENLY SWALLOWS, SLIGHT PAUSE.
HE PUTS HIS HAND UP TO HIS THROAT.

CUT TO
CAMERA:

Extreme C.U. of his face.

FX: Timpani - slow four monotonous beat
     on alternating timpani.

Camera de-focuses and focuses
as required.   PETER: (GROANS AND GASPS)

FX: Sounds of him banging into furniture.

INLAY
CAMERA:

Top right hand corner. One
of cast staggering around back to camera (obscure lighting)

CAMERA	VISION	SOUND

PETER: (pre-recorded) Thru' my entire body ran a pain so vicious I felt as if I were being torn in two. I reeled around the room - I felt my collar grow suddenly tight - I was gasping for air - I lost count of time - then suddenly......

ALL MUSIC AND NOISE STOPS.
INSET FIGURE WALKS NORMALLY.
FOCUS BACK ON TO LAB. TABLE.   ....it all stopped....I felt

PETER WALKS INTO SHOT -   different - very different....I walked
BACK TO CAMERA - HOLDING A
MIRROR. HE TURNS TO FACE   back to the table....found a mirror
CAMERA. HIS FACE HAS
CHANGED. HE HAS INSERTED
FALSE TEETH TO MAKE HIS LIPS
AND MOUTH PROTRUDE IN CHIMPEAN
FASHION. HE HAS ON A BLACK WIG,
WHICH GIVES HIM THE APPEARANCE OF
HAVING A GORILLA'S HEAD. HE HOLDS
UP HIS HANDS - THEY ARE COVERED
IN HAIR

PETER: (Evil - different voice) Ha ha ha ha....it's gone wrong...I've got rid of my good self......me?....I'm all evil... ha ha ha...(WITH DETERMINATION) Now what do evil men do - of course - Hyde Park, I'll take my mac, the grass may be damp..... ha ha ha ha.

he exits.

GRM: Three shock chords.

CUT TO
CAMERA: Caption - "Hyde Park" -
       "Notice to Public
    It is dangerous to approach
    Guardsmen during the mating season"

    PETER WITH TOP HAT AND CAPE - ENTERS -
    HE IS LOOKING AT THE NOTICE.

PETER: Curse - a band. (HE EXITS)

ROLL
FILM: Cartoon film of marching band.

CAMERA	VISION	SOUND

CUT TO: GRAHAM AS TRAMP LYING ON PARK BENCH, COVERED WITH NEWSPAPERS.
BACKGROUND OF BUSHES. AT NIGHT. GAS LAMPS BEING LIT.
ENTER PETER. HE GOES TO STRANGLE TRAMP, BUT TURNS HIS BACK
AS POLICEMAN APPEARS. (VAL)

POLICEMAN GOES UP TO TRAMP.

> VAL: Here you
>
> GRAHAM: Oh yus officer?
>
> VAL: If I were you I'd get out of this
> park, there's been a woman attacked.
>
> GRAHAM: I ain't done it mate.
>
> VAL: Come on now...move along.
>
> GRAHAM: Right mate.

THE WHOLE BENCH MOVES OUT OF SHOT.
COP EXITS. TART APPEARS. OUT DROPS
PETER. LIZ.   DUMMY

> EXTRA: Oh, you cheeky thing.

mix to
CAMERA: Photo of smiling Peter.

> PETER: (pre-recorded) So it went on — by
> day I was the respected Dr. Jekyll — but
> night — after drinking the potion — I became
> the terrible Doctor Hyde and attacked
> women......I had hundreds of proposals.
> Then came the reckoning. One night I had
> just done one of my most fiendish murders...

CUT TO
CAMERA: PETER ENTERS SHOT IN HORROR
MAKE-UP, TOP HAT and CAPE. EXHAUSTED.

> FX: Police whistles — distant.

BEHIND PETER A DOOR IS CARRIED INTO
PICTURE BY KEN (DRESSED IN A DEERSTALKER
WITH MEERSCHAUM PIPE AND LIFE JACKET).

VAL(AS POLICEMAN) stands at DOOR —
HE KNOCKS.

CAMERA	VISION	SOUND

PETER: They mustn't find me like this...
coming.....I'm coming...

STARTS TO DRINK THE DRAUGHT.

CAMERA DE-FOCUSES AND FOCUSES FX: Timpani beat as before.

FX: Knock on door. (BECOMING MORE PERSISTENT)

PETER RETURNS TO NORMAL   PETER: Who's there?

KEN: The Police

PETER: Go away!

KEN WALKS FROM DOOR TO PETER. KEN: Open that door at once.

PETER WALKS BACK TO DOOR - OPENS.

PETER: I say!

KEN WALKS BACK   KEN: Ah Dr. Jekyll.

THREE SHOT.   KEN: I saw a light in your street so we
came in

PETER: Oh yes, come in.

KEN: I'm Sherlock Bling - Detective!

PETER: Never heard of you!

KEN: You remember the murders in the bath?

PETER: Yes

KEN: I did them.

PETER: I see, why was this?

KEN: I have a fear of drowning.(LOUDER)
Now then Dr. Jekyll - tonight in Hyde
Park, Lady Mingely was attacked....

PETER: Well?

CAMERA	VISION	SOUND

KEN: She wants to put the man under contract ....we trailed the man to <u>this</u> street...

PETER: What are you suggesting?

PETER STARTS POURING A POTION.

KEN: Dr. Jekyll - or should I say...Mr. Hyde....I must ask you to accompany me to the Police Station

PETER: Why?

KEN: I'm scared to go alone.

PETER: Before we go - a drink.

KEN: Thankyou....(DRINKS) cheers!

Focus and de-focus as before. FX: Timpani as before.

While CAMERA IS OUT OF FOCUS -
PATTI DRESSED IDENTICALLY AS
KEN WAS - SHE IS CLUTCHING HER
 THROAT'

VAL COMES RUNNING.   PATTI: Constable.

VAL: Yes...Inspec......Ohhhh.....

PATTI: Sergeant, arrest him, he just tried to poison me. Sergeant, you've never stared at me like this before.

VAL: Inspector, you've never <u>looked</u> like this before.

PATTI: Let me go! (STRUGGLES OFF)

PETER: James?

ENTER GRAHAM AS CHAUFFEUR. GRAHAM: Sir?

PETER: Drive me home.

GRAHAM STICKS SUCTION
STEERING WHEEL ON HIS
HEAD AND DRIVES HIM OFF

ROLL
FILM: Cartoon marching film.

Silly Verse for Kids: 1959

Silly Verse for Kids was Spike's first children's poetry book.

Hipporhinostricow

Such a beast is the hipporhinostricow
How it got so mixed up we'll never know how;
It sleeps all day, and whistles all night,
And it wears yellow socks which are far too tight.

If you laugh at the Hipporhinostricow,
You're bound to get into an awful row;
The creature is protected you see
From silly people like you and me.

Today I saw a little worm

Today I saw a little worm
Wriggling on his belly.
Perhaps he'd like to come inside
And see what's on the Telly.

Teeth

English Teeth, English Teeth!
Shining in the sun
A part of British heritage
Aye, each and every one.

English Teeth, Happy Teeth!
Always having fun
Clamping down on bits of fish
And sausages half done.

English Teeth! HEROES' Teeth!
Hear them click! and clack!
Let's sing a song of praise to them –
Three Cheers for the Brown Grey and Black.

The Milligan Book of Records: 1975

They say he was a contortionist and he died in the middle of a trick.

Of course this doesn't necessarily mean you'll paint like Toulouse-Lautrec.

"It looks like a booby trap sir"

A Spike Milligan
World War II Joke

Puckoon: 1963

Chapter Three

Spike's first novel. It took him four years. Three times he gave up on it. Thankfully he persevered.

The pub door flew in and a fast stream of silent drinkers moved into position. The air was immediately machine-gunned with a rapid series of orders – 'Guinness – Whiskey – Stout – Gin – Beer – Rum – Port – Beer – Stout – Stout –'. There followed a silence as the day's troubles were washed away with great liver-crippling draughts of alcohol. Stock still they stood, waiting the warming glow that makes us acceptable to all men and vice versa. The first one to feel a powerful benefit was blind George Devine, a thin white El Greco figure with two sightless sockets.

'Good evenin' all,' he said, 'it's been a lovely day, has it not?' He spoke with the authority of a man who had seen it all. Blind since his sixth year, he could just remember the shapes and colours of the countryside. Those fragile memories were all he had to relieve his Guinness-black darkness. Still vivid was that last seeing moment. His sister on the swing, him pushing her away, mother calling 'Tea-time, children'. He had turned to say 'Coming Mum', meeting the full force of the oncoming swing at eye line.

O'Brien was rattling the bar with his empty glass.

'A drop of the real hard stuff now lad,' he instructed the spotty thin potboy. O'Brien was the head man round these parts. He ran the village grocery and took bets. He also had money in the bank, a cousin in America and a girl in the family way. Forty years old, though a little puffy in the face, he was still a handsome man. Like all men in Puckoon, he was married but single after six at night. When the war started he had, in a fit of drunken patriotism, joined the Connaught Rangers, gone to France, caught the crabs and won the V.C. Arriving home on leave, he was greeted like a hero, given a presentation casket of blue unction and then thrown into jail for having obscene French postcards in his haversack. Constable Millikudie had confiscated the offending pictures, and slaved all night duplicating another hundred. Disguised as a tout, he later sold them to visiting Americans. 'Genuine Dublin night life,' he told the startled tourists. As a result two American warships were crewless for a month while the sailors searched Dublin for the like.

O'Brien was joined by his friend, Dr Sean Goldstein. So Semitic did he look, that even at all-Hebrew parties people would say, 'Who's that Jewish-looking feller?' He had just come from the ailing Dan Doonan, where the patient had been complaining of a slight improvement.

'He's dying, for sure,' said Goldstein, parting a Guinness with his nose, 'It's a coronary condition. I give him the best drugs but, tsu, it's just a matter of time, which I suppose is the sentence we're all under.'

O'Brien lit a cigarette. 'I sometimes think,' he said, mixing his words with smoke, 'it would be kinder to do away with incurables.'

'Oh, nobody's incurable,' Goldstein was quick to reply. 'It's just that we don't know the cure, and remember, what's good for the dying is sometimes bad for the living.'

'Eh?'

'Well, if he dies I'm worse off. Work it out for yerself.'

'Oh, you're a hard man tell me, what's your feeling about abortions den?'

'You're a Catholic. You know the answer to that.'

'True, but what's your opinion as a medical man?'

'Murder.'

'How about that London surgeon? The girl had been raped and he took it away. Was he right or wrong?'

'I'll ask you the question which goes before that. Was the child right or wrong?'

O'Brien noticed a heated tone creeping into Goldstein's voice.

'Well Doc, at the time it wasn't *really* a child.'

'If it wasn't *really* a child O'Brien, what was all the fuss about?'

'Well,' began O'Brien, but was shut up by Goldstein –

'It's a bloody cosy little argument that, for the likes of get-rich-quick abortionists. It's not a child, it's just formed, it's just – it's just – just *anything* they want to call it to ease their bloody consciences! A mother sees her child born deformed due to some drug she took during pregnancy and has the child put to sleep! What *right* have we? When a man is mutilated in the war we don't kill him! *We* are the cowards. We can't stand seeing a deformed child. That child could grow up and enjoy life. Happiness is a state of mind, not body.

O'Brien paused, then drank his drink, thoughtfully.

'Oh yes, oh yes, I was in der fightin' all of der way.' Little Mister Pearce in the corner was holding forth. From a parchment dry face, locked under a flat cap, twinkling blue eyes peered through heavy pebble glass lenses, giving him the appearance of a goiterous elf. Both his weathered hands rested on a walking stick. 'In all the fightin' and the English never caught me.' He was speaking rapidly to a Mr Foggerty.

Foggerty wore a long, foul, ragged black overcoat, which seemed to have grown on him. It was secured round the middle with repeatedly knotted string, from which hung various accoutrements, mug, hairbrush, spoon, fly-swat, tin opener. An outsize greasy brown trilby, set low on his forehead, gave him the appearance of having no top to his head, which in fact he hadn't. Son of a long line of camp followers, he had been relieved of his post as lighthouse keeper at the shale rock when he drew the blinds, to 'stop the light shining into the poor sailors' eyes'. The light was closed down, and these days ships have to find their own way on to the rocks. His father had been drowned after a brawl on the edge of a whisky vat, not that he couldn't swim; he tried to drink his way out. Alcoholic poisoning was the Coroner's verdict.

'I tell you, he was so beautifully preserved, it seemed a shame ter bury him,' said the amazed mortician.

'Yes,' went on Mr Pearce, 'I was wounded twice, once by me own side.' He said it with the same surprise as when it happened, and moved his biddy pipe to the other corner. 'You see, the Tans and the police was lookin' fer rebels; we was hid up in Clontarragh Street. One night we could hear them searchin' the places, all drunk. Finally they breaks into our place, they smashes up the furniture and lets fly a few rounds into the ceiling, me in the loft I gets it in the leg. In a few days it goes gangrene, so they smuggles in Goldstein and he offs with it. It was bloody murder, you should have seen the bill he sent me. Still, I survived.' He tapped his wooden leg with his pipe. 'It's hollow. ... You know why?'

'No,' said Foggerty, nodding his head.

'It's hollow because I *made* it so. You see,' he puffed his pipe and looked up at the nicotined ceiling, 'Michael Leary wanted someone ter smuggle hand grenades out through the police cordon, so, I hollows me leg and I travels the bombs in that. And,' he laughed, 'they never caught me.'

Foggerty looked at Mr Pearce. Pearce looked at Mr Foggerty. It appeared to Foggerty that Mr Pearce had finished.

'Oh!' he said.

'Oh?' said Mr Pearce, 'Oh? I tell you a tale of Irish courage and hero-ism and all you can say is, Oh?'

Foggerty seemed to struggle with his mind. Gradually a pathetic smile spread over his face. 'Fish!' he said.

'Fish?' said Pearce, 'Fish? What about fish?'

'Well, it's different from "Oh".'

Mr Pearce just looked at Foggerty. There was something amiss in this lad. Only that day someone had said 'Good morning' to him, and he seemed at a loss for a reply. Then again, Foggerty was the only one who had been a failure during the boom.

'You'da been in real trouble if dem bombs had gone off in yer leg, mate. Yer arse would ha' been half way up yer back.'

The voice came booming from Thomas Rafferty who stood six foot square. The pockets of his dark green jacket were congealed with blood, fur and feathers. When he wasn't poaching he was writing bits of poetry, but he lived by the trap. There was nothing like it. To sit on the banks of the Puckoon, eating a whole fresh salmon when the nobs in London were payin' ten shillings a slice for it. To walk on a silver cold moonlight night, in ankle-deep mist swirling in from the Atlantic; the repetitive crunch of boots on hard frost, hearing a barn owl shriek from the soot-black line of the venal trees, and the best of all the barking of a dog fox across the winter-tight countryside.

'Yarowwwww!' he gave an imitation. 'If that sound doesn't give you a thrill, youse dead,' he grinned, then upended a box of dominoes on the table.

'I'll give you a game,' said Foggerty, eagerly.

'No you bloody well don't!'

'I beat you last time.'

'I know you did and I haven't lived that down! Being beat by you is an admission of insanity, you stupid bloody idiot! No offence meant, mark you.'

Behind the bar, Mr O'Toole was speaking to the pig-of-a-face that was his wife. He had married her twenty years ago, but still woke up white and sweating. On leave from France, he had come out of a drinking-hole in Sackville Street and bumped into a girl. It was dark, he was drunk, she was keen. He awoke next morning to find her in bed with him. He ran screaming from the house, her purse under his arm. He didn't get away with it. Seven weeks later, a giant of a man, seven foot high and smothered in red hair, walked through the door holding her by the hand. The monster lifted O'Toole off the floor and told him to get ready 'for marriage or death'. He had started to object, whereupon the monster had started to hit him with great bone-crunching knuckles. All he remembered was birds twittering and her shouting 'Don't ruin him for the honeymoon, hit him above the waist.' Leaving a trail of broken teeth he was dragged to the altar in the grip of two monsters who looked like kinfolk of Grendel.

Finally, when the priest asked 'Will you take this woman –' a hired ventriloquist from Cork said, 'I do.' And he was done. The marriage hadn't turned out too bad, well, actually it had, but otherwise it wasn't too bad. The red monster, her father, had died mysteriously of heart failure after falling under a train but not before willing them the Holy Drinker.

'Where's the Milligan tonight, Maudie?'

'I don't know. He was here this morning trying to cadge a drink,' she replied, looking over his shoulder at the handsome O'Brien. She had, in moments of dreaming eroticism, imagined herself clutching his members under the sheets. Whenever she saw a sign 'Members Only' she thought of him. The pub door opened, and in bore a podgy police uniform carrying the body of Sgt MacGillikudie. There was a rush for the door. He held up a calming hand but was knocked flat by the exodus.

Arising, he dusted himself.

'I'll be glad when dis town gets prison cells with locks on. Now –' he felt in his breast pocket, '– I'm here to read a brief notice.' He removed his helmet and inadvertently placed it over Blind Devine's beer. 'To all Citizens of the Free State,' he commenced.

His speech was hesitant and clipped; a black Lord Kitchener moustache cut his face in two. 'Next week military and civil members of the Ulster Boundary Commission will be passing through this area. Any hostility towards them will be penalized with fines from a shilling up to death. Ah, tank you –' he accepted a free beer from O'Toole. 'Cheers!' he said and drained it to eternity. Blind Devine was groping.

'Some thievin' swine's stolen me beer!' he shouted angrily as only the blind have courage to.

'You might ha' drunk it.'

'I never forget any beer I drink!' shouted Devine. He flourished his stick, striking Foggerty a sickening blow on the shin.

'Owwww!' screamed Foggerty, clutching his elbow.

'Here, man,' said O'Toole, giving Devine a beer, 'drink this on the house and calm down.'

'Well, I'll be on me way now,' said MacGillikudie, picking up his helmet.

'What's this, then?' said O'Toole, pointing to the glass of beer revealed.

'Oh, dat's mine,' said Foggerty, who was not such a fool after all.

'Come on, Stan lad,' said O'Brien, 'give us one of yer love songs, one of dem with all the strains.'

The spotty lad gave Mrs O'Toole an appealing look.

'All right then, we're not too busy.'

Despite the absence of a piano player, the lad came and stood dutifully by the mute instrument.

'Ladies and Gentlemen –' he began.

'Order, please.'

'Silence for the singer.'

'Is it free?'

The lad went on: 'I should like to sing the late J. Collard Jackson's lovely song "*Eileen, My Eileen.*" '

He raised the lid of the beer-saturated piano, struck a note and started singing a different one. The lad opened a raw red mouth, revealing great harp strings of saliva. At first no sound came, then, welling from the back of his body there came a quivering, tense, tinny sound, like a tram issuing from a tunnel. With the arrival of the first uncertain note, the lad's eyes glazed over, as though a stricture of the bowels was imminent; the singer's body went rigid, a series of stomach convulsions ensued, then the whole body quivered. It even frightened Dr Goldstein.

'Eileeeeeeeeeeeeeen!
Yooooou arrree my Queeeeennnn …'

The agonized notes seemed to swell up from the thorax and pass hurriedly inwards towards the back of the head, where they were apparently trapped and reduced by a three-inch cavity skull; rebounding, they escaped by struggling down one side of his clogged nose at strength three.

'My Queeeeeeeeeeeeenn
    The finest I've ever seeeeeeeeeeeeeen ...'

Puzzled spectators observed that his lower jaw, unlike yours or mine, remained static; it was the *top* of his head that moved. On high notes it was so acutely angled, most of the time was spent looking up the singer's nose, a terrible sight to behold. He indulged in an orgy of meaningless gestures, even the word 'it' was sung, trembling with catarrhal ecstasy; time and again he raised his skinny arms to heaven, revealing a ragged armpit from which protruded tufts of brown hair. Veins stood out on his forehead, and sweat ran down his face as, purple with strain, he braced himself for the last great note; bending his knees, clenching his fists, he closed his eyes and threw back his head. In that tacit moment the observant Foggerty spoke:

'Hey, Mister, you got a bogey up yer nose.'

The last great note burst and was lost in a sea of irreverent laughter. Red-faced, tears drowning his eyes, he returned to the bar. The world of music was safer by far and J. Collard Jackson stopped turning in his grave.

The air outside was still and humid. Without warning, the sky lit up in a moment of fluorescent anger: a fistful of thunder racketed over Puckoon. 'God save us all from the Protestant thunder,' gasped two wax-white old biddies, clutching their bedclothes and making arthritic signs of the cross. 'Quick, Millie, the Po,' gasped the elder sister.

'Coming, coming, Sarah!'

'Too late, Millie, too late.' The reply came in a long, damp moan.

Cool spindles of long-fingered rain came racing to the eager ground. Earth gurgled under the delicious assault, the attarahent smell of earth and water wedded came wafting from the ground. Heavier and heavier it fell. Even at this late hour, ducks on the village pond could be heard acclaiming the deluge. The whole sky was a cullender of water. Again and again lightning hurried across the sky, blossoming like electric roses; the temperature fell, the closeness split, a great song of silence followed.

Millie was changing the bed linen, spiders tested their webs and a drunk called Hermonogies K. Thuckrutes lay face down in a gutter, singing softly.

'Good, we could have done with that little lot,' said O'Brien, looking out the pub window.

Outside there was a strange muffled sound. The pub door opened slowly, and there, reeling, smoke-blackened, and smelling strangely of burnt rubber and singed flesh, was the near-carbonized figure of the Milligan. The whole pub turned inwards as he entered. Someone made the sign of the cross.

'Is it the devil?' said Blind Devine, hiding his matches. Milligan took his still smouldering cap and hurled it the length of the room.

'Struck by lightning! That's all I needed was to be struck by bloody lightning!'

'Are you all right?' asked Dr Goldstein, handing him his professional card.

'It was only the rubber tyres on me bike saved me from being electrified. It struck the roots of a tree, bounced on ter me legs then travelled up to me head! Me hat, look at me hat!' he said, picking up the charred relic.

'Here,' said Mrs O'Toole, 'drink this.' She handed him a small measure of cheap whisky. Even in moments of charity there was no need to be uneconomical.

Through all this commotion, through all the thunder, singing and drinking, from the opposite wall two humans stared unwinking at each other, eyes choked with mutual hate, fury and frustration.

She was Mrs Cafferty, he was known to her as Mr Cafferty, and there's no divorce in Ireland. But enough of this. Elsewhere important things were happening.

A Book of Milliganimals: 1968

Toucans

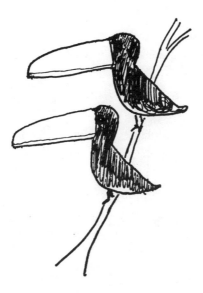

Onecan

Strawberry Moose

Idiot Weekly: 1958

ABC Australia commissioned Spike to write a comedy show. This was it. It was a huge success.

Note. This time he was given a credit for writing it.

Idiot Weekly No. 1

"IDIOT WEEKLY".

NO.1

Recorded: 20/5/ 58

Broadcast: 1/6/58

C.ST:

SPIKE MILLIGAN:	REG GOLDSWORTHY
BOBBY LIMB:	RAY BARRETT
JOHN BLUTHAL	JIMMY PARKINSON

MICHAEL EISDELL

JIM GUSSEY & THE A.B.C. DANCE BAND.

SCRIPT: SPIKE MILLIGAN   SUB-EDITOR: MAX GREEN.

ORK: THEME

STUDIO ANN: The A.B.C. presents Spike Milligan in the IDIOT WEEKLY

ORK: CONCLUDE THEME:

ANNOUNCER: This is the A.B.C.   We present a programme for people
    without trousers.

SPIKE   *Keep up your moral colibers.*

REG: For those who have to leave early, here is the end.

ORCH: ALTO SAX BACKED RHYTHM.   "LAURA".

SPIKE: Cynthia? Cynthia? Where are you darling mm?

CYNTHIA: Oh Rupert, you're back, you've come back.

SPIKE: Yes, I've been a blind fool about you, I've realised that
this thing is bigger than both of us.

CYNTHIA: What thing's bigger than both of us?

SPIKE: It's in this parcel.

FX: FURIOUS FAST UNWRAPPING PARCEL.

CYNTHIA: Oh it's an elephant. Darling, you shouldn't have.

SPIKE: Yes darling, I'm not waiting any longer, we're going to be
married.

RED: And sure enough, that night Spike Milligan married an
elephant. Now read on.

ANNOUNCER: We present "The Idiot Weekly", price tuppence.

LIMB: "The Idiot Weekly", the paper with the moron appeal. Put
it in the fridge and it will keep indefinitely.

SPIKE: ~~The show especially sent by Queen Victoria to her new colony in Australia.~~

ANNOUNCER: Those appearing will be, Hubert Dilly.

LIMB: Hello.

ANNOUNCER: Gormless T. Outcast.

BARRETT: Hello.

LIMB: Parp, Parp, beep, beep. Page five, Sports Flash Motor
             Racing. In the years following the war contentinental
             drivers were supreme. The Italians ran with all the prizes
             sometimes before the race even started.

REG: Last year Australia entered the field and despite shortage
             of money took part in the Le Mans Grand prix .

BARRETT: Yes. Will never forget the end of that race....

GRAMS: GRAND PRIX ATMOSPHERE. CARS APPROACH AND FLASH PAST THE
             MICROPHONE.

REG: And here at the winning flag the first three cars are all
             Italian Spaghettis and they're all driven by Juan Fangio,
             next comes the German Maladies fourth fifth and foofth
             and a long way behind in last place t he Australian entry.

FX: CLOP CLOP OF COCONUT SHELLS TO SIMILATE OLD CART HORSE.

BLUTHAL: (BUSH AUSSIE) Woah Daisy Woah back. Woah back.

ANNOUNCER: Woah back he says, I wonder if you can Woah forward?

REG: Stand aside Pommy, the Idiot Weekly proudly presents a story
             of Australia's glorious past.

SPIKE: This is the story of a most gallant episode which actually
             never happened in the desert of Lybia .

BLUTHAL: The story of the Tumbarumba Scots Brigade.

ORGH: THREE OR FOUR DRAMATIC DRONE CHORDS WITH BAGPIPE THEME ON
             WALTZING MATILDA.

GRAMS: DISTANT ARTILLERY FIRE. FADE UNDER.

SPIKE (SCOT) Arr! It were in the year 1942 , and we of the Tumbarumba
             Scots Brigade were all dug in around the Wadi of El Ywant

FX: PHONE RINGS. OFF HOOK QUICKLY. (REMEMBER IT'S URGENT)

BARRETT: (ROUGH AUSSIE) Hello? Wadi El ya Want?

1 BLUTHAL: (SCOTS) (DISTORT)   Hello this is Sgt. MacKness of B
               Company, we've just been heavily shelled by a German
               armoured car.

2 BARRETT: Did you get his number?

               busts out of season.

3 BLUTHAL: No, but we got him for parking without lights.

FX: KNOCK KNOCK ON DOOR.   (RAPID)

4 BARRETT: Come in.

5 LIMB: (DRY) I am in.   I'm knocking to get out.

6 BARRETT: Very funny, Private Limb.   I've got bad news for you.

7 LIMB: Private Limb?   I'm a Captain.

8 BARRETT: Aye.   That's the bad news.   Now - what's the trouble.

9 LIMB: I have a secret message for the Commanding Officer.

10: BARRETT: Right, I'll give you a letter of introduction (WRITING)
               Dear C.O., see this man immediately.   There!

11 LIMB: Thank you sir.   By the way, who is the C.O.?

   BARRETT: (I am.)

13 LIMB: Good, I have a letter for you.

14 BARRETT: Splendid, then I'll see you immediately.   Now, what's
               the trouble?

FX: DOOR BURSTS OPEN

15 SCOT: Surr, Z-urgent request from the line, the Tumbarumba
               Scottish Brigade want permission to change from their
               kilts into trousers.

16 BARRETT: Why?

17 SCOT: The Germans are playin' a dirty trick.   They're attacking
               with feather dusters.

but this is a ticklish problem

1 BARRETT: Permission granted.
But

ORK: LOW SUSTAINED CHORD:

GRAMS: DISTANT GUNS:

2 ANNOUNCER: At first light the Germans launched an offensive with
                armoured toasting forks, - a three pronged attack.

3 REG: Major!   The Germans are breaking thru everywhere.

4 BARRETT: How are the Tumbarumba Scottish faring?

5 REG: Their line's been cut.

6 BARRETT: (FURIOUS)   Oh dear all their washing in the mud again.

7 REG: They fought gallantly sir, they held firm for over two
                seconds, then they were sent reeling.

8 BARRETT: A Scots reel.

FX: DOOR BURSTS OPEN:

9 SCOT: (SPIKE)   Surrr, terrible news, the Germans have captured
                the Bagpipes of the Tumbarumba Scots, and we're all
                surrounded.

   BARRETT: Don't panic.   Remember how we escaped at Tobruk?

11 OMNES: Arrrrr (Scottish Aye)

12 BARRETT: You think you could do it again?

13 OMNES: Arrrrrr.

14 BARRETT: Right then.   Off you go.

OMNES: Arrrrrr ARRRRRR ARRR (THEY GO INTO AN IMPRESSION OF A MOTOR
          BIKE DRIVING AWAY)

ORCH: A FEW DEPARTING SAD CHORDS.

ANN: (STERN) The loss of the Bagpipes demoralised the Tumbarumba
          Scots.

SCOT: Aye, as a sign of mourning the men wore their kilts at half mast.
          Many suffered from exposure.

ANN: But help was on the way. As the next bit shows.

SPIKE: Knock knock.

BLUTHAL: Come in Knock-knock.

SPIKE: Brigadier Sir, this letter has just arrived from Government House
          Canberra.

BLUTHAL: Canberra? We'd better read it kneeling down. Mmmmmm, strange
          all it says is to Brigadier Bluthal.

SPIKE: Nothing else?

BLUTHAL: No, unless...

SPIKE: Unless what.

BLUTHAL: Unless there's something inside the envelope.

FX: LETTER RIPPED OPEN BUT DON'T HALT THE DIALOGUE FOR IT.

BLUTHAL: I was right - there's a letter inside.

SPIKE: A letter inside? Curse and I can't speak a word of side.

BLUTHAL: Mmm (READING) From Australian War Office. Imperative that you
          recapture Tumbarumba Brigade Bagpipes. Cost unimportant find
          enclosed Postal Order for sixpence. Signed Field Marshall Slimm.
          18 stone 3lbs.

SPIKE: As last - action (FADE SELF) Now this is the plan - the e is
          silent as in...

REG: The Brigade we've brought back to Australia and trained for a
           secret operation....

OMNES: JABBER JABBER:

LIMB: Eyes front, ears at the side and legs down. Commanding Officer.

BARRETT: At ease. Now, you men of the Tumbarumba Scots, I'm about to
           reveal a secret attack plan, first an oath of secrecy, say after
           me. I swear to keep secret.

OMNES: & ORCH: "I swear to keep secret.

BARRETT: All that is said in this room.

OMNES: All that is said in this room.

BARRETT: Right, now you can all sit down and have a smoke.

OMNES: Right, now you can all sit down and have a smoke.

BARRETT: This is the plan, we attack Rommell's HQ under cover of daylight
           and recapture your bagpipes, alive. Now any volunteers?

           PAUSE.

OMNES: EMBARASSED SINGING. La de da da.

BARRETT: Come now men, remember, your doing this for Australia.

REG: Can't we think of a better reason? Like er money?

BARRETT: Money isn't everything.

REG: No but it's the nearest thing to it mate.

BARRETT: Very well, we'll draw lots for it, Limb? Write your name on
           ten pieces of paper and put then in a hat.

LIMB: Right. — there .

BARRETT: Now draw one out.

LIMB: Er, Mrs. Elsie Smith.

BARRETT: You forger!

ECCLES: (OFF AND APPROACHING) Help let me go let me go.

BLUTHAL: (TOUGH SGT) Come on legs eleven.

ECCLES: No, No No I don't want to fight.

BLUTHAL: Keep movin' soldier!

ECCLES: Take your filthy hand off my filthy armmm Owwww no (I'm a coward
          I don't want to fight I got bad legs dats it bad legs. Ow! Ow!

BARRETT: Sgt who is this man.

BLUTHAL   Tell him who you are.

ECCLES: I'm a volunteer.

BARRETT: Brave man, you'll get a decent underground funeral for this.

ECCLES: Supposin' I don't die.

LIMB: (DRY) You'll get   a funeral wether you die for not.

REG: Pardon Captain mate, the meteoroligical officer says that tonights
          weather should be ideal for operations.

BARRETT: Splendid, I'll have my appendix out. The rest of you will board
          the H.M.A.S. Spon and proceed with Operation Bagpipes.   But
          first our 1887 Dixieland Pensioners will play from a tree.

DIXIELAND BAND   "AT THE ZAZZ BAND BALL"

ANNOUNCER: That was a recording of the band, the protagonists not wishing to risk actually being caught playing that stuff. In the distance I see the Tumbarumba Highlanders aboard the *HMHS.* SPON, hugging the coast of Lybia.

I say this is Thrilling

GRAMS: SEA SOUND, THROB OF SHIPS ENGINES. HEAVY WIND THRU RIGGINGS

bang of the Spon

LIMB: January 1st: Heavy seas. First mate washed overboard, second mate washed *overboard,*, third mate washed overboard,....overboard now spotlessly clean.

REG: Look Capn'! A ship on the *forward* port bow.

SPIKE: Gad it's a battleship, and it's wearing a German helmet.

GRAMS: TERRIFIC SALVO OF INCOMING SHELLS AND MG FIRE?

LIMB: Think they've seen us.

SPIKE: They're heaving to.

Well don't stand here

LIMB: ~~Well!~~ Let's heave two back at 'em.

GRAMS: EXPLOSION

ECCLES: Captain , Captain Barett, there's a fire in No. 1 hold.

BARRETT: Oh good! I'll come down right away my cabin's freezing.

SPIKE: Don't understand! We've been hit ! There's a hole in the ship's wall.

BARRETT: Ship's wall? Bulwarks to you.

ECCLES And Bulwarks to you, too.

REG: German ships closing in from all directions.

LIMB: We'll use evasive action.

REG: How?

LIMB: We'll pretend we're out. Put empty milk bottles on the doorstep.

REG: Are all your family clever.

LIMB: Very clever, they're all back home in bed.

GRAMS: SHELL EXPLODES. *Scream*

BLUTHAL: Did that shell hit anybody?

LIMB: Yes, *who* you.

BLUTHAL: Oh! They got me. Gather round and bend over me lads,
preferably facing inwards. Now, according to information I've
received , I'm finished.....Ohhh (DOES HAM ACT) Ohh shot
down in my prime I' Ohhhhhhh *any others hit* .

LIMB: (DRY) ~~Don't overdo it.~~ *Yes 10 but you were hit first.*

BLUTHAL: *At last Top of the hit parade.* ~~Well, it's the first time I've ever been killed and I want to
make the most of it.~~

REG: Admiral! *tender* Are there any last requests before we go to lunch?

BLUTHAL: Ah yes, lad! When I die, don't , don't bu**ry** me at sea.

REG: Why not?

BLUTHAL: I, I can't swim.......Ring Ring Ring Ring. Ah! The phone,

BARRETT: Hello? ~~HMS~~ *HMAS* Spon here?

SPIKE: (DIS) Achtung? Is zat zer Captain ya?

BARRETT: Yes Captain Ya speaking.

SPIKE: Hands up! I am zer Kaptain of the German Battlecruiser.

BARRETT: You swine. How did you get the phone number of my *battle* ship?
A spy gave it me he lives in a cottage pie

~~BARRETT~~ SPIKE: *Ah cottage pie* ~~I won it in a raffle.~~ *After that terrible burn.* Now, I call on you to surrender, or I'll
reverse the charges.

BARRETT: A Captain of the Royal Australia Navy, surrender? Never!
I'll never surrender.

SPIKE: Ach! I can't wait that long, my last tram goes at midnight,
I give you until the end of the war to surrender , then I

- 1) -

```
FX:        CLICK:

BARRETT:   Limb, battle stations, and full speed ahead.    in all directions

LIMB:      (CALLS) All hands on the splonters and splinge.  the wargal.

BLUTHAL:   (OLD SALT OFF) Aye aye surrr.

LIMB:      Stretch yer neck and bend yer ears backwards.

BLUTHAL:   Ahe ayesurrrrrrrr.

LIMB:      Strike yer shins,mangle yer nose and tear yer hair out by the
           roots.

BLUTHAL:   Aye aye surrr.

LIMB:      (AMAZED) I don't know how he does it.  But he's always so
           willing.

BLUTHAL:   Aye aye surrrr.

BAND:      DRAMATIC CHORDS:

LIMB:      At midnight the Tambarumba Scots raiding party slid ashore
Ann        with their teeth blacked out   20 miles behind the German
           lines.

GRAMS:     SOLDIERS.  TRUDGING WEARILY OVER ROCKY DESERT GROUND.

ECCLES:    How much furder to this place.

REG:       Thirteen miles exactly.

ECCLES:    Ohh Ohhhhhhh.  Thirteen is unlucky.

REG:       Oh fourteen miles then

ECCLES:    You see?  Dat thirteen was unlucky .

REG:       How?

ECCLES:    Well!  We're a mile furder away now.
```

Aye Aye Si

LIMB: Sir! We've been marching for ten hours, the men are all in.

BARRETT: Right! *Sgt* We'll have a short rest. Company halt. *SPIKE*

GRAMS: REGIMENT COMING TO A SMART HALT.

SPIKE   (IMMEDIATELY) Quick march.   ) one smooth
) go.
GRAMS: MARCH OFF AGAIN.   )

OMNES: MOANS.

BLUTHAL: Phew, that sun's hot.

SELLERS   Well, you shouldn't touch it.

LIMB: Er , Captain I think the Germans are within ear shot.

BARRETT: Why?

LIMB: They just shot one of my ears.

BARRETT: (DRY) How eerie. (Not long now folks.) Men ! I need a
            volunteer to scout ahead, Goldsworthy?

REG: Not me! You wouldn't risk the life of a man with thirty eight
            kids?

BARRETT: You got thrity eight children?

REG: No, but all I ask is a little time   -

LIMB: He's a coward, sir? I'm not afraid to die for my country.

BARRETT: You mean that?

LIMB: (DRY) No, but I had you fooled there for a moment.

BARRET: Cowards, all of you.

BLUTHAL: I object to that remark.

BARRETT: Do you deny it?

BULTHAL: Mmmmm , No, but I object to it.

LIMB: Me too, I'm no coward, *I want a chance to prove I'm a* what do you think I got these models men
            for.

BARRETT: ~~What?~~

~~LIMB:~~ ~~10/ the lot.~~

GRAMS: DISTANT SOUND OF SOLO BAGPIPES.

SCOT:: Hear that surrrr? The pipes of the Tumbarumba Scots being
~~played by~~ the Germans, in their dug out.

Washington in its cannon Sir

BARRETT: But not for long, we'll hide in this handy family sized Arab
farmhouse which the script writer has provided for us. At
dawn we'll attack. ~~All in new....(FADE TALKING)~~

GRAMS: (FADE UP) DISTANT HOWLING OF DOGS.

~~REG.~~ Will these wild dogs never stop howling?

LIMB: They're always like that in the desert - no trees. *Just cactus*

~~BLUTHAL:~~ ~~What's the time , Limb?~~

LIMB: My ~~watch~~ *calendar* says midday .

BLUTHAL Strange mine ~~says midnight~~ *slow it says February*.

~~LIMB:~~ ~~Ah! Yours must be twelve hours slow.~~

BLUTHAL: ~~Oh, I'll just put it forward. There, that's better, fancy,
I've been walking around in the dark when all the time it
was daytime. Huh. I must have been mad.~~

how men

BARRETT: ~~Yes! Now we're in~~, we must put a sentry on duty outside.
Eccles, ~~out you go.~~ *me outside*

ECCLES: Is'nt dat dangerous?

BARRETT: Only for you. It had to be you, you see you're the only single
man here.   Any requests before you go?

what

ECCLES: Yer ^ marrry me.

BARRETT: ~~I'm sorry I've borrowing an elephant in the~~ Get out, and stay out there until dawn! ~~opening~~ .

ECCLES: O.K. -   until dawn.

FX: DOOR CLOSES:

GRAMS: ALL HELL LET LOOSE MACHINE GUNS FIRING. SHELLS EXPLODE.ETC.

FX: DOOR OPENS AND SLAMS.

ECCLES: Morning everybody. This letter just arrived for us.

BARRETT: Let's see - Mmmm - Quickly turn the lights off!

LIMB: Why? What is it?

BARRETT: Our electricity bill.

LIMB: *Swine* That means somebody's given our position ~~away~~ *current*

BARRETT: *I wonder* Give me my binoculars - *imaginary* just see what ~~Jerries~~ *the Bosch is* up to.

REG: I bet those Germans are as thick as flies.

BLUTHAL: They must be thicker than that or their trousers would fall down.

BARRETT: Ahhhhh, I can see 'em . There's two sentries guarding Rommel' Bind Quarters.

LIMB: *you mean Head Quarters.*

BARRETT: NO. He's got his back to me -

FX:GRAMS: TWO SHOTS COCHETED NEAR BY.

LIMB: They're shooting at us *But there going* Bang, bang, bang

BARRETT: *But theyre allowed to* Bang, bang, bang? ~~Soon, they'll be~~ *Therefire* firing at us in English. This could mean war! Bugler? Sound the alarm.

REG: BUGLE CALL WITH MOUTH.

LIMB   *must get that boy a bugle*

BARRETT: ~~Must get that boy a bugle.~~ Now ~~men, in the back and~~...... Eccles what have you got in the cardboard box? *light the gas tove, well make things hot for the Gereys*

ECCLES: ~~If I meet a German I'll make things hot for him.~~ *BULLETS*

BARRETT: ~~What's in it?~~

LIMB / BARRETT   *we better get out of here — why*

ECCLES: A gas stove. *that last one came from the Audience*

BARRETT: ~~We can't win.~~ Now listen men, this is the plan, ~~it's no good making a frontal assault.~~ *Shhh!*

ECCLES: Yer no good.

BARRETT: If we can get round the back there's a Sand dune that overlooks
             the German position.

ECCLES: Yer, yer.

BARRETT: Shut up. It will mean a detour of twenty miles to get there.

FX: BANGING ON DOOR.

REG: (GERMAN) open zer door, or we break it in . Ve know zere is
             someone in there. Ker blunten gerzitchitz, Berlin alles
             Bompen . Ya ya ya achtung der Dusseldorf Hitler Zeig Heil
             Deuscheland Uber alles.

ECCLES: It's a German.

BLUTHAL: What, quick everyone swallow their uniforms.
             (Chewing)
LIMB: Wait! Ahem! (DOES IMPRESSION OF A CHICKEN.

REG: Ah! It was a chicken,Hans!

BLUTHAL: But there are no chickens in Lybia, Fritz.
             nor ducks.
LIMB: DOES A DUCK.

REG: And I know for a fact there are no ducks, Hans!

LIMB: DOES A DOG:

REG: Dogs don't exist out here.

ECCLES: Let me try. DOES LONG MAD NOISE
             PAUSE

ECCLES: That fooled 'em.

LIMB: Are you sure?

ECCLES: I'll find out (CALLS) Hey dat fooled you didn't it?

GERMANS: ENRAGED SHOUTS:

GUNS: OUTBURST OF MG FIRE.

ORCH: ORCH. DRAMATIC CHORDS. THEN AN INSISTENT TIMP. BEAT

           REPRESENTING ~~FEET SLOGGING THEIR FEET IN BLISTERING HEAT~~

           in the fight that followed the Tchumbergnafer

ANN: ~~In the burning hell of a noon day Lybian sun the heroic~~

           Spike Milligan and Company

           ~~Australians marched to the attack.~~

BARRETT: *But at Sunset we attacked again*

           ~~Yes,~~ grim faced we advanced, purposeful, every soldier with

           but one thought in mind.

LIMB: Desertion.

BARRETT: Shhhh, Good news, men, - by skipping two pages we've taken

           the Germans by surprise, Ya, we were all ready for you on

           page 15, when suddenly we look around and there you were on

                   page 17, Alles Kaput. Oww alles Kaput. Mit alles

                   Gerbunden. Schalzena! *Splosh.*

LIMB: You do, and you'll clean it up.

BARRETT: Come on ! ~~There's the Rumba~~ *You German devils / where are our bagpi—* Bagpipes.

BLUTHAL: In zis cell. *Gagged & bound .*

FX: KEY IN LOCK CELL DOOR OPENS:

BARRETT: Ah! At last - ohhh no!!!! There's been a fire, everything's

           tartan
           burnt, and those ashes....those are the ashes of our beloved

           bagpipes ~~OWWWWWWWWWWW~~ .

           2nd moan
LIMB: Who did ~~this~~ *dreadful deed .*

TEETH: My name is Bertram Teeth, last night I fell asleep and left

           a fag burning by my bed side -

ORCH: MILITARY MARCH (COMRADES OF COLONEL BOGY.)

ANN: That was Idiots Weekly......Bertram Teeth is now appearing

           at Sydney Cemetary.

ORK: REPEAT THEME CHORDS :

ANN: You have been radio-reading THE IDIOT WEEKLY, written
                        by Spike Milligan. Cartoons were provided by Ray,
                        Barrett, John Bluthal, Bobby Limb and Reg Goldsworthy, with
                        headlines by myself, Michael Eisdell. Sub-editor,
                        Max Green. Musical illustration by Jimmy Parkinson and
                        Jim Gussey and the A.B.C. Dance ban d. Don't forget
                        to be waiting next week for the second edition of
                        IDIOT WEEKLY , reduced, by popular demand, from
                        tuppence to a penny ha'penny.

ORK: THEME TO CLOSE _

The Bedside Milligan: 1969

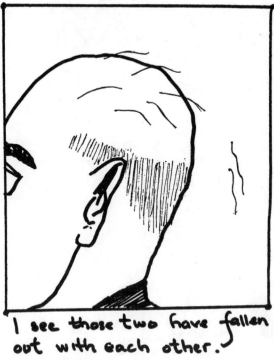

I see those two have fallen out with each other.

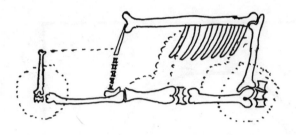

Skeleton of Prehistoric Car

Brontacycle

The Bedside Milligan: 1969

Paris Paree

Written in Paris when I went last time.

Paris! Paree! What pictures of gaiety those two cities conjour up, down, and sideways, Paris, city of Napoleon, the Revolution, the Mob, the blood, the head rolling. Alas, those happy days are gone, yet, Paris, the Queen of cities calls us all. Last week it called me, 'Cooee!' it said and I responded. Travel allowance being only £50, I saved by taking sandwiches and a Thermos of Tomato Sauce. I saved further on the air fare by travelling second class non-return tourist night flight, all you had to do was sign a Secret Enoch Powell form saying you were an undesirable coloured alien with incurable bed-wetting. At the airport, there was the carefully disguised panic rush to get the back seats in the plane. On take-off I fastened my safety belt, read 'How to inflate Life Belt', swallowed a boiled sweet, made the sign of the cross and read the *Times*. One hour later coming in to Orly I fastened my copy of the *Times*, made the sign of the seat belt, swallowed my boiled life belt and inflated myself for landing. Through to Customs and out! At the airport my taxi drew up in a cloud of Garlic, and the driver leapt out and gesticulated in a corner. Arriving at the Hotel, the porter raised his hat and lowered his trousers. Real French hospitality! The Hotel had been built in 1803 – in 1804 they added a west wing and in 1819 it flew away. Next morning I was up at the crack of noon shouting 'Apres moi le deluge' and whistling Toulouse Lautrec, I hurriedly swallowed a breakfast of porridge and frogs and a steaming bidet of coffee. I next joined a crowd of impoverished British tourists on the 30 centimes all-in English punishment Tour. A great herd of us assembled at the Place du Concord, from there we were force-marched to the Notre Dame, beaten with sticks and made to climb the great Bell Tower. Sheer physical agony! On the way up we passed many who had perished in the attempt and never made it. Fancy! 600 steps! No wonder Quasi Modo had a hump on his back when he got to the top! From the top I took several lovely photos of the Eiffel Tower. At Midday, we were led to a Cafe 'Le Gogo Plastique', the establishment bore the indelible stamp of the British tourists –

[Menu]
'Escargots and mash ...'
'Bisque d'Homard, bread and butter'
'Pate de Fois Gras and Chips'
'Lobster Thermidor, 2 Veg., Boiled Pots. etc.'
'Crepe Suzette Flambe and Custard'

The lady next to me had Frogs' legs, her friend's weren't much better. It's all that walking, I suppose. I was served by a waiter who made it perfectly clear he held me personally responsible for a) The loss of Algeria b) Waterloo c) Edith Piaff. Just so they didn't think I was an oaf, I ordered the whole meal in French – I was brought a hip-bath, a silk tie, a coloured pencil and a small clockwork Virgin Mary that whistled Ave Maria every hour, made in Hong Kong. I spent the rest of the afternoon sketching the beautiful Eiffel Tower. There's always something to do in Paris! Carefully following my Baedecker's Paris I walked up the hill to the Cemetery of Pierre Lachaze, I saw the very spot where Moulin Rouge lay buried, and above me gleaming white was the Sacred Cur, now used as a church. I had been walking some three hours and as a quick calculation showed me that I was exactly six miles from the lovely Eiffel Tower, I took a taxi back to the Pension; to my horror he asked for 13 francs, I was about to have a show down with him, but, rather than ruin the evening, I paid him. It ruined the evening. I freshened up in my room, taking a shower and a foot-bath in a very low basin with a rather dangerous water jet that took me completely by surprise. The evening would be dedicated to Art, I always wanted to see the French Impressionists so I booked for the Folie Bergere where a man was doing imitations of Maurice Chevalier, Josephine Baker, and many others. What a show! Women uncovered from the waist up, and yet there was a cover charge! Watching women with naked bosoms is unsettling, but eventually they grow on you. If they grew on me I'd go to the pictures alone. The Grand Finale was called 'Salute les Anglais', the band played a Pop version of God Save the Queen while a French queer wearing a Prince Philip mask juggled with three Plastic Busts of the heir presumptive. It was good to see that we were still a country to be respected. If only we had their Eiffel Tower there'd be no stopping us.

Silly Verse for Kids: 1959

This is the most requested poem for anthologies.

My Sister Laura

My sister Laura's bigger than me
And lifts me up quite easily.
I can't lift her, I've tried and tried;
She must have something heavy inside.

Denis Norden's favourite poem written by Spike.

Rain

There are holes in the sky
Where the rain gets in,
But they're ever so small
That's why rain is thin.

Down the stream the swans all glide

Down the stream the swans all glide;
It's quite the cheapest way to ride.
Their legs get wet,
Their tummies wetter:
I think after all
The bus is better.

Granny

Through every nook and every cranny
The wind blew in on poor old Granny;
Around her knees, into each ear
(And up her nose as well, I fear).

All through the night the wind grew worse,
It nearly made the vicar curse.
The top had fallen off the steeple
Just missing him (and other people).

It blew on man; it blew on beast.
It blew on nun; it blew on priest.
It blew the wig off Auntie Fanny –
But most of all, it blew on Granny!!

I'm not frightened of Pussy Cats

I'm not frightened of Pussy Cats,
They only eat up mice and rats,
But a Hippopotamus
Could eat the Lotofus!

The Bedside Milligan: 1969

An Ear passed me
        the other day
And silently
        went on its way
I wonder who
        that ear can be
And has it ever
        heard of me?

Said the mother Tern
        to her baby Tern
Would you like a brother?

Said baby Tern
        to mother Tern
Yes
One good Tern deserves another.

Sent to Chislehurst & Sidcup College

Brave New World

Twinkle Twinkle, little star
How I wonder what you are
Up above the sky so high
Like a diamond in the sky.

Twinkle Twinkle, little star
I've just found out what you are
A lump of rusting rocket case
A rubbish tip – in outer space.

Values '67

Pass by Citizen:
>   don't look left or right,
Keep those drip dry eyes straight ahead.
A tree? Chop it down.
>   they're a danger to lightning
Pansies, calling for water?
>   Let 'em die – the queer bastards!
Seek comfort in the scarlet plastic
>   labour saving rose
Fresh with the fragrance of Daz.
Sunday. Pray citizen:
>   pray that no rain will fall
>   on your newly polished
>   four wheeled
>   God.

Bad Jelly The Witch: 1973

My favourite children's story. This is the fairy-tale Charles Curran refers to in the letters that follow this extract.

IIII

Back at the childrens home their mummy was crying "Oh my poor children, where are they?" Their daddy said "I've looked every-where I think some animal in the

forest must have eaten them". Poor
mummy. "I'll never be able to play the
trombone to them again", she said.
By now Dinglemouse had reached
the tree where Jim the giant eagle
lived Jim. was fast asleep. when he
heard Dinglemouse calling "Help, Wake
up Jim! Jim was a beautiful eagle.
with brown feathers on his body, white
feathers on his head and a big yellow
beak and blue eyes and he was
nearly as strong as God. "Hurry,
the witch is going to eat the
children when the sun comes up!"
So Jim the Eagle quickly took off his
pyjamas, Dinglemouse jumped on
Jim's back and away they

flew "Faster, Faster Jim, the sun will soon be coming up" shouted Dinglemouse.

V

Back in their prison room the chil-dren were looking out the window. "Can you see the eagle coming Tim" said Rose "No," said Tim. "Look" said Rose "The sun is starting to come up! And listen, I can hear the witch coming up the stairs" "Step - step - step Im coming to get you" screamed the witch. They could see her through the keyhole, and she had a big sharp knife! Rose said "Look out the window

I can see Jim the Eagle coming" The witch was starting to open the door. Now Jim the Eagle flew up to the window "Quick children get on my back". But the witch was opening the door! The children were getting on Jim's back "Stop them"! screamed the witch, but the children were on the mighty eagles back, and awayyy they flew away from the terrible witch. She was so angry she screamed "Stinkypoo to all of you! Then she jumped on her fastest broom stick and started to chase after the children, and she took a magic powder to throw on the

children and turn them into big
black sausages. Jim the Eagle flew
up and hid inside a cloud, the
witch flew round and round the
cloud waiting for Jim and the
children to come out, just then
God came along, and when he saw
what the wicked witch wanted
to do to Jim and Rose he told the
witch to go away. "No I won't" said
the witch, and tried to scratch Gods
eye out, so God pointed his finger at
the witch and Berooom-Bang-Spiddl-
e-deee! The witch burst like a bomb and
disappeared in smoke, and her broom
stick turned into a sky-snake that
flew to the moon. When Jim the Eagle

saw that Badjelly was dead he
flew the children back to the witches
castle to look for Lucy "There
she is" said Rose, and there chained
to the wall was poor Lucy. Quick
-ly Jim flew down next to her, she
was so pleased to see the children
she went Moooo - Moooo, and
cried. Jim the Eagle broke her chain
with his beak, but then the back
door of the castle opened and
out came Dulboot the giant "Get
away from that cow, it belongs to
me, shes my dinner" he said, and he drew
out his sword and he tried to chop
the childrens heads off but Jim
grabbed the giant by the hair

while Dinglemouse jumped on the giant, nibbled his belt and down came the gia-nts trousers! 'Oh help' said the giant I'm showing my bottom!" and he ran away and never came back. "Now we're all safe" said Tim "Yes, thanks to Dinglemouse and Jim" and she gave them both a kiss. Then Jim got the children and Dinglemouse on his back then he flew up, grabbed Lucys horns in his strong claws and flew them back to their home. When their mummy and daddy saw them fly down on the back of a giant eagle. with Lucy hanging underneath, they ran inside the house and hid "Don't be frightened Mummy and Daddy,

Jim is a kind Eagle and saved our lives". Up popped Dinglemouse "So did I help save them too" he said So Mummy and Daddy came out with a big bag of Jellybabies and gave them to Jim + Dinglemouse, then they all played Ring-a-Roses, and then they blindfolded Lucy and played blind mans buff, and lived happily ever after until the next time.

The End

Tim and Rose   (SM)

PS. Badjelly the Witch is now available on a Polydor record!

The Bad Jelly The Witch Saga: 1975

To: Sir Charles Curran,
British Broadcasting Corporation   *21st May, 1975*
Dear Sir Charles,

T he B.B.C. programme Let's Join In, want to do a fairy tale of mine, and in it they want to excise the word God, they say its 'policy principle does not allow the mingling of fact and fiction.' Anyhow, I cannot contribute to such stupidity, and I am writing to let you know the B.B.C. Departmental laws, and I have refused to allow the word God to be cut out. The attached letter is self-explanatory.

I am writing to you because I thought you might change this silly rule.

Hope you are well Charles, and all goes well with you and your wife.

Love, light and peace,
Spike Milligan

Broadcasting House, London W1A 1AA
5th June, 1975

Dear Spike,

T hank you for your letter of 21st May, earlier acknowledged by my secretary. 'Let's Join In' is a Schools programme intended for infants and the producer wanted to avoid conveying the impression to them that God existed on the same level of reality as goblins, witches and giants. Neither you nor I believe that. There is no policy against mingling fact and fiction, only in this instance a wish not to confirm some children's belief that God and His powers belonged to the world of magic. As a believer, I think you will recognise that there is a serious point here, and I do hope you will reconsider your decision not to allow the broadcast to take place.

Yours ever,
Charles
Director-General

Spike Milligan, Esq.

To: Sir Charles Curran

9th June, 1975

T hank you for your letter – you are a good man to take time to write letters, they are so important in giving one an insight of the writer.

Part 2. God versus Goblins.

My dear Charles,

I believe in Goblins *and* God; I think the combination is absolutely marvellous, of course, I like to get it very clear that all my Goblins are Roman Catholics, that's why when you go into confession, if you look on the floor you will find a long thin ladder leading up to the confessional window.

I refuse to give in Charles, but I am sure God will forgive you for not believing in Goblins.

I must go now, there is a fairy tapping on my window pane – wait a minute I think it's a Protestant, so I won't open it.

Love, light and peace,
Spike Milligan

P.S. I will give in, but only because you are all so unenlightened, I will allow the word God to be stricken from the record, but don't forget Charles, on the Great Day, when God says 'who told you to remove my name from that story?', you know who I will be pointing at.

Broadcasting House
London W1A 1AA
10th June, 1975

Dear Spike,

    Thank you for your covering letter of 9th June, which is nice about me. Why am I not nice to Goblins – or, at least, not as nice as you are?

    Well, simply because I am a Director-General, which means that I am only allowed to believe in things that other people tell me. Of course, as me – Charles Curran – I am perfectly free to believe in Goblins, even in the Confessional. And like you, I am quite sure that they are all Roman Catholics and that when we come out of the Confessional they carry away our sins in little bags and put them in the collecting boxes, where, of course, they turn into buttons! (You always knew, didn't you, that it was not little boys who put buttons in the box?)

    And if God asks me on the great day, 'Why did you take my name out of that story?' – I shall say, 'Not me! Blame the BBC – like everybody else does!'

    And thank you for being so generous about allowing God to be invisible in your story. He really is, you know.

Yours ever,
Charles
Spike Milligan, Esq.   *Director-General*

Small Dreams of a Scorpion: 1972

For Korea, read Iraq. Times don't change.

Korea

Why are they lying in some distant land
Why did they go there
Did they *understand?*
Young men they were
Young men they stay
But why did we send them away, away?

A Book of Milliganimals: 1968

Spike was working on this book when I first started at Orme Court.

A baby Sardine
Saw her first submarine:
She was scared and watched through a peephole.

'Oh, come, come, come,'
Said the Sardine's mum,
'It's only a tin full of people.'

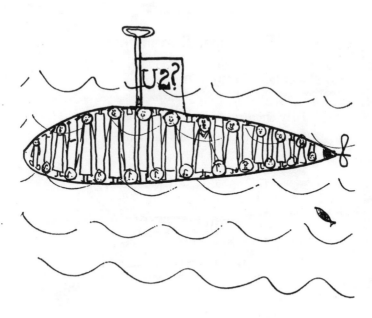

The Lion

A Lion is fierce:
His teeth can pierce
The skin of a postman's knee.

It serves him right
That, because of his bite,
He gets no letters you see.

Tiger, Tiger Burning etc.

Tigers travel stealthily
Using, first, legs one and three.
They alternate with two and four;
And, after that, there are no more.

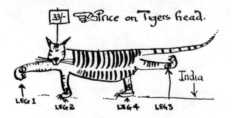

Envoi
Tiger, Tiger burning bright.
Look out! You'll set the jungle alight.

A Dustbin of Milligan: 1963

Porridge

Why is there no monument
　　To Porridge in our land?
If it's good enough to eat
　　It's good enough to stand!

On a plinth in London
　　A statue we should see
Of porridge made in Scotland
　　Signed 'Oatmeal, O.B.E.'

(By a young dog of three)

'Tis due to pigeons
　　that alight
On Nelson's hat
　　that makes it white.

Puckoon: 1963

Chapter Nine

Life is a long agonized illness only curable by death. Ruben Croucher lovingly and delicately dusted the coffins displayed in his parlour. They were such beautiful things. Stately barques that bore us across the Styx into the eternal life beyond. All was peace and calm within. The only sound was the endless buzzing of a lone fly, who shall remain nameless. Ruben Croucher walked with crane-like dignity across the black cracking lino to the window. His long thin nose pointed the way; a million rivers of tiny ruptured veins suffused his cadaverous face, two watery eyes like fresh cracked eggs in lard looked out from a skull-like head. It had got dark early and he had lit the gas, which cast a sepulchral glow along the neatly arranged coffins. With a cloth he wiped the condensation from the sightless windows. Business was bad, it seemed people couldn't afford to die these days. But, what was this?

Two ragged-arsed men were approaching, both smoking the same cigarette. They were pulling a cart and heading rapidly for the shop. Pausing only to open the door, they entered. When Lenny saw the face of Mr Croucher, he reverently took his hat off. Croucher bowed ever so slightly from the waist up.

'Good morning,' he said, then after some thought added, 'Gentlemen.' After all they could be eccentric millionaires.

Shamus coughed. 'We are eccentric millionaires,' he said. 'Do you sell coffins?'

Mr Croucher nodded. 'Yes, we do, sir,' and as a try on, 'how many do you want?'

'Oh, just one to start with.'

'Good, good. Who is the deceased?'

'Oh.' Shamus hadn't thought of this, but he was a man of some guile. 'It's for me friend here,' and he pointed at Lenny. 'You see,' he went on, 'he hasn't been well lately, and we thought just to be on the safe side we'd have one now.' Mr Croucher, though puzzled, pressed on. 'Ahem. Well, I suppose this method will save normal post mortem mensuration.'

'Eh?'

'Measuring him. Now he can – well – try one for size.' Mr Croucher indicated the coffins. Shamus and Lenny ran their hands over several. 'We'll have that one.' Shamus pointed.

'Ah, a black one. A very wise choice, sir, it won't show the dirt.' Mr Croucher withheld a whimper of joy. It was the most expensive coffin in the shop.

Lenny slid over the side and lay back in the pink satin padding.

'It feels real fine!' he said. 'Dis is really worth dying for.' He squirmed to make himself more comfortable.

'Now let's try the lid on,' said Mr Croucher.

Carefully he lowered the lid over Lenny's little white face. Shamus raised his voice.

'How's dat feel, Lenny?'

'Very nice,' came the muffled reply.

'Right,' said Shamus addressing Mr Croucher. 'We'll have this one.'

Ruben rubbed his hands with professional pleasure, the dry skin crackling like parchment. Forty years he had sold coffins, but never as quickly as this. His father, the late Hercules Croucher, O.B.E., had founded a fine parlour at Shoreditch. King Edward the Seventh and his ten mistresses were on the throne when the young Ruben was given a black suit for his tenth birthday, that and a scale model replica of the famous Geinsweil Coffin. It awakened in him some deep-rooted instinct; he buried it. Other boys felt girls and played conkers, but little Ruben watched local workmen digging, digging, digging.

'Now sir,' Ruben said, 'if you will step into the office we'll conclude the financial side.'

'You stay there a while,' said Shamus rapping on Lenny's coffin.

In a small room at the back Mr Croucher slid behind an order book and perched on a fountain pen. His black tail coat hung from his shoulders like tired wings. Neatly he took down details in his book. All was silent save the scritch-scratch of his Waverley nib on ruled foolscap.

A great pot of steaming hot Irish stew was heading for the shop at seven miles an hour. It was carried lovingly in the hands of Mrs Ruben Croucher, ex-shot-put champion of Ireland. She walked with a brisk bouncing athletic step, a step forty years younger than her husband's. It had been a most successful marriage. He couldn't do it, and she didn't want to. They had one child. He didn't take after either of them. He did it all the time and walked with a stick. Into the shop bounded the ex-shot-put champion.

'Cooooooooeeeee! Are you in there, darling?'

The lid of Lenny's coffin rose up. 'Hello, little darlin',' said Lenny cheerfully.

An Irish stew struck him between the eyes. Mrs Croucher ran screaming from the shop.

'There's your receipt, sir,' said Mr Croucher after carefully counting and recounting thirty-eight carefully forged pound notes.

'We'll take the coffin back on our cart,' said Shamus, standing up.

The culinary arts of the world are varied and a blessing to the sensitive innards of the gourmet, but never in his tour of the globe had Mr Croucher seen a man in a coffin, unconscious and covered in Irish stew.

That night Ruben lay abed cooing through his shrunken gums. A thirty-eight-pound coffin sale. 'Bless us and thank thee, oh Lord, for the merciful benefits thou bestowest on us.' He crossed himself on his homemade prayer, turned slowly on to his good side and fell into a deep peaceful thirty-eight-pound dream. At three o'clock in the morning he died in his sleep. The cost of his funeral came to exactly thirty-eight pounds. His puzzled wife was now in the county jail for passing forged currency. Without her restraining hand her onanistic son now walked with two sticks and a stoop.

Autumn, season of mists and mellow fruitfulness.

'That's a lot of rot,' said Milligan, examining his fingers for frost bite. He scraped the jigsaw of leaves into little funeral pyres. He stooped to light one and warm his hands. The shrill elastic whistle of a robin came clear through the misty morning.

'Awww, shut up, yer idiot!' Milligan was in no mood for nature.

His wages were two weeks overdue and his wife was three.

'I say, Paddy.'

Milligan looked up. Webster was outside the Customs tent beckoning him.

'Me name's not Paddy,' he replied defiantly. He hated Englishmen who called Irishmen 'Paddy'.

'Would you like a cup of tea Paddy?'

'Paddy' Milligan dropped his rake and arrived before it hit the ground.

'It's der first time I had tea with der Customs!'

'Like a dash of whisky?'

'I'll accept dat, sur.'

'Say when.'

'I certainly will not!'

'Found this bottle on a mourner at Dan Doonan's funeral.'

'Oh well, some of dem needs it. Especially the bereaved. I knew a feller so bereaved he could hardly stand.'

In the face of such hospitality, Milligan felt a twinge of conscience, just below the knee. For the last three weeks they had let him through the border without even searching him; in return he had spent his time surreptitiously loosening the earth round Dan Doonan's grave in preparation for the event. All that remained now was for Father Rudden to give the word.

Father Rudden was all ready to give the word but for the unexpected arrival of two ragged-arsed men both smoking the same cigarette and pushing a coffin. Strange. He'd not been notified of a funeral.

'Please, Father,' said Shamus, 'we are poor illiterate farmers, we can't read, write, or post letters. We have pushed the coffin of our grandmother a hundred miles for this burial. We would be grateful if you would officiate.'

Father Rudden was about to refuse when Shamus produced a wad of pound notes. 'Father, we would like to donate dis to the church ...'

Before Shamus had finished, the priest, never taking his eyes off the money, sprinted backwards to the vestry and returned fully robed with the book open at the service.

One hour later, the customs were examining the beautifully forged passport of the late Mrs Eileen Ford. There followed a solemn burial of two hundred and eighty pounds of T.N.T. Amen.

It was dark when Constable Ah Pong had followed the poacher Rafferty to the vestry of the church. Peering slant-eyed through the window he saw five men donning ragged clothes and whispering. So! Rafferty was the leader of a poaching gang. Disgrace to Ireland! The men were putting pliers and knives down their socks, two were coiling ropes round their waists; their blackened faces made identification impossible. By removing his helmet, remaining still, silent and sub-servient, Ah Pong could hear the conspirators' conversation.

'It will take five of us to lift it.'

Ah Pong was puzzled – even more difficult, he was puzzled in Chinese.

'What is it poachers caught that took five men to lift?'

He would wait and see. He ran to a tree as the vestry light went out and five shadowy figures came silently from the back door. Goldstein was tying a handkerchief over his face.

'I got to wear it,' he said. 'If anyone sees my nose Rabbi Brody will have me up fer helpin' Catholics.'

Commando-like they tiptoed noisily towards the barbed wire and were swallowed up in the night. His boots round his neck, Ah Pong tiptoed after them.

Chapter Ten

How he'd got on to the wrong side of the border was beyond the com-prehension of the idiot Foggerty. He'd been dancing happily alone at the Halloween Ball in the Corn Exchange. Everyone was dressed as a witch or a banshee. Him never having seen either was put to improvis-ing. Foggerty had whitened his face, stuck three chickens' feathers in his hat and painted the sleeve of his overcoat yellow; as an afterthought he stuck little balls of cotton wool on his trousers and boots. He hadn't won a prize but people *had* pointed him out. He was well pleased. He had gone outside to relieve himself when the country gas supply had failed. In the dark he lost his direction and sprayed all over a man called Flood, who gave chase with a stick. For an hour now he had been stumbling oaf-like across unfamiliar territory.

'Helloooooo!' he wailed. 'Helloooooooo! I'm getting the hang of this,' he chuckled.

There was no moon; even with it, Foggerty would have been none the brighter. So, collecting evening dew in his hat and calling 'Hello!' he wandered into Northern Ireland, a strange and awesome sight. Even a hungry black panther skulked to the safety of the trees. In his flight Foggerty stumbled over two bodies on the ground. 'Opsss, sorry,' he said, disregarding the rock they threw at him. They waited till he had gone, then continued in their practice of the noble art of nudism, or sunbathing as some say. These two were coming to the end of a long hard day.

On this dark night the sun tan oil glistened on their undulating skins. Locked in a passionate embrace they rolled hither and thither, backwards and forwards through the bushes, drenched with rain, their bodies adhered with passion and clay. They had travelled some thirteen miles like this, not ideal travel but economical.

Watching from the safety of a tree was a man called D. H. Lawrence. He made a hurried note. 'This will make a damned good novel,' he said and hurried off to his Queen's Counsel.

The two sunbathers were now ecstatically groping each other and travelling up a slight incline. For several pubic hours they had fought to extricate all the animal pleasures that were locked in their heaving bodies. Mutual steam was rising from their loins, and the nearest fire brigade ten miles away! Oh, for a bucket of water! Her protruding breasts were pressed flat between his body and hers. He had felt them, he had fondled them; he lifted them, he pressed them, he weighed them, he valued them, he counted them, he massaged them, he stood back from them, he pulled them, he sat on them and picking up a banjo he played them. She clawed at the grass, she clawed at her hair, she clawed the air, she dug her nails into the earth, she dug them into his buttocks. 'Ouch!' he said. Their two mouths were locked in the vacuum of a kiss taut with pulling tongues. Their buttocks tightened and relaxed in never-ending bursts of uncontrollable thrusts of hot coursing gyrations. Inside her, great earthquakes of seminal delight were coursing through her body. He took her nipples in his mouth and drew them into pulsating erection. 'Naughty!' she said. How she loved him, how she worshipped him, this silly old soft-hearted one-eyed negro Lascar off a coaling ship at Belfast. Now the black piston of Africa was helping to cement black-white relationships. He could return to Kenyatta and say the white people love us, let's go back for more. It was over. They lay back gasping.

Next day she took him to meet 'Daddy', the Marshal of the County, Lord Cecil Kasingbroke, V.C., D.S.O. It was the first intimation he had of his daughter's colour blindness. Umboko had run from the stately home, his yellow suit shattered by gun-fire and bull mastiffs, the tribal seat pulverized with buck-shot. For weeks he was unable to sit down, even worse, he couldn't stand up. It did, however, prevent white members of the crew having recourse to a certain unsavoury sailor habit.

The heavy metal cutters minced through the barbed wire. O'Brien had cut close to the wooden posts. Father Rudden at his side gave the thumbs up sign. Through the gap, the five men crawled towards the grave of Dan Doonan, rapidly becoming the most travelled corpse in Ireland. Milligan, in the van, cast anxious eyes towards the sentry three hundred yards to their left. A light from the guard hut glinted on the soldier's bayonet. The five men moved to the temporary shelter of an ancient mulberry. Only one hour before two ragged-arsed men had hid in the self-same place. They too had felt for the grave with the loose earth. Soon they were digging up the coffin of Dan Doonan.

'Strange dis T.N.T. doesn't feel so heavy now,' said Shamus.

'No, it doesn't,' said Lenny struggling manfully alone under the weight of the coffin.

Father Rudden led his men forward, his hand too felt for a grave with loose earth.

'Funny, I could have *sworn* it was over there,' said the Milligan as the shovels set to work. Soon the coffin of 'Mrs Eileen Spoleen' with its 200 lb. of T.N.T. was rising.

'Freeze!' said Goldstein.

The party stood, knelt and lay transfixed as a soldier came suspiciously forward. He held his rifle at the ready, he came closer. He stopped, looked cautiously left and right, placed his rifle against a tree. … The dirty swine! No wonder the place was starting to smell. They heaved on ropes, sweat was pouring down Milligan's arms.

'Freeze!'

The bloody sentry was coming back; the diggers, gasping, lay flat and still, the ropes cutting their hands.

'Anybody out there?' called the soldier. 'If there's anyone out there say so and I'll fire.' He raised his rifle.

Milligan looked imploringly out of the page.

'For God's sake don't let him shoot, Mister.'

The soldier about-turned and marched away. Milligan grinned.

'God, you got all the power in this book.' He stroked the stubble on his chin. 'You havin' the power of de author, can I have a request?'

'Yes.'

'Dat dirty soldier that nearly pissed on us, make him do something that will get him into trouble.'

The soldier returned to his post, sloped arms, fired three rounds in the air, dropped his trousers and sang Ave Maria. The Sgt of the Guard came hurrying from his tent.

'Private Worms?' he shouted, 'You're under arrest.'

A powerhouse raspberry was the reply.

'What's going on here?' said Lt Walker, arriving pyjama-clad on the scene.

'I'll show you, sir,' said the sergeant, and inexplicably launched into a series of cartwheels, back somersaults and impressions of Al Jolson in Maltese.

'Both under arrest for being drunk and disorderly. Turn out the guard.'

At the command, the guard assembled and watched him, the Lieutenant, return to his tent with a series of animal noises and great backward leaps on one leg. What would his father Field Marshal Walker, M.C. and Bar, say? Nothing; at this self-same moment he was performing the same feats before his puzzled sovereign at the Passing Out Parade at Sandhurst.

Milligan watched the Lieutenant's antics with a great piano-keyboard smile.

'By Gor, you got the power all right. I wish I was a writer.'

O'Mara put his great shoulders to the rope and pulled the coffin towards the church. 'God, he's heavier since he died, it must suit him.' They all headed for the church leaving Milligan to fill in the grave.

Ah Pong lay lynx-like and silent in a tree of his own choosing. He was about to descend when two shadowy ragged-arsed figures carrying another box headed in the opposite direction. Shamus and Lenny heard a sneeze above them and were hit by a bare-footed falling Chinaman. Running with a coffin-cart they disappeared, firing their pistols in all directions. Ah Pong replied with a burst of whistle-blowing, took a pace backwards and disappeared into an empty grave.

The guard turned out and opened fire. 'The I.R.A.!' went up a cry. A bewildered bugler in underpants blew the lights out and put the whole camp in darkness. Webster leapt from his bed into the po. Barrington fainted in his sleep. Father Rudden and Co. dropped their coffin and ran like hares for cover. Incendiary bullets criss-crossed the night sky, verey lights burst in the darkness. Private Dawson saw a gamboge Chinese face arising from a grave and promptly did in his trousers what cascara takes 24 hours to do.

'Halt, who goes there?' he said, hurriedly tearing up a newspaper.

Quaking with fear the Chinese answered in Pekinese and was immediately fired at in Gaelic. The shot knocked the top off his truncheon. Hysterically he walked up the grave wall and ran chattering into the night. 'Sod that for a lark,' he said. He really was getting a grip on the language.

It was 4.32. The firing had died away. There was an uneasy silence. The soldiers strained their ears. Then from the distance came the unmistakable sound of an unidentified noise. 'Helloooooooo!' it went. The voice was strange to them, but not to Foggerty. The corporal made a signal to his men.

'This might be a trick, hold yer fire till I give three short blasts on me whistle.'

'Hellooooo!' It was coming closer. Running. Ah Pong tripped over Milligan's shovel. Heroically he blew three blasts on his whistle, and Foggerty received the full ballistic weight of B Coy's fire power.

The moon came out, its silver beams streaming through the bullet holes in Foggerty's trousers and hat. Life is a matter of majorities, either you have one or you haven't. Right now Foggerty was outvoted.

The dawn came up like thunder out of China across the bay. It didn't do that in Ulster. Shivering and swearing, Lenny and Shamus scraped the hoar frost from their faces and pushed Dan Doonan's coffin into the bushes.

'We can't hang around here, Lenny, they'll be looking for us on both sides now. What bloody bad luck. We'll leave this T.N.T. there till the hooha dies down.'

Lenny nodded woefully as he arranged the bracken on top of the coffin. Sad yes, this little lot was supposed to blow up that police station at Durragh. The sound of a bugle being bugled broke the morning silence. Lenny hid behind Shamus.

'Is that the Military?' he said.

'I don't know, it cummed from over there.'

The two men climbed to the lip of a hill and peered cautiously over. A fine sight met their eyes; gleaming white in the morning sun were the tents of that knobbly-kneed society, the Scouts.

It was the Ulster Annual Jamboree. For weeks past, hundreds of spotty-faced herberts, with yodelling voices and chin fuzz, had tied three million knots, started ten thousand twig fires, and completed six hundred leaf shelters; perfect training for round about 3,000 BC but

bloody useless in the twentieth century. Where were their geiger coun-
ters? Their strontium detectors? Their books on how to bury ten million incinerated children? Be prepared? Ha! Ha!

Shamus could just read the sign, 'Scout Store. Rekitting Section.'
Scouts of all sizes were lining up for a fine breakfast of burnt eggs and
carbonized toast when two ragged-arsed men slipped unnoticed under
the flaps of a marquee. Chief Scoutmaster Theobald Dring looked on
approvingly. What a fine bunch of lads. He felt fine too. He examined
himself. He was fine. He looked fine. Fifty-seven fine years old, tall,
erect, clear skinned, fine broad shoulders, slender hips; fine muscular
arms, short bow legs. He had overcome this latter handicap by stuffing
newspapers down the inside of his hose, and thus managed to build up
the calves sufficiently to match the extensive outward curve of the leg.
It did however give him the unfortunate appearance of a man with 29-
inch calves, and a man with 13-inch thighs can't do that sort of thing.

He yawned and rose from his sapling and sheepshank bed. Strange,
he thought as he searched for his shaving kit, it was there last night.

Two cleanly shaved scouts in new but ill-fitting uniforms enjoyed
the pleasure of an alfresco breakfast without payment.

'Oh-ho,' said Lenny, 'dis is a stroke of luck, no one but Baden-
Powell would tink of lookin' for us here.'

Shamus nodded in agreement, his mouth moving relentlessly on a
slice of dead pig recumbent on a sea of porridge.

'Pardon me, sir,' said a small scout sitting opposite, his face held
together with pimples, 'what troop are you from?'

'The 3rd Puckoon Rangers,' said Shamus, licking his lips, plate,
knife, fork, spoon, fingers and thumbs.

Twelve miles north of Puckoon, set in rolling acres, rose the delicate
Georgian facades of Brent Lodge, built in an age when craftsmen loved
the excitement of creation, be it only brick upon brick. Now it lay open
to its greatest enemy, the twentieth century. The proportions were for
all to see, uncrowded, with an eternal grace culled from Ancient Greece.
Soane had built it for the Dukes of Munster, who, falling short of

money and an heir, willed it to the people of Ulster in perpetuity. In the hands of the local council, it had been reduced to 'Units of Housing'. Aged gentlefolk, retired Colonels and widowed matrons now lived out their lives in the grim indifference of local government. The tall, beautiful, curved glass windows looked out on once topiaried hedges, now long untrimmed; lily ponds and choked fountains graced the lawns the local council had recently officially 'cut', with a bread knife it would appear. There it now stood, a masterpiece of yesterday, ignored by the bureaucratic barbarism of today. Soon, the Chairman of the Council Planning Committee would gather strength from statistics, revenue, and a chorus of 'Ayes' from his sycophantic minions, and order it to be 'pulled down'. To the press he would issue a well-thumbed paper '– too expensive to maintain, etc., etc., etc., make way for etc., etc., etc., sentimentalism must not stop progress etc., etc., etc.' Bureaucracy was the counterpart of cancer, it grew bigger and destroyed everything except itself.

Before this monster stood Brent Lodge. The wind was blowing flakes of paint from its lintels and pediments. Occasionally a refined old face would part the heavy, long, faded velveteen curtains, then slowly recede into the oblivion of the great house. The two tall, double-fronted, mahogany wood doors with their unpolished brass handles were reached by twelve gently ascending marble steps, flanked by Venetian balustrades; on top, supported by two slender columns, was a portico surmounted by a Greek frieze. On the doorstep stood a half-pint bottle of grade 2 milk. A thick veiny but refined hand withdrew it into the hall.

The youngest member of this ageing community was ex-variety artiste, Patrick L. Balls. Fifty-nine now, he spent out his remaining years pulling a rope lift and bottling fruit. He had once whistled Ave Maria for Queen Victoria. She wasn't present at the time, but nevertheless that's who he was whistling it for.

Today would be very busy. No whistling for him. Today was the Concert. Once a year the scouts came and 'did a concert of talking'. Tonight they would perform in the Hydro Hall a drastically cut version of 'The Immortal Bard', *Julius Caesar*.

The indoor plunge bath in the Hydro was boarded over, and the great French windows were folded back to make way for the temporary stage that backed on to the garden. Behind this, jacked up on its back axle was the 1909 de Dion, whose yellow wheels drove the power for the footlights. Slowly now, the hall was filling with the spectre-like audience. The sisters, Agnes and Millicent Grope, walked mincingly down the aisle on Minny Mouse legs, fox furs around their long, thin white necks.

'It's *Julius Caesar* again then,' said Agnes, taking her seat.

'It was *Julius Caesar* last year, Agnes.'

'Oh? I suppose this is an encore,' smiled Agnes, opening her programme. Preparing themselves in the orchestra pit were the Patrick Furg 'Refined' Trio. A doddering trinity of febrile musicians, led by a bent, thin violinist. The piano keyboard lay staring up at Mrs Auraulum Murphy, a short, tubby, middle-aged lady with amber beads and a dropped womb. She clipped her music to the stand with clothes pegs, a present from a musical laundry man. Behind her, supporting herself on a 'cello was Madame Elsie Mooney, who ran her resin listlessly across the hairs of her bow; her long stringy neck and pendulous jowls gave her the appearance of a plucked turkey. She was dressed carefully in a sea of brown Majorca lace; brittle white hair escaped in all directions from its prison of hairpins; she turned her lizard-like gaze at the stage. A small, hastily made-up, roseate face appeared from the wings. 'Psssstt, ready in two minutes,' it said and disappeared. Madame Mooney prodded Patrick's stern with her bow.

'Don't do that Madame Mooney!' he said. 'It pleasures me not any more.'

'They'll be ready in two minutes, Patrick.'

'Oh.' Patrick checked his music. 'Did you hear that, Miss Murphy?' She nodded her head.

'A tuning A please.' He plucked the sagging strings to order, then in a jocular mood, drew the bow fiercely across the bridge with all the fire of decay. 'How's *that*!' he said.

'Out!' shouted an old cricket fan in the audience.

Miss Murphy tittered at him. He had proposed to her thirty-seven times in ten years and been refused. Last week she had proposed to him, and he was now considering it.

Both conversation and the house lights went down; a few exhibition coughers voiced their bronchial ego; the silence that followed was shattered by two loud thumps of Patrick Furg's boots, and the refined trio launched shakily into several bars of obscure music. 'Good God!' said a music lover finally, 'It's – it's William Tell.'

Slowly the front curtain rose rapidly, stuck and crashed down again. It rose rapidly. Got stuck and stayed stuck rapidly. It revealed a forest of anonymous legs. Two embarrassed Scoutmasters with overcoats hastily donned over togas, shuffled on the stage. With sticks and whispered orders, the obstinate curtain was raised. Fronting four and twenty Roman spearsmen were three steps covered in army blankets; flanking this stood two canvas and lath Doric columns painted on brown paper. The programme note: Rome. The steps of the Imperial Palace. How the old place had changed. Standing on this noble pile, the figure of an eight-year-old Cassius was speaking; proud and erect he stood in his white bed-sheet and cardboard laurel leaves, in his pocket a complete set of great footballer cigarette cards. To the refined ear, trained for euphony, Shakespeare rings most comforting; to a Roman spearsman named Shamus Ford it brought a mental remark, 'What the hell's this all about?' To his left Lenny was thinking that he didn't look too bad as a Roman soldier. Cassius raised his hands to silence the mob. The great curtain crashed to the stage. This time the Patrick Furg trio were ready.

'Emergency One,' said Patrick to his trio. Off they went, reducing in three minutes a reputation Rossini had taken one hundred years to establish. After further sticks, pushes and shouts the curtain rose again. The same scene plus, at no additional cost, happily smoking Centurion. Shamus snatched the cigarette from Lenny's mouth.

From back stage there was a metallic clang. ... The silencer had fallen from the generator car and the ensuing noise of the open exhaust forced the young actors to shout, causing one Roman's nose to bleed. A change of wind was now blowing smoke from the long carbonized car engine, up through the cracks in the stage; the cast were now reduced to shouting *and* coughing. 'Beware the Ides of March,' said the sooth-sayer, losing his beard in a fit of coughing. The smoke obscured the players who all moved forward to the footlights. Unaffected, the Furg trio were playing the Hall of the Mountain Kings, with a difference; the rising warmth of the thermal waters below them was gradually lower-ing the pitch of their instruments; gradually the Hall of the Mountain Kings slid chromatically from C Major down to B Flat Minor.

'Crazy, man,' whispered Patrick.

The smoke had caused a disturbed deaf member of the audience to phone the fire brigade. 'Come quick, Brent Lodge is in flames, thou-sands are trapped!' was the simple message.

In the front row was guest of honour, Inspector Tomelty. For ten minutes he had been wrestling with the face of a certain Roman soldier. Suddenly he clicked his fingers. 'Shamus Ford! Excuse me,' he said, pushing along a row of creaking arthritic legs. Soon two Black Marias thundered in the night, during which time the audience were treated to the spectacle of six men in brass helmets dashing on a smoke-filled stage with hoses; they immediately set about the floor with hatchets and with the first stroke three toes came off. Smoke now obscured the cast from the audience. Groping forward, a fat Julius Caesar tripped and fell on to the piano; eighteen stone of Julian flesh was all it needed to send the instrument crashing through the floor beneath; with a splin-tering groan the Patrick Furg Trio, all playing valiantly, slid majesti-cally into the warm waters of the hydro pool below. A chain reaction followed as the temporary floor broke into sections, everywhere were floating rafts bearing the trapped, shouting, aged audience. The De Dion had fallen off its blocks and ripped the backcloth away, revealing twenty scouts in various stages of undress. Hoses were starting to douse the last remaining actors. Police whistles announced new arrivals. Shouts of help came from the marooned audience.

'Let's beat it,' said Shamus pulling Lenny with him.

They reached the first floor with the police at their heels. The lift!

A gift from above! Slamming the gates, Shamus gave the ancient rope the pull of its rotting life. It snapped. The ancient lift hurtled down the shaft, hit the rubber buffers in the basement and hurtled up again. It hovered at the third floor 'twixt momentum and gravity, *just* long enough for an unsuspecting chambermaid to step in and hurtle down again.

'Have we got the electric on?' she smiled at the terrified òccupants.

Patrick Balls not wanting to spend his remaining years yo-yoing in a lift, grabbed at the end of the frayed rope as it came within reach and was left hanging as the lift hurtled down again. Rocketing up, Shamus and Lenny judged the pause and leaped out at the second floor.

Cries of 'Send help!' came from the plummeting gentlefolk. Colonel Carrington-Thurk R.A., Retd., awoke from his slumbers, heard the cacophony, and leapt from his bed; sabre in hand he opened the door and fell over a fire hose.

'Take that, you Indian swine!' he yelled, slicing through the pulsating canvas; a deluge of water from the hose jack-knifed him back into the dumb waiter which descended at speed to the kitchen.

On the end of the ruptured hose, Fireman Mortimer Wreggs suddenly held a lifeless bronze nozzle in his hand. 'Bugger!' he said, 'Oh bugger, bugger, bugger!' and lay face down on the floor threshing his legs in temperamental spasms. This emotional outburst was of deep Freudian significance; had not Adler, Freud and Jung all agreed that the seeds of hereditary ambition are passed on through successive generations until fulfilment? So was it with young Fireman Wreggs. His great-great-grandfather had *almost* extinguished the greatest and most expensive fire in the history of Ireland, but alas, in the best traditions of British services had arrived too late!

That fearful conflagration was a mighty story in the annals of the family Wreggs. The disintegration of the Austro-Hungarian Empire hit many people, especially those who had disintegrated with it. The Count Nuker-Frit-Kraphauser was one such notable. In the hiatus that followed the assassination of the Archduke Ferdinand, and the collapse of the Empire, he had fled his native Hungary in the jade of a revolutionary night with nothing save a small suitcase with three million pounds and some silly old crown jewels, but this fortune meant nothing; his greatest loss was having to leave the great and majestic family Easence. The greatest toilet in the western world and the only consecrated one in the Holy Roman Empire.

The Count Fritz Von Krappenhauser had fled to Northern Ireland, bought Callarry Castle, ten thousand acres, and a small packet of figs. For years he brooded over the loss of the ancestral abort. Finally worn out by indifferent, and severe wood-seated Victorian commodes, he decided to build a replica of the family's lost masterpiece here in the heart of Ulster's rolling countryside. He employed the greatest baroque and Rococo architects and craftsmen of the day, and every day after; seven years of intense labour, and there it now stood, a great octagonal Easence. No ordinary palace was this; from the early stone Easence of Bodiam Castle to the low silent suite at the Dorchester is a long strain, but nothing equalled this, its gold leaf and lapis lazuli settings gleaming in the morning sun, on the eight-sided walls great ikons of straining ancestors, a warning to the unfit. Through a Moorish arch of latticed stone, one entered the 'Throne Room'; above it, in Gothic capitals the family motto, 'Abort in Luxus'. From the centre rose a delicate gilded metal and pink alabaster commode. Six steps cut in black Carrara marble engraved with royal mottoes led up to the mighty Easence; it was a riot of carefully engraved figurines in the voluptuous Alexandrian style, depicting the history of the family with myriad complex designs and sectionalized stomachs in various stages of compression. The seat was covered in heavy wine damask velvet, the family coat of arms sewn petit-point around the rim in fine gold thread. Inside the pan were low relief sculptures of the family enemies, staring white-faced in expectation. Towering at the four corners, holding a silk tasselled replica of the Bernini canopy, were four royal beasts, their snarling jaws containing ashtrays and matches. Bolted to the throne were ivory straining bars carved with monkeys and cunningly set at convenient angles; around the base ran a small bubbling perfumed brook whose water welled from an ice-cool underground stream.

Gushes of warm air passed up the trouser legs of the sitter, the pressure controlled by a gilt handle. By pedalling hard with two foot-levers the whole throne could be raised ten feet to allow the sitter a long drop; and even greater delight, the whole Easence was mounted on ball-bearings. A control valve shaped like the crown of Hungary would release steam power that would revolve the commode. There had been a time when the Count had aborted revolving at sixty miles an hour and been given a medal by the Pope.

White leather straps enabled him to secure himself firmly during the body-shaking horrors of constipation. Close at hand were three burnished hunting horns of varying lengths. Each one had a deep significant meaning. The small one when blown told the waiting household all was well, and the morning mission accomplished. The middle one of silver and brass was blown to signify that there might be a delay. The third one, a great Tibetan Hill Horn, was blown in dire emergency; it meant a failure and waiting retainers would rush to the relief of the Count, with trays of steaming fresh enemas ready to be plunged into action on their mission of mercy and relief. With the coming of the jet age the noble Count had added to the abort throne an ejector mechanism. Should there ever be need he could, whilst still in throes, pull a lever and be shot three hundred feet up to float gently down on a parachute. The stained glass windows when open looked out on to 500 acres of the finest grouse shooting moor in Ulster. He had once invited Winston Churchill to come and shoot from the sitting position. In reply Churchill sent a brief note, 'Sorry, I have business elsewhere that day.' From his commode, the Count could select any one of a number of fine fowling pieces and bring down his dinner. Alas, this caused his undoing. The boxes of 12-bore cartridges, though bought at the best shops in London, had sprung a powder leak. Carelessly flicking an early morning cigar, the hot ash had perforated the wad of a cartridge.

But to the day of the calamitous fire. It had been a fine morning that day in 1873. The Count had just received his early morning enema of soap suds and spice at body heat; crying 'Nitchevo!' he leapt from his couch. Colonic irrigation and enemas had made his exile one internal holiday. Clutching a month-old copy of *Der Tag*, and contracting his abdomen, he trod majestically towards his famed Imperial outdoor abort bar. A few moments later the waiting retainers heard a shattering roar and were deluged, among other things, with rubble.

'Himmel? Hermann? What did you put in the last enema?' queried the family doctor of the retainers.

Flames and debris showered the grounds and there, floating down on the parachute, came the Count. 'People will look to me when I die,' he had once said. His wish had come true.

In that fire had perished Fireman Wreggs. Now his great-grandson lay there crying on the floor of Brent Lodge House. The pandemonium had snowballed and perfectly good friends were hitting each other.

'*There is no fire!*' a very angry Scoutmaster was saying, his paper columns flattened with water. 'There is no fire!' he repeated as three firemen poured eighty gallons a minute over him. 'You're ruining our costumes!' he shouted. They silenced him by increased water pressure, at a hundred gallons a minute he was sluiced backwards into a choked lily pond.

'Three troop to the rescue!' he shouted through his umbrella of water lilies.

Solitary and floating alone in her row 'D8' chair, its planks awash, was stone-deaf Miss Penelope Dingley-Smythe, her hearing aid turned to zero. She snored oblivious of the hydro waters that lapped at the soles of her little Victorian high-button boots. The Brigade were being severely hampered by two things, a lack of water, and a lack of fire. Of the thirteen hoses only six were at full pressure. Frantically lighting fires as he went, Fire Chief Muldoon discovered a rusty verdigris board covered in turncocks. 'Hallelujah!' he exalted as he turned the lot on. There was a rumbling sound under the earth. Long forgotten fountains lived again, eroded pipes burst in all directions, streams of water shot from under many an unsuspecting victim. Thirty great jets hurled a screaming scoutmaster twenty feet in the air, ripping his boots and socks from his feet. Once gentle bidets suddenly gushed up unsuspecting old females, giving a mixed feeling of fear and joy. The delightful

Junoesque fountain Naiad, her innards clogged this many a year, suddenly burst. Old Admiral Munroe under his shower was flattened by the increase in water power. The ancient brass geyser was trying to consume the new rate of intake and remain intact; with steam everywhere, it started to boil and fall apart. As the Admiral took to his heels, it exploded and hurled him naked into the corridor right on to the teatray outside the door; seated on it like an aged Puck, he slid powerless down the steps shouting 'Foreeeeeee!' Tightly holding the edge of his slender craft it hurtled down the wet stairs into the hall, and finally shot out the front doors on to the lawn at the feet of Mrs Grimblenack. 'Madame!' roared the quick-witted Admiral, 'Get out of my bathroom!' But she would have none of his finesse. 'If you don't go to my bedroom at once I'll scream!' she said. He fled into the countryside and later was found dead from indecent exposure.

Correspondence with Marty Feldman: 1972

Marty was one of Spike's favourite people. This reflects that.

from –

a man posing as Superjew
Feldman, last seen sitting
by a pool in a flash
hotel, getting angry
about being rich.

MARTY FELDMAN

Sunday July
30th

Dear Spike,
     I'm up up and on with to America,
America, which you may recall is a country
based on a novel by Elia Kazan, Elia Kazan.
I'll be grubbing for dollars for the next
month or so and infesting the Chateau
Marmont Hotel – Beverly Hills – lolling
poolside, between gigs, supping sparkling
vintage meths from ageing starlets surgical
boots. Please write!
If you don't write, I will.
If you don't answer my letter, fuck you, I
won't bother to write in the first place.
My best to you & yours; my second best
to them & theirs – the rest to be
equally divided among the needy.

         Yours in extremis –

         Marty

9 Orme Court,
London. W. 2.
16th August, 1972

Marty Feldman Esq.,
The Chateau Marmont Hotel,
Beverley Hills.
California.
U.S.A.

O.K.

       Love

P.S. Don't say I haven't written to you.

The Bedside Milligan: 1969

At Orme Court we employed a multi-talented office boy, Philippe le Bars. Spike gave him his first break (follows), then wrote a poem for him (below). Spike never could spell his name.

Phillip le Barr
Was knocked down by a car
On the road to Mandalay
He was knocked down again
By a dust cart in Spain
And again, in Zanzibar
So,
He travelled at night
In the pale moon-light
Away from the traffic's growl
But terrible luck
He was hit by a duck
Driven by – an owl.

The Spike Milligan Army Show: 1965

An early radio show.

HOUNSLOW GARRISON AND SPORTS CLUB

DRAMATIC SECTION

PRESENTS

A L L   S T A R   V A R I E T Y

FRIDAY 8.0 P.M. 28th MAY 1965

at

GARRISON THEATRE, CAVALRY BARRACKS
HOUNSLOW

ARTISTES APPEARING

The World Famous Dagenham Girl Pipers
    The International Band
(By kind permission of the Directors)

VERDINI - Continental Magician & Shadows Act

GEORGE, PAT, TOMMY & CO - Musical Artists - Accordians, Harmonicas etc.

EDDIE CLIFF - Comedian on the Brighter Side

YURI GRINDNEFFS - Comedy, Uni-cycling & Juggling

BARBARA NEWMAN - Comedienne, British, Bright & Breezy.

VIOLETTE-DE-SAXE - Come Sing along with me - Vocalist Modern & Old Tyme

Under the Patronage of
and in the presence of

LIEUTENANT-GENERAL SIR GEORGE COLE, KCB, CBE
AND LADY COLE

ALL PROCEEDS FROM THIS SHOW ARE TO BE GIVEN TO THE HANDICAPPED
CHILDREN AND ARMY WIDOWS AND ORPHANS FUNDS

Admission: 4/-   (Forces in Uniform 3/-)

BOOK NOW: Tickets may be obtained from the following:-

        Mr GARDNER - CAMP COMMANDANT   Tel Ext 15

        Mr DU PARC - COMMAND PAY OFFICE   "   508

        Mr LUNGLEY - LAD REME, Beavers Lane Camp   "   194

        Mr MARTIN - MPBW   "   208

        Mr BAMPTON - EC FINANCE BOARD   "   89

        ORDERLY ROOM - 10 Signal Regt,
                    Beavers Lane Camp

Spike Milligan

Army Show

THE SPIKE MILLIGAN ARMY SHOW

with

JOHN BLUTHAL
BARRY HUMPHRIES
JOHN BIRD
RODDY MAUDE-ROXBY
ALAN CLARE
PHILLIPE LE BARS

-------oooOooo-------

Script by Spike Milligan
Produced by Charles Chilton

REHEARSAL: SUNDAY, 16TH MAY 1965:   PLAYHOUSE

1000-2030   REHEARSE F/X, CAST, ETC.

2030-2130   RECORD.

TAPE NO: TLO 520/721

1.

1. GRAMS:	SOUND OF EL ALEMEIN GUNS. CLASHING OF MEN AT ARMS. SCREAMS AND SHOUTS. BUGLE CALLS

2. ~~ANN.~~ *Roddy* Good evening / Welcome to Frorces Fravourites. You have just been listening to a record of World War Two requested by Gnr. J. Sponk, ~~for his wife, his mother and his mistress, all at Gladys Road, Bexhill.~~ I will now hand you over to Captain Fumbling Grope, V.C., M.C., D.S.O., G.-

3. BIRD: Alright Sarnt Major, no need to spell it. At ease. Now, you men are possibly wondering what you were all detailed to come here this evening for. (PAUSE) In 1949, just after the war finished, sad thing it did too, I was so enjoying it, anyhow, in March of that year, the BBC under the command of Eric 'Balilika' Maschwitz sent War Office the following memo.

4. GRAMS: IN THE BACKGROUND. TYPEWRITER.

5. MAN: (SPIKE) We are at present, desperately short of studio audiences. Would you consider recruiting an audience of military volunteers. Signed Shrilibriolm (mumble)

6. RODDY: But, we at War Office wanted more gen. than that. My word yes, and we replied:

7. GRAMS: DISTANT MORSE CODE UNDER NEXT SPEECH

2.

1. MAX: **BARRY**   (SPIKE) Agreed in principle, but do you want
audience drawn from one particular Regiment?
Would they be expected to laugh? If so would
the officers and NCOs be allowed to laugh first.
Signed: Lt. Draws Colletus, M.G.M.

2. RODDY: and they replied:

3. GRAMS: BACKGROUND TYPEWRITER. AS LAST WORD IS SPOKEN.
TYPEWRITER BELL.

4. MAN: (SPIKE) And as as much as there to.
Nevertheless, where as para three is agreed,
we think that in so far as to say, notwithstanding
forthwith and scrimpscanson scrampson on the
scrans and twergled by inches three.

5. RODDY: To this, we agreed. We decided to step up
recruiting with new and exciting posters.

6. PHILLIPE: (COCKNEY) Join the British Army and get free
seats to the BBC!

7. RODDY: The result was sensational!

8. SPIKE: Nobody joined.

9. RODDY: We tried using subtlety. Such as interviews
ON BBC.

10. BLUTHAL: And in the studio we have - your name?

11. BIRD: G. Rifleman Eric Kak. 007.

3.

1. INTERVIEWER: Well Mr. Rifleman Eric Kak, why did _you_ join the Army?

2. BIRD: (UPPER CLASS COCKNEY) Well, I saw a poster saying join the modern army and travel to far away places. I was fed up with Civvy Street at the time, I was a white spotty faced clerk in foggy London. I thought I've had enough, and so, I joined the Irish Guards. [~~I have been with them now for six years~~]

3. INTERVIEWER: [And thanks to the Army _And anyone_ you are now **what**.

4. RIFLEMAN: I am now a white spotty faced Guardsman in Foggy London.

5. SPIKE: Somehow, that didn't do us any good either, then we thought of using a poster by Cecila _Marget Pon_ ~~Beaton~~. It read.

6. FAIRY: _Roddy_ Boys, join the Regular Army, its lovely.

7. SPIKE: We didn't get the right sort of man with that one. However, with the sudden drop in unemployment, the fear of working for a living suddenly drove hundreds _of English language_ to join. Soon the Army was at full strength.

8. BLUTHAL: (COMMENTATOR) On October the Thurnth Nineteen Fafty Tune, at a secret place called Salisbury plans, plains, were made to train men as BBC studio audiences.

4.

1. BARRY: The plan had the code name, Training with
                    Infantry Tactics, or, T.W.I.T.'.

2. OMNES: MURMERS

3. GRAMS: 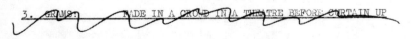 MADE IN A CROWD IN A THEATRE BEFORE CURTAIN UP

4. OMNES: MURMERS

5. BLUTHAL: Eyes and nose front. You may smoke. Now pay
                    attention.

6. R.S.   You will shortly be called up to laugh in the
                    face of a comic assault. The nature of what is
                    simple. You will march to map reference 380.960.
                    A wellknown BBC Studio. You will then sit in
                    chairs facing a stage. On the stroke of 1800 hrs.
                    (PRONOUNCED HERS) an entertainment will then
                    commence. Two men of the rank of comic will
                    then deliver a witticism or joke. So: First
                    Comic: Why did the Chicken cross the road?
                    Second Comic: To get to the other side. Now
                    a demonstration by Rifle O'Shaggs and Gnr.Bules.

7. SPIKE: Can a lady with a wooden leg change a pound note?
    (GNR.BULES)

8. BLUTHAL: Can a lady with a wooden leg change a pound note?
    (RIFLE O'SHAGGS)   Yes.

9. SPIKE: No.
    (GNR.BULES)

10. BLUTHAL: Why not?
    (RIFLE O'SHAGGS)

11. SPIKE: She's only got half a knicker.
    (GNR.BULES)

5.

1. ~~R.S.M.~~ *Bluthal*   Now, on the line <u>Half a Knicker</u>. You will
immediately sit at attention and then say,
ha ha ha ha. Repeatedly until I will silence
you so *FX Whstl* - now laughing in time - begin.

2. OMNES: Ha ha ha ha.

3. F/X: FOOTBALL WHISTLE

4. BLUTHAL: Very gude. Very gude indeed. The entertainment
will be divided into two parts, one and two,
and in that order. The first part is to be
laughed at, and the second part, music for
the listening to of, will be clapped. This can
be done by bringing the palms of the hand
together in a crisp movement make the sound.
So -

5. F/X: HAND CLAP

6. BLUTHAL: Any questions? Gude. Now Rifleman Len O'Shaggs
will sing the last bar of a known melody, after
which you will applaud. Rifleman Shaggs?

7. SPIKE: Sah?

8. BLUTHAL: One pace forward singing, commence.

6.

1. SPIKE: SINGS A SONG

                  My darling little baby

                  What will 'ee grow up to be

                  The Prime Minister of England

                  Or the King of Hitalyeeee

                  Hai waited thirty years or more

                  To see what he would be

                  Hes now a dustman in Wapping

                  Oh dearie dearie meeeeeeee.

God bless you and keep you mudder- Mc'Cree! eee

2. OMNES: BRITTLE CLAPPING

3. F/X: WHISTLE

4. BLUTHAL: Very gude very gude.

5. GROPE: (RODDY) Well there you have it, that is the
                  story behind why you are all here today. Any
                  questions?

6. PHILLIPE: (FROM AFAR) Yerst!

7. RODDY: Sarnt Major? Put that man on a charge. Now,
                  to start the Military Entertainment we now hand
                  over to the Official BBC Spokesman.

8. SPIKE: (NARRATOR) Good evening. Tonight, for the
                  first time, we tell the little known story of →

9. GRAMS: SOFT ROLL ON TYMP.

7.

1. BLUTHAL: Operation Sporran! *Hairy* Festang!

2. GRAMS?   TYMP ROLL INCREASES INTO A DRAMATIC CRASH OF
                    EXCITING CHORD THEMES WITH A SCOTTISH SOUND,
                    WITH THE DISTANT DRONE OF A BAGPIPE.

3. BLUTHAL: (AMERICAN) This is the story of brave men
                    who volunteered to act these parts, for money
                    alone.

4. BARRY: (NARRATOR) It was Nineteen Forty One in England,
                    but still only 1887 in Japan, such was the
                    difference between these two great notions,
                    Fertang!

5. GRAMS: FADE IN DISTANT GUNFIRE. NOT TOO HEAVY, BUT A
                    GOOD MIXTURE OF ARTILLERY. MACHINE GUN FIRE
                    AND SPORADIC RIFLE FIRE.

6. OMNES: BOOM! BANG (WITH THE SOUND)

7. BLUTHAL: (AUSSY) One day, in Organ the second, the
                    Island of Singapore fell under the auctioneers
                    mallet of the Japanese Army.

8. SPIKE: Singapore going once, twice. Sold to Japan
                    for certain .18 Bamboo pounds.

9. F/X: GAVEL BANG ON DESK.

10. BIRD: Damn these tiny yellow fiends. of Grown:

11. BLUTHAL: (SGT) That was Major Startling Grope, VC and Pin.
                    When all seemed lost, he rallied us round the
                    White Flag.

8.

1. BIRD: (MAJOR) Yes, rather than surrender, we gave
                ourselves up.

2. GRAMS: FADE IN MARCHING OUT OF STEP (JUST A PRONOUNCED
                MUDDLE OF UNDISCIPLINED MEN WALKING WITH BOOTS
                ON)

3. BLUTHAL: (Aus) From there we was marched two 'undred miles
                to the jap prison camp of Bitza Khazi.

4. BIRD: (Major) Thus penetrating deep into enemy
                territory, unarmed as well. That night I
                gave myself a couple of quick V.C's.

5. BARRY: (SANDY) My name? Humphries, Captain Sandy
                Humphries. I'm an Australian cobber. I was
                in the prison camp the day the Major Fumbling
                Grope and his men came in, and listened to the
                camp commandant.

6. GRAMS: OUTDOOR ATMOSPHERE. OCCASIONAL TROPICAL BIRD CALL

7. JAP: (SPIKE) Now you listen me. My name General
                Fred Fertang! You come my camp. All plisoners
                work.

8. OMNES: GASPS OF HORROR AT THE MENTION OF WORK

9. MAN. Blu   (BIRD) Work!

10. MAN 2 Roddy (BARRY) Never!

11. MAN 3 Bluy Bowy Fiends.

/Mr Spike 4   Swin

9.

1. ~~MAN 4~~ *Spike* (~~BLUTHAL~~) ~~Swines~~.

2. MAJOR: (BIRD) Japanese fiend! You mustn't frighten
                 my men like that. Have you not read the
                 Geneva Convention?

3. JAP: Have not read Geneva Convention. Am waiting
                 till they make film. You all worlork!

4. BLUTHAL: I'd rather die than worlk sir.

5. BIRD: (MAJOR) That was Sgt. Thud. Brilliant
                 Regular Soldier. Gave himself up, three years
                 before the war.

6. ~~SPIKE~~ *(Wog. Barry)*   *In the YWCA high Comma'*
                 What we didn't know was, when the Nips captured
                 Singapore they also captured the Sacred Bagpipes
                 of the Third Scots Hairies.

7. ~~BARRY~~ *Spike: Fife Ro*   (COMMENTATOR) When the loss was discovered,
                 a runner was despatched.

8. F/X: SHOT

9. SPIKE: SCREAM

10. BARRY: And arrived wounded at The Scots Hairies H.Q.
                 in Poona.

11. ~~ECCLES~~ *Spike Wog.*: Knock Knock on door sir.
11ᵃ *ALEX*   *Whus that*
     Wog   *Short Wog who can't reach the kno*
12. ALEX: *Roddy*   (FIFE ROBERTSON) What do you want knock *short way who a*
                 knock on door sir.

10.

1. ~~ECCLES~~ **Wog**:   A message for you sir.

2. ALEX: Slide it under the door.

3. ECCLES: UGHHHHHH. UGHHHHHHHH. It won't go under.

4. SCOT: Why not.

5. ECCLES: I got it in my head. It says that the Bagpipes
               of the 2nd Scots Hairies have been captured.

6. SCOT: Mac Ohhhhhh. Ohhhhh

7. GRAMS: BAGPIPES DEFLATING

8. OMNES: GREAT SCOTTISH GROANS

9. SCOT: (SPIKE) Oh it was terrible noos. Kilts were
               worn at half mast - many suffered from
               exposure!

10. COMMENTATOR **Blu**: Meantime, back at Bitza Kazhi.

11. GRAMS: JUNGLE SOUNDS   }
                                                    } VERY QUICK
12. OMNES: LIGHT MURMURED CONVERSATIONS   }

13. ~~BARRY~~ **Spike**:   . Eyes front. *& back again,*

14. BIRD: (MAJOR) Now, Captain Humphries, why have you
               called me at this late hour, I'll miss ITMA .

11.

1. BARRY: Sir, several of us want to get out of here.

2. BIRD: (MAJOR) Is it something I've said?

3. BARRY: It's nothing personal, it's just that we
              want to escape.

4. BIRD: (MAJOR) Escape? From here? Are you mad?

5. BARRY: I have a certificate.

6. BIRD: It means certain death.

7. BARRY: Yes, its a death certificate.

8. BIRD: Who else.

9. ECCLES: Me sir.

10. BIRD: The voice came from a malodeous something,
              wearing a finely shredded coal sack and one
              heavily blancoed boot!

11. BARRY: This is Field Marshall Eccles.

12. OMNES: GASPS OF 'NO'

13. BLUTHAL: (MAN 1) Impossible   ⎫
                                                      ⎬
14. ~~ASHY~~ Reddy: (MAN 2) Can't be true.   ⎬   VERY FAST
                                                      ⎬
15. SPIKE: (MAN 3) We'll lose the war.   ⎬
                                                      ⎬
16. BARRY: (Man 4) Typing mistake.   ⎭

12.

1. BIRD: How did you ever become a Field Marshall?

2. ECCLES: A clever mother. I was baptised Field Marshall
               Eccles.

3. BIRD: I've changed my mind. It's the duty of <u>every</u>
               British soldier called Field Marshall Eccles
               to try and escape. First the M.O. wants a word.

4. ALEX: (SCOT) Yes. If ever, if ever you get into a
               tough spot, and there's no way out, take one of
               those little black pills; three times a day.

5. ECCLES: GULP. Ah. What are they?

6. M.O.   (ALEX) Concentrated liquorice. They give a
               man something.

7. ECCLES: Thanks Doc, I'll never forget you for this.

8. M.O.   (ALEX) Indeed you won't. Now off you go.

9. ECCLES: Right. Captain you go first, I'll follow.

10. BARRY: When?

11. ECCLES: After der War.

12. ORCH: ?   DRAMATIC LINKS   *Phillip* : *Dramatic Music - then sound of a River*

13. BARRY: By dawn we reached the River Karpetee.

14. GRAMS: TWO SPLASHES AS THEY DIVE *Phillip & plase. splase*
               Dived in, and then made a <u>terrible</u> discovery.

13.

1. ECCLES: We couldn't swim.

2. BARRY: We'll have to build a quick Queen Mary. I tell 'ee
                Eccles have you any knowledge of trees?

3. ECCLES: I was born in one.

4. BARRY: Good, see that one about a mile away. Think
                you could chop it down ?

5. ECCLES: Not from here.

6. BARRY·   Alright, you wait here I'll bring it back.
                (FADING OFF) run run run run run run.
                (RUNS SELF OFF TALKING AND THEN GOING INTO AN
                INSANE GABBLE)

7. BLUTHAL: Within weeks three, the two men reached the
                British lines where they finally recovered
                from the treatment they got in the Military
                Hospital.

8. ALEX: Immediately they were driven to HQ Scots Hairies.

9. GRAMS: FADE IN A JEEP DRIVING ALONG.

10. BARRY: Coughs. Gad these jungle roads are dusty.

11. BLUTHAL: I can't understand it sir, we only had 'em
                dry cleaned last week.

12. SPIKE: (SENTRY) HALT!

14.

1. GRAMS: JEEP STOPS DEAD

2. SPIKE: (SENTRY) Who goes there? Friend or Foe?

3. F/X: THREE PISTOL SHOTS

4. BLUTHAL: Wounded friends.

5. SPIKE: (SENTRY) Advance wounded friends and be
               rec-konagised.

6. F/X: RUSTLING OF PAPER.

7. BARRY: Here is my permit.

8. SPIKE: (SENTRY) This permis is for a dog.

9. BARRY: BARKS.

10. SPIKE: (SENTRY) It appears to be in order. You'll
               find Lord Louis FleaBitten behind this next
               knock'.

11. PHILLIPE: KNOCK KNOCK. DOOR OPENS. ~~SLIGHT~~ CREAK OF
               UNOILED HINGE. ~~MORE VERBAL SOUND EFFECTS TO FOLLOW~~

12. SPIKE: Ta! Ahh, Captain Humphries, come in, pull up a
               chair.

13. BARRY: I'd rather stand.

14. SPIKE: Stand on a chair then, we respect Australian
               customs. Now, you are familiar with Camp
               BlitzaKharzi.

15.

1. BARRY: Well not familiar, shall we say, just good
                friends.

2. SPIKE: In your report you say that the Bagpipes of
                the 2nd Scots Hairies are being held prisoner. *again*
                then Wills

3. BARRY: Yes.

4. SPIKE: Don't be evasive. We want you to neuteralise
                those before the ~~Japs~~ *Japan* learn how to play them .
                back at us. If a Scots man ever saw a Jap
                playing the pipes - well it doesn't bear thinking
                about ,

5. PHILLIPE: RUSTLING OF MAP   TAP TAP. *TOP OF FINGER*

6. ~~ANNOUNCER: These recurring verbal sound effects have been
                put in to show the dexterity of the actors.
                It also shows that the BBC sound effects man
                hasn't turned up.~~

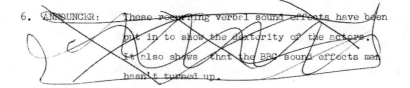

7. SPIKE: Here are the plans of a Bagpipe, this is the
                Chanter which <u>must</u> be removed and the Pipes
                destroyed. Boom ker thull powwww. Blatt.
                That or, Ferdanggg Kerunddd, thuck blammee.
                One of those two combinations should prove
                fatal.

8. BARRY: But this sounds like a Scottish affair, I'm an
                Australian.

9. SPIKE: I know old Cobbler, but this raid will be
                dangerous, and if anybody gets killed -

16.

1. BARRY: Yes?

2. SPIKE: We want it to be <u>you</u>. ~~You'll take charge of~~
                 the raiding ~~party and leave at dawn.~~

3. ~~BARRY:~~   But its half ~~day early closing.~~

4. SPIKE: I know but remember, we're doing it ..... for
                 England.

5. BARRY: Can't you think of a better reason?

6. SPIKE: (TAKEN ABACK) Er no ... Any last request?

7. BARRY: Yes I'd like to hear Gunner Milligan sing
                 Roses and Lollipops for Ethel, Gladys and
                 Alice, and all the other officers in the
                 Horse Guards. —

8.   ROSES AND LOLLIPOPS   Duct bin

9. PHILLIPE: Sounds of steaming jungle in day time, occasional
                 bird calls howler monkeys .

10. GRAMS: <u>BRING IN MEN HACKING THROUGH VEGETATION</u>.
                 <u>FADE JUNGLE NOISES INTO BACKGROUND</u>.

11. ALEX: The raiding party left at half past dawn.
                 Eight Burmese Village girls carried the lighter
                 loads while we men carried the heavier stuff
                 like the piano, the telly ~~and~~ ...

17.

1. ~~ECCLES~~: *Bluthal*   Why did we have to bring a piano along.

2. SPIKE: My dear, when you've been in the army as long
as I have you'll realise the value of the piano
in Jungle Warfare. Ever seen a man struck by
a piano? Its not a pretty sight. ~~By jove~~
~~there's a nip in the air this morning.~~

3. BLUTHAL: Through the long day we marched thru a dense
jungle. Towards evening we came upon a dense plain.

4. SPIKE: Halt. We'll camp here for the night. Put up
tents for the men and a three story Georgian
Mansion for the officers.

5. BARRY: *(Neil Sands)*   (APPROACH) Ah! Orders sir, we've got to get
to Bitzakharzi by May Tenth. According to
American intelligence and British stupidity,
that's nine days time.

6. SPIKE: I don't know how they get the information.

7. BARRY: They captured a Japanese calendar, alive.
Under pressure, it spoke:

8. SPIKE: *ham knee medal*
Brilliant. You'll get the Charing Cross for
this. Now men gather around this map of a
calendar.   You'll see that we are .....

9. PHILLIPE: TAPPING. *OF FINGER*

10. SPIKE: ..... here on the 1st of May, we've got to
head straight for May tenth. Here.

18.

1. PHILLIPE: More tapping.

2. OMNES: LIGHT MURMERS OF UNDERSTANDING.

3. SPIKE: Any questions.

4. PHILLIPE: (OFF) Yerst, why do I only get 5 fags a week
                 and you get a hundred cigars?

5. F/X: PISTOL SHOT. THUD. GROAN.

6. SPIKE: Any more questions. No good. Now, Sgt.
                 Bluthal where are the Burmese girls?

7. BLUTHAL: They are bathing in the River Karpartee, Sir.

8. SPIKE: Oh? Where's Field Marshall Eccles?

9. BLUTHAL: He is minding their clothes with a pair of
                 binoculars.

10. SPIKE: The swine, it was my turn for that, I'll have -

11. GRAMS: DISTANT SCREAMS OF WOMEN

12. LT.JYMPTON: (RODDY) (APPROACH OUT OF BREATH) Quick a Jap
                 Patrol have spotted the girls.

13. SPIKE: What-we must get there before the Japanese
                 Sunday Papers. We mustn't use rifles. Too
                 noisy. We'll have to use knives.

14. RODDY: Oh, I Ive never used a knife before, sir.

19.

1. SPIKE: You lie. I saw you eating peas off one at
               lunch. You'll use a knife, and like it. Ha.ha.ha.

2. RODDY: Sir, you must have ice in your veins.

3. SPIKE: I know, and its damned cold in here. Come on.

4. PHILLIPE: A RUSH OF DEPARTING BOOTS
               DRAMATIC MUSIC: OF ORK. DRAMATIC MUSIC.
               SCREAMS AND SHOUTS OF A FIGHT.
               THUDS OW BLAT. OUCH IN JAPANESE. ETC.

5. RODDY: (BREATHLESS) We polished off the Japs, the
               last was done by Lord Louis. He sliced the
               Nips braces, and the fellow died of indecent
               exposure.

6. SPIKE: It wasn't a pretty sight.

7. RODDY: Now, ah Eccles (WORRIED) Eccles? the - the
               Burmese girls?

8. ECCLES: You're too late - they've dressed.

9. SANDY: Time for your VC sir.

10. RODDY: Thank you Mrs. Aster. You'll be mentioned in
               despatches.

11. SANDY: So there is a Father Christmas

20.

1. RODDY: As the raiding party drew nearer, the
                    Prisoners, at Bitzakharzi got news of it on
                    the grape vine, which they had secretly grown
                    in a blacked out haversack.

2. MAJOR: (BIRD) Hear that men. We just got news of
                    it on the grape vine grown in a blacked-out
                    haversack. Now listen, the raiders are going
                    to try and dynamite the bagpipes, our job is
                    to cause a diversion. So, I've told General
                    Itchikutchi, that we are going to give a camp
                    concert on the night of the do. At the end
                    we will sing God Save the King very loud.
                    Any questions?

3. MATE: Yers, 'ows the tune go?

4. MAJOR   (BIRD) Er, I er, er, see .... well ....
                    don't worry the Japs are <u>bound</u> to know it.
                    Meantime behave like true British Prisoners
                    and don't dance with Jap privates. Any
                    questions?

5. PHILLIPE: Yers. Why do I only gets -

6. F/X: PISTOL.

7. PHILLIPS: SCREAM

8. MAJOR   (BIRD) Any more? Good, now remember, if this
                    raid succeeds, it will shorten the war by three
                    foot six inches.

21.

1. BBC ANN: We should like to assure listeners of a
                 nervous disposition that Japan and England
                 are <u>not</u> really at war again, this is merely
                 a temporary half hour war done under licence
                 for the BBC.

2. BLUTHAL: (R.S.M.) Sah. We now rejoin the official
                 entertainment in which the raiding party
                 arrive at the Banks of the River Karpathi.

3. PHILLIPE: SOUND OF RIVER IN AND THEN OUT.
                 DISTANT JUNGLE OUTDOOR SOUND.

4. LT.   (RODDY) I'm calling for three brave volunteers
                 to go on the last leg.

                 PAUSE

5. LT.   (RODDY) Alright three cowards then.

                 PAUSE

6. OMNES: NERVOUS SINGING STARTS THEN GETS OUT OF HAND.
                 You're all to beautiful -

7. RODDY: Stop. There's only one way. Field Marshall
                 Eccles? Write your name on three pieces of
                 paper and put it in this hat.

8. ECCLES: MMMmmmmmmmmm. There sir!

9. RODDY: Right. Draw one out.

10. ECCLES: Oh!

22.

1. RODDY: What does it say.

2. ECCLES: Mrs. Gladys Scrubber of Leeds.

3. RODDY: No we can't send her, she'd never get here in
                 time. Take your hat off, bend forward.

4. PHILLIPE: SOUND OF WATER POURING OVER A ~~HEAD~~ AND BEING
                 man not
                 CAUGHT IN A TIN BATH. -

5. RODDY: (VICAR STYLE) Field Marshall Eccles, I baptise
                 theeee Mrs. Gladys Scrubber of Leeds.

6. GRAMS: <u>DISTANT SOUND OF A CHOIR SINGING GERMAN
                 NATIONAL ANTHEM</u>

7. SGT.   (BLUTHAL) Listen (_   )   the signal.
                 They're singing ..... 'ere, that's the <u>German</u>
                 National Anthem.

8. SPIKE: When will you all learn, that is the <u>British</u>
                 Anthem disguised as the German Anthem. If the
                 Japs heard ours they'd capture it and play it
                 behind bars. Lt. Roddy I want you to go with
                 Captain Humpheries and Eccles.

9. LT.   (RODDY) Right sir and sir -

10. PHILLIPE: ~~SYRUPY HOLLYWOOD VIOLIN SOLO IN BACKGROUND~~.

11. LT.   (RODDY) Sir, if anything happens to me, I want
                 you to give this, to my wife.

23.

1. SPIKE: Your cheque book.

2. RODDY   Yes, she always wanted it.

3. SPIKE: Don't worry, Lt., I'll get it to her if I
               have to cash every cheque myself. Off you go.

4. GRAMS: THREE SPLASHES. ONE LAPPING.

5. GRAMS: DRAMATIC MUSIC. WITH A BAGPIPE THEME

6. BARRY: We three brave idiots dived into the cold
               waters of the River Karpati.

7. ECCLES: Yer and deres nothing worse than a cold
               Kar pa tea. (AD LIB) Especially when
               it doesn't get a laugh.

8. OMNES: DRAMATIC MUSIC WITH A BAGPIPE THEME.

9. ANN: But disaster had struck at man, beast and
               duck. The Japs had got suspicious. They
               wanted to know what the Bagpipes were, and used
               torture.

10. MAJOR: (BIRD) Nooo, nooo, no more. One step nearer
               and I'll set fire to this Bhaddist. *Secret*.

11. SPIKE: (JAP) Major Grope, you speak'. Or I give you more.

12. MAJOR: (BIRD) No no I can't stand any more.

13. JAP: I raise it to five pounds, ten shilling.

24.

1. MAJOR   (BIRD) Alright I give in I can't hold out
                 any longer. Those are the Bagpipes of the
                 second Scots Hairies.

2. JAP: Ha ha ha ha ha ha. **Keep Japan Yellow.**

3. PHILLIPE: DRAMATIC JAPANESE FIENDISH DEVIL MUSIC.

4. OMNES: PLINK AND PLONK ETC.

5. BARRY: Had the Japs triumphed? Not a bit of it, a
                 mere half hour before, we had removed the
                 chanter and substituted a plastic duplicate,
                 inside which was ten thousand tons of dynamite.

6. BLUTHAL: While at Base Camp, Lord Louis and another
                 person awaited the return of the raiders.

7. BARRY: Tell me Lord Louis, is this what English
                 call embarrassing position.

8. SPIKE: (LOUIS) No. More uncomfortable I'd say.
                 I mean what would people think? Me half way
                 up a mango tree dressed as Mephistopheles
                 and you down there bottling fruit in a transparent
                 plastic kilt. It would never do.

9. GIRL: (BARRY) Come let us dance.

10. GRAMS: OLD GRAMOPHONE RECORD OF A TRIO PLAYING LA PALOMA

11. SPIKE: (LOUIS) What a strange sight we made Tangoing
                 thru the steaming Jungle, the silence only broken

25.

1. GIRL: (BARRY) Oh, I only had eyes for him, and
                 he only had eyes for me.

2. SPIKE: We fell over a cliff.

3. RODDY: (APPROACH OUT OF BREATH) Sir, sir, we've done
                 it, and so have you by the look of it.

4. SPIKE: Good work!

5. RODDY: *If you say so.* We've fixed the Bagpipes so that the moment the
                 Japs ~~try and~~ play them, kerboom.

6. GRAMS: DISTANT LONE BAGPIPE.

7. RODDY: Listen. They've taken the bait!

8. BARRY: Any minute now ... ha ha ha ha ... if only
                 ~~they~~ knew ... ha ha ha ha ha ha ha .

9. OMNES: ALL LAUGH. SILENCE.

10. GRAMS: SOUND OF DISTANT BAGPIPES.

11. ECCLES: Ha ha ha ha ... if only he *dad Jap* knew what was coming
                 to him ... ah (ad lib)

                 SILENCE. LONG SILENCE. DURING WHICH THE
                 BAGPIPES CONTINUE.

12. OFFICER: *That appears to be the end of the adventure* ~~Alien~~ - any questions.

26.

1. MATE: Yes. Why ain't the bagpipes exploded.

2. F/X: PISTOL SHOT.

3. MATE: Ahhhhhh.

4. OFFICER: Any more questions. Company start clapping.

5. GRAMS: MASSIVE CLAPPING

                FADE OUT

                FINI

If short Sing it all again

A Book of Bits, or a Bit of a Book: 1965

Great Feets of Strength

Casabazonka

Coat of arms

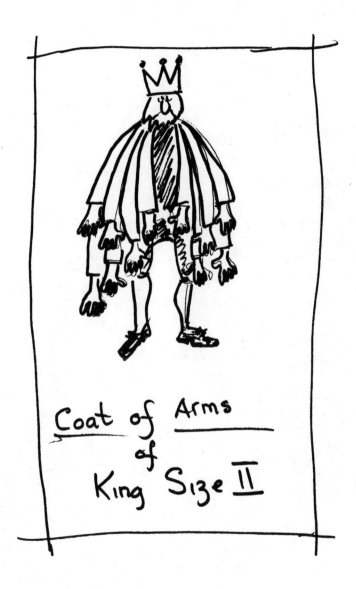

2

Milligan Flourishes

Q5 Script No. 2: 1969

The germ of an idea soon became a reality. I was always amazed how quickly Spike scribbled the first idea for a script and within hours it was completed.

Second in a series of 'Q' shows. Q5, show 2. The first show was called 'Oh in Colour'.

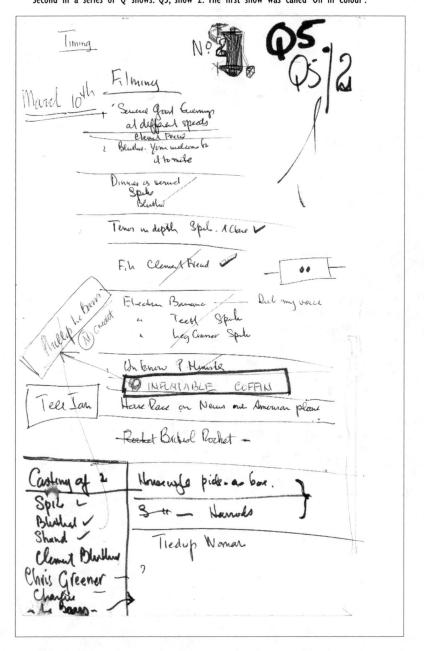

Q5 Script No. 3: 1969

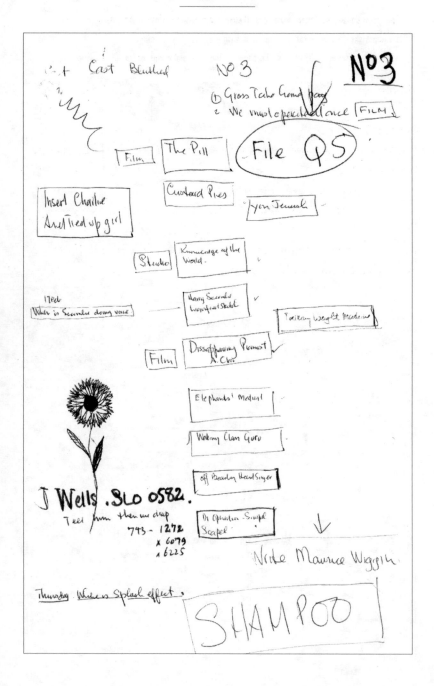

More Spike Milligan Letters: 1984

Spike was devastated when his friend Marty Feldman died. This is the letter he wrote to Loretta, Marty's widow.

To: Mrs Loretta Feldman   *14th December, 1982*

My dear Loretta,

As you know words are bloody useless at a time like this, but you know how I feel.

When you come over, please see me.

It was a terrible loss for me, God knows how much it was a loss for you.

He wasn't just a funny man, he was a bloody nice fellow. If life is a game of cards, somebody is cheating.

Love,
Spike

To: The Rt Hon. Mrs Margaret Thatcher, PM
10 Downing Street,
London SW1   *7th December, 1982*

Dear Mrs Thatcher,

I had a sighting of your reply to the R.S.P.C.A.'s letter of the 18th October, 1982 regarding the seal ban. You quote that you and your Government would only consider a ban on seal products if it shows that the species is proven to be endangered.

I hate to draw this parallel but whereas the human race is not an endangered species, you showed a remarkable amount of compassion, and even shed tears of concern at the thought of even the loss of one of them, namely your son, Mark Thatcher. Dare I say, what would you have done if you had to wait for a Scientific Committee to sit in judgement for a decision on whether he was worth saving. Basically the argument is a moral one. Man is the only creature who has a chance to show compassion through his morality.

I speak prophetically, the human race can no longer continue the course of believing that animals have to give way to them. When you consider the sheer slaughter and massacre of the Jews by the Germans, and even nearer to date, the slaughter of innocent Palestinians, by what are laughingly called 'Christian' Phalangists in the Lebanon.

I beg you to have some compassion in your judgement, and not rely solely on committees. Don't be like Pontius Pilate and wash your hands of the matter.

Meanwhile, I take this opportunity of wishing you and your family a very Merry Christmas.

Love, light and peace,
Spike Milligan

To: Messrs. Jack Hoy & S. Mitchell,
Issue,
(Furtherwick Park School Newspaper)   *10th January, 1972*

Dear Lads,

Basically, here is the dilemma:

COPULATION EQUALS POPULATION EQUALS POLLUTION.

ANSWER: BIRTH CONTROL.

Sincerely,
Spike Milligan

BMA Review: Undated

This is one of the many commissions Spike had to write for magazines and newspapers.

Medical Experiences

I have been asked to write 800 words on my experiences at the hands of the medical profession. Well, it started in distant Hyderabad in Sind as a child when I was stricken with fevers. Despite blood tests, the RAMC doctors couldn't diagnose the illness. Finally, after years they decided on 'clinical malaria' and dosed me with quinine; it didn't ever cure the fever but it gave me tinnitus.

Then there was my tonsils, for this I was operated on in a tent in Poona. It was the days of chloroform – I remember the anaesthetist soaking a cotton wool pad and saying 'We're going ninny byes', then placing it over my mouth and nose.

Returning to England in the Ramsay MacDonald days, my clinical malaria seemed to pass. My next confrontation with doctors came when during a weight training session I 'did something' to my back. It was in fact a slipped disc, something then unknown to the medical world. My doctor, Dr O'Brien, put me in Lewisham General with suspected rupture. 'I can feel the rupture coming,' he said, inserting obstetrical fingers into my groin. No rupture came but specialists did, I was suffering from specialists. They prodded me and advised an intravenous pyelogram as they thought I had stones in the kidney. It all proved pointless, they never diagnosed the slipped disc which was gradually finding its way back into place. No, I was to become an outpatient who, every Monday, had to strip to my underpants, get into a bath-like apparatus lined with light bulbs which were switched on; this was called heat treatment. Apart from sweating profusely and losing half a stone, nothing happened except World War II started. I and my bad back were called up and I took with me a recommendation from Dr O'Brien that I needed further heat treatment. On joining my regiment I handed this recommendation to Captain Bently, the Battery doctor, who took it with these words, 'You won't be needing this any more, the marching and fresh air will soon have you better.'

Next I reported that I had night blindness. On guard at night I'd say, 'Halt, who goes there?' When they 'advanced to be recognised', I couldn't see to recognise them. I told Captain Bently, 'I can't see in the dark sir.' He said, 'Nobody can see in the dark. With all the marching and fresh air you will soon be better', and that was that. I still can't see in the dark. I bumped into Captain Bently after the war; he was wearing pebble-lens glasses. I wanted to say 'what you need is marching and fresh air'.

Another great diagnosis was the military doctor at Herstmonceux Hospital. 'That's Dhobis itch,' he said with the nearest dhobi ten thousand miles away. A nurse applied my groins with gentian violet until my willy looked like a painting by Picasso, but much more valuable.

From the war came my first contact with psychiatry. During the battle for Cassino some German, totally unknown to me and without warning, fired a mortar bomb that blew me up – in retrospect, I should have stayed up; alas, I hadn't mastered gravity and I came down again. Crying and stammering (I was also wounded in the leg), I remember, after my wound was dressed, being in a tent with a stern captain psychiatrist who, after asking me to sit down, snapped, 'You're going to get better you understand.' It was a version of 'all the marching and fresh air will make you better'. Despite crying and stammering, I wanted to laugh. He then reeled off this statistic: 'It takes the Germans fifty thousand shells to kill one man.' I wondered who this resilient man was.

Several soldiers, all 'bomb happy' like me, were loaded into a RAMC ambulance. We travelled in stern silence for half an hour, then an Irish soldier said, 'I tink they're querying us.' Eventually we arrived at No. 2 General Military Hospital Caserta, where I came under the care of a Major Palmer. He was the psychiatrist who introduced the revolutionary narcosis treatment for battle fatigue. The patient, in this case me, was given sodium amytal which put me to sleep for three days. In moments of consciousness one was on a sort of high; I remember asking an aged Italian lady cleaner to marry me. Finally, when the effect wore off, Major Palmer saw me, he told me I was an anxiety state chronic, the very name was depressing; I could never return to the battery, I would be confined to bare depot work.

It seems now that illness has governed my life. I have spent the last thirty-five years going from psychiatrist to psychiatrist. From the early days I've noticed a change in their approach. There was a distant aged one, Dr Harry Bramwell, now passed on, his was to 'pull-yourself-together-snap-out-of-it-all-the-marching-and-fresh-air-will-do-you-good'. I thought he was on the verge of prescribing Horlicks three times a day.

Since then I've been under dozens of psychiatrists, but I'm still an anxiety state chronic; perhaps, after all, I need marching in the fresh air. I must close now, my Surmontil is calling.

More Spike Milligan Letters: 1984

Spike wrote a letter to *Private Eye* objecting to the mosque in Regent's Park. He received a reply from Helen Slyomovics and Barry Wilkins saying he was a racist. His answer to their accusation was his opinion on racism. He never altered his views.

To: Helen Slyomovics & Barry Wilkins   *23rd August, 1977*

Dear Helen and Barry,

I am not a racist, the word is used too easily these days, one can blaspheme at the English (Pommie Bastard), at the Irish (Irish jokes about them being stupid), etc. etc. – no one says racist, but it becomes almost an automatic reaction to shout racist to anybody who says anything about Pakistanis, or negroes, etc.

Well, absorb very carefully what I am about to write, and you may understand my letter in Private Eye.

So, I object to a Mosque in Regents Park, to you this means I am a Racist, O.K. I also object to Gothic Churches that have been built in India, does this mean I am a racist as well, if so, then I also hate the English. If you say 'yes', to the last mentioned, don't read any further.

Because, like many people you have become over sensitised, like the people who say, that even if proven and a black murderer is judged guilty, and the jury happens to be white, there are those creeps who shout the jury are racist.

One cannot arrest coloured people anymore, even justifiably without creeps shouting out 'he's a racist'. I am all for each race surviving, I volunteered to fight in the Six Day Israeli War, not to be overwhelmed by the Arabs. Likewise, I also stood for a homeland for the Palestinian people, but what I object to is the destruction of the environment by architecture, which has no harmony with the surroundings. I think a Mosque in the middle of London looks bloody awful, and if you don't think so, then you have no eye for beauty, and we have absolutely nothing in common. Obviously you would like a Zulu

Resting Camp in Hyde Park, so I hope one day they will build one there, so it will please you.

Sincerely,
Spike Milligan

Who once stood on the lines at Whitechapel against Oswald Mosley in 1933.

Adolf Hitler: My Part in His Downfall: 1971

The first volume of his war memoirs. Originally titled 'It'll be all over by Christmas' because that's what his father used to say. We disagreed on the title and he came up with Adolf Hitler: My Part in His Downfall.

How it all started

September 3rd, 1939. The last minutes of peace ticking away. Father and I were watching Mother digging our air-raid shelter. 'She's a great little woman,' said Father. 'And getting smaller all the time,' I added. Two minutes later, a man called Chamberlain who did Prime Minister impressions spoke on the wireless; he said, 'As from eleven o'clock we are at war with Germany.' (I loved the *WE*.) 'War?' said Mother. 'It must have been something we said,' said Father. The people next door panicked, burnt their post office books and took in the washing.

Giant troop-carrying submarines

Almost immediately came the mournful wail of the first Air-Raid Warning. 'Is that you dear?' said Mother. 'It's a Jewish Funeral,' said Father, 'Quick! Put out the begging bowls.' It was in fact the Bata Shoe Factory lunch hooter. It caused chaos until it was changed. Uncle Willie, a pre-death mortician, who hadn't worked for years, started

Giant troop-carrying airships

making small wooden mushrooms. He sent them to Air-Marshal Harris requesting they be dropped on Germany to prove that despite five days of war, British craftsmanship still flourished. They were returned with a note saying, 'Dropping wooden mushrooms during raids might cause unnecessary injury.' My brother Desmond too, seized with pre-pubic patriotism, drew pictures of fantastic war machines. He showed Father: 'Son,' he said, 'these inventions will be the salvation of England.' They wasted no time: carrying the portfolio of drawings in a string bag, they hurried to Whitehall by 74 tram. After several arguments and a scuffle, they were shown into the presence of a curious nose-manipulating Colonel. He watched puzzled as Father laid out drawings of Troop-Carrying Submarines, Tank-Carrying Zeppelins and some of Troops on Rocket-Propelled Skates, all drawn on the backs of old dinner menus. 'Right,' said the Colonel, 'I'll have the brown windsor, roast beef and two veg.' Father and son were then shown the door, the windows, and finally the street. My father objected. 'You fool! By rejecting these inventions you've put two years on the war.' 'Good,' said the Colonel, 'I wasn't doing anything!' Father left. With head held high and feet held higher, he was thrown out.

He took the war very seriously; as time went on so did Neville Chamberlain, he took it so seriously he resigned. 'Good! He's stepping down for a better man,' concluded Father, and wrote off for the job. One Saturday morning, while Mother was at church doing a bulk confession for the family, Father donned an old army uniform and proceeded to transform the parlour into H.Q. Combined Ops. Walls were covered in tatty maps. On the table was a 1927 map of Thomas Tilling's bus routes. Using wooden mushrooms as anti-tank guns, Uncle Willie placed them at various points on the map for the defence of Brockley. My father told the early morning milkman, 'That,' he said tapping the map, 'that is where they'll start their attack on England.'

'That's Africa,' said the puzzled Milkman.

'Ah yes!' said Father, quick to recover, 'But that's where they'll start from – Africa – understand?'

'No I don't,' said the Milkman. Whereupon he was immediately nipped in the scrotum, thrown out, and his horse whipped into a gallop. 'Only two pints tomorrow,' Father shouted after the disappearing cart.

Next morning a Constable arrived at the door.

'Ah, good morning Constable,' said Father raising his steel helmet. 'You're just in time.'

'In time for what sir?'

'In time for me to open the door for you,' said Father, reeling helplessly with laughter.

'Very funny sir,' said the Constable.

'Knew you'd like it,' said Father, wiping tears from his eyes.

'Now what can we do for you, a robbery? a murder? I mean times must be bad for the force, why not slap a writ on Hitler?'

'It's about these barricades you put across the road.'

'Oh? What's wrong with them? We're at war you know.'

'It's not me sir, it's the tram drivers. They're shagged out having to lift them to get through, they've got to come down.'

'You're all fools!' said Father, 'I'll write to Churchill.' He did. Churchill told him to take them down as well.

'He's a bloody fool too,' said Father. 'If he's not careful I'll change sides.'

My father, Leo Milligan   Grandfather William Milligan

I was no stranger to Military Life. Born in India on the Regimental strength, the family on both sides had been Gunners as far back as the Siege of Lucknow. Great-Grandfather, Sergeant John Henry Kettleband, had been killed in the Indian Mutiny, by his wife, his last words were, 'Oh!' His father had died in a military hospital after being operated on for appendicitis by a drunken doctor. On the tombstone was carved –

> R.I.P
> In memory of
> Sgt. Thomas Kettleband.
> 954024731.
>
> Died of appendicitis
> for his King & Country.

Now apparently it was my turn.

One day an envelope marked O.H.M.S. fell on the mat. Time for my appendicitis, I thought.

'For Christ's sake don't open it,' said Uncle, prodding it with a stick. 'Last time I did, I ended up in Mesopotamia, chased by Turks waving pots of Vaseline and shouting, "Lawrence we love you in Ottoman".'

Father looked at his watch, 'Time for another advance,' he said and took one pace forward. Weeks went by, several more O.H.M.S. letters arrived, finally arriving at the rate of two a day stamped URGENT.

'The King must think a lot of you son, writing all these letters,' said Mother as she humped sacks of coal into the cellar. One Sunday, while Mother was repointing the house, as a treat Father opened one of the envelopes. In it was a cunningly worded invitation to partake in World War II, starting at seven and sixpence a week, all found. 'Just fancy,' said Mother as she carried Father upstairs for his bath, 'of all the people in England, they've chosen you, it's a great honour, son.'

Laughingly I felled her with a right cross.

I managed to delay the fatal day. I'll explain. Prior to the war, I was a keep-fit addict. Every morning you could see people counting the bones in my skinny body at Ladywell Recreation Track, as I lifted barbells. Sometimes we were watched by admiring girls from Catford Labour Exchange; among them was one with a tremendous bosom. She looked like the Himalayas on their side. The sight of this released some kind of sex hormones into my being that made me try to lift some impossible weight to impress her. Loading the barbell to one hundred and sixty pounds (about $70) I heaved at the weights, Kerrrrrrrissttt!! an agonised pain shot round my back into my groin, down my leg, and across the road to a bus stop. Crippled and trying to grin, I crawled, cross-eyed with agony, towards the shower rooms. Screams of laughter came from the girls.

'Ohhh yes,' said our neighbour Mrs Windust, 'you've got a rupture comin'. My 'usband 'ad one from birth. Orl fru our courtin' days 'e managed to keep it a secret, 'course, on our 'oneymoon 'e 'ad to show me, and then I saw 'e was 'eld together wiv a Gathorne and Olins advanced leather truss. 'e 'ad to 'ave it remodelled before we could 'ave sectional intercourse.'

Terrified, I hied me to my Hearts of Oak Sick Benefit Hindu Doctor,

Tommy Brettell's Ritz Revels. Yours truly, extreme right, front row

who had a practice in Brockley Rise. 'Oh yes Milligan! You are getting a rupture! I can feel it!' he said inserting curry-stained fingers like red hot pokers in my groin. That diagnosis from a son of the B.M.A. was thirty-five years ago. I'm not ruptured yet. Perhaps I'm a late starter. Rupture! the thought filled me with lumps of fear, why? For three years I had been trumpet player with the Ritz Revels, a bunch of spotty musicians held together with hair oil. They paid ten shillings a gig;* of this I gave Mother nine, who in turn gave seven to the church for the Poor of the Parish. I couldn't understand it, *we* were the Poor of the Parish.

Blowing a trumpet puts a strain on the groin up to chest height, so, every time we did a gig I improvised a truss. I stuffed rags into an old sock until it was packed tight. I then placed it in the predicted rupture spot and attached it to my groin with lengths of tape and string, this gave me a bulge in my trousers that looked like the erection of a stallion. Something had to be done, I mean, if some woman saw it, I could never live up to it, so I tried to reduce the bulge by putting leather straps round me and pulling them tight; nothing happened except my voice went up an octave. It still looked obscene, but Mother came to the rescue; she sewed on an additional length of dyed black curtain

* A one-night stand

which covered the bulge but brought the jacket half way down my thighs. Embarrassed, I explained it away by saying, 'This is the latest style from America, Cab Calloway wears one.' 'He must be a cunt,' said the drummer.

I had bought the evening dress from my Uncle Alf of Catford for thirty-eight shillings, the suit was tight, but so was money, so I bought it. For weeks I played in my leather harness trussed up like a Turkey.

After a month I got saddle sores and went to the doctor, who passed me on to a vet, in turn, he reported me to the police as a Leather Pervert. The pain in my back persisted, sometimes I couldn't move for it. What I had was a slipped disc, a condition then unknown to the world of medicine. But to get a 'bad back' at the same time as your call-up rings as hollow as a naked wife in bed with the lodger saying the laundry's late. (In my case it was true, the laundry was late.) I was put in Lewisham General Hospital under observation. I think a nurse did it through a hole in the ceiling. Specialists seeking security in numbers came in bunches of four to examine me. They prodded me, then stepped back to see what happened. 'He's still alive,' said one. They then hit me all over with rubber mallets and kept saying to each other 'what do you think?' Days later a card arrived saying 'Renal Colic'.

The old man in the next bed leaned over and said in a hoarse voice, 'Git aht of here son. I come in 'ere wiv vericose veins and they took me 'pendix aht.'

'Thanks,' I said, 'my name's Milligan.'

'Mine's Ethel Martin,' he said.

'Ethel? It says Dick on your chart.'

'I was when I come in, somewhere between there and 'ere.' He pointed in an obvious direction.

'The unkindest cut of all?'

'They got me mixed up with someone who wanted to be sterilized. How do you tell your wife you ain't what she thinks you are?'

'Don't tell her, show her!'

'I'll think about it.'

'From now on that's all you will be able to do about it.'

Those sons of fun at the hospital, having failed to diagnose my ailment, discharged me with a letter recommending electrical treatment, and headed 'To whom it may concern' – I suppose that meant me. It was now three months since my call-up. To celebrate I hid under the bed dressed as Florence Nightingale. Next morning I received a card asking me to attend a medical at the Yorkshire Grey, Eltham. 'Son,' said Father, 'I think after all you better go, we're running out of disguises, in any case when they see you, they're bound to send you home.' The card said I was to report at 9.30 a.m. 'Please be prompt.' I arrived prompt at 9.30 and was seen promptly at 12.15. We were told to strip. This revealed a mass of pale youths with thin, white, hairy legs. A press photographer was stopped by the recruiting Sergeant. 'For Christ's sake don't! If the public saw a photo of this lot they'd pack it in straight away.' I arrived in the presence of a grey-faced, bald doctor.

'How do you feel?' he said.

'All right,' I said.

'Do you feel fit?'

'No, I walked here.'

Grinning evilly, he wrote Grade 1 (One) in blood red ink on my card. 'No black cap?' I said. 'It's at the laundry,' he replied.

The die was cast. It was a proud day for the Milligan family as I was taken from the house. 'I'm too young to go,' I screamed as Military Policemen dragged me from my pram, clutching a dummy. At Victoria Station the R.T.O. gave me a travel warrant, a white feather and a picture of Hitler marked 'This is your enemy.' I searched every compartment, but he wasn't on the train. At 4.30, June 2nd, 1940, on a summer's day all mare's tails and blue sky we arrived at Bexhill-on-Sea, where I got off. It wasn't easy. The train didn't stop there.

Small Dreams of a Scorpion: 1972

Spike's first serious poetry book.

Death Wish

Bury me anywhere,
Somewhere near a tree
Some place where a horse will graze
And gallop over me.
Bury me
Somewhere near a stream,
When she floods her banks
I'll give her thanks
For reaching out to me.
So bury me – bury me
In my childhood scene;
But please –
don't burn me
In Golders Green.

Italy 1944

Oberon

The flowers in my garden
grow down.
Their colour is pain
Their fragrance sorrow.
Into my eyes grow their roots
feeling for tears
To nourish the black
hopeless rose
within me.

Nervous breakdown
Bournemouth
Feb 1967

My favourite.

The New Rose

The new rose
   trembles with early beauty
The babe sees the beckoning carmine
   the tiny hand
   clutches the cruel stem.
The babe screams
The rose is silent –
Life is already telling lies.

                  Orme Court, London
                      Feb 1967

Love Song

If I could write words
Like leaves on an Autumn Forest floor
What a bonfire my letters would make.
If I could speak words of water
You would drown when I said
'I love you'.

Adolf Hitler: My Part in His Downfall: 1971

Dieppe

On August 18th, 1942, we were learning how to shoot Bren and Vickers machine-guns at Fairbright. The range was on the cliff facing out to sea. Our instructors were from the Brigade of Guards. We stood at ease while a Grenadier Guards Sergeant told us the intricacies of the 'Vickers 303 Water-Cooled Machine-Gun. I will first teach yew which is the safe end and which is the naughty end. Next, I will show ew how to load, point and fire the weapon. Following this, I will dismantle the gun and reassemble it. It's not difficult; I have a three-year-old daughter at home who does it in six minutes. Anyone here fired one before?' I had, but I wasn't going to fall into the trap. Never volunteer for *anything* in the army. So the day started. It was worth it just to hear the military repartee. 'What's the matter with you man, point the bloody gun at the target, I've seena blind crippled hunchback shoot straighter than that! Don't close yer eyes when you pull the trigger! Remember Mummy wants you to grow up a brave little soldier, doesn't she? You're firing into the ground man! We're supposed to shoot the Germans not bloody worms! Steady, you're snatching the trigger, squeeze it slowly, like a bird's tits. Left-handed are you? Well, I'm sorry we can't have the weapon rebuilt for you, you'll have to learn to be right-handed for the duration.' Then, to little Flash Gordon, who got in a hopeless mess trying to load the Bren. 'No no son, tell you what, you go and stand behind that tree and say the Lord's Prayer and ask him to tell you to STOP WASTING MY BLOODY TIME!' The day was alive with these sayings.

It all ended badly for me. As we climbed on the three tonner to go back to Billets, Driver Jenkins slammed the tail-board on my right hand. It came up like a balloon and I don't mind saying I was cross-eyed with agony. They took me to Hastings, to St Helen's Hospital, to have it X-rayed. I had no broken bones. They bandaged the hand up and put my arm in a sling. What a bloody hang-up. I was going on leave the next day.

By now my father had rejoined the army as a captain in the R.A.O.C., and the family were living at Linden House, Orchard Way, Reigate. I arrived home after dark, having had difficulty getting a lift from the station. My mother and father were not given to drinking in pubs, so after dinner I went into the Bell, which stood at the crossroads near our house. Of course this was the day of the raid on Dieppe and its heroic failure. It was in the papers and on the radio. Some of the Battery trucks had been commandeered to pick up some of the survivors at Peacehaven. Lance Bombardier Lees drove one truck and told me of seeing the survivors come home. They were all silent, their faces painted black; they came ashore with hardly a word said; some of the badly wounded had died on the way back. What can anyone say? Anyhow, that evening when I walked into the pub with my hand all in new white bandages I was on to free drinks for the night. An elderly, dignified man came across and said to me, 'Would you care to have a drink with me and my friends?' I said 'Yes', and, seeing it was free, I had a Scotch. After a few words of conversation the elderly man said, 'What was it like, son?'

'What was what like?' I said.

'Oh come on son. No need to be modest.'

'Honestly, I don't know what you mean.'

The elderly man winked at his friends and nodded approvingly towards me. Then it hit me. Dieppe. Had I been to Dieppe? If I said no, the chance of a lifetime to drink free all night would be thrown away. Yes. I had been to Dieppe, a whisky please, yes, we went in and, Cheers, I was in the last wave, another whisky please, anyhow I crawled towards this pill-box, a brandy then, and ...

That night my mother put me to bed; for two hours I had been a hero, something I had never been before and would never be again.

A Book of Goblins: 1978

Norris Pigdrench
A Nothing Goblin

Please tell me the way to Nowhere,
 That's where I want to go!
For somewhere out in Nowhere
 There's a Ying Tong Iddle I Po.

I have come from Somewhere
Which is something miles away;
Perhaps when I get to Nowhere
 The Fonnies will be at play.
 Now, if I'm going Nowhere
 I must carry a posey of dill
And the way to get to Nowhere
Is to hurry and stand quite still.

I'm on my way to Nowhere
Where the Golapins fill the air
And at the speed I'm standing still
By golly I'll soon be there.

Tim O'Prafer
A Catholic Goblin

'Oh earnest clerical Goblin
How do you get so holy?'
'By saying my prayers in bed at night
And eating roly-poly.'

'Oh earnest clerical Goblin
How long have you been a vicar?'
'No, I'm a Catholic priest', he said,
'Promotion there's much quicker'.

The Spike Milligan Letters: 1977

This was in 1968. How prescient! Spike hated the nanny state. Imagine the barrage of letters had he been alive today.

5th June, 1968

Dear Miss Hewitt,

Thank you for your letter which confirms that dictatorship exists in our lives. I find it becoming increasingly unbearable to accept England as a democracy.

We are all gradually being seduced from freedom by laws.

You realise that when citizens in a country are tied down at every level by unending laws, it is just an inversion of Communism and Fascism.

You are (the GPO), in fact, telling me what kind of furniture I should have in my office.

If you don't find this outrageous, then obviously you have been thoroughly indoctrinated into the system.

There is no need to send your engineers because the antique phones have *not* been connected.

However, I intend personally to get the law changed. Somebody has got to fight against this monstrous thing called State.

I am throwing in my lot with the students.

Respectfully,
Spike Milligan

Spike bought me an antique phone for my office.

To: Inspector Haines,
Harrow Road Police Station,
London W2   *16th May, 1972*

Dear Sir,

Milligan versus Dog Shit
Case Number 2.

On Sunday the 7th May at about 11.30 am. a large black dog defecated on the pavement, I called the creature and said 'Come here Darling', and saw that its label bore the address – Burnham Court, Moscow Road, and the dog's name was Liz. A fitting Royal name for a debasement of the Royal city.

Would you please prosecute?

Sincerely,
Spike Milligan

After his haemorrhoid operation.

To: Dr Philip H. Moore   *27th March, 1972*

Dear Dr Moore,

Ｈow dare you send me a bill. I was conscious throughout the operation and my screams were recorded as far away as Houndsditch.

Signed: Bottomless Milligan

P.S. Charge me all that money, you must think my purse is bottomless, well it's not anymore.

To: The Editor,
Rand Daily Mail,
Johannesburg   *20th August, 1976*

Sir,

Ｉ have just received an incredible cutting from your newspaper,
showing two porcupines, one called Spike and one called Milligan.
You realise that this has turned me into a bisexual schizophrenic.
You will be hearing from my solicitor in the morning.

                                                   Sincerely,
                                                   Spike Milligan

P.S. My solicitor is called Harry Secombe, and he is two Aardvark.

For me, this is a typical Milligan.
Spike had made friends with a Father Patrick Fury. They had corresponded quite
frequently, until this letter.

28th March, 1975

Dear Father,

Just a brief note to ask how you are and whether the post-operative
condition is satisfactory.

I did enjoy my stay in Rhodesia, and of course that miraculous quality called sunshine was everywhere, but never in the shade.

I saw a wonderful panorama of wild beasts and I, deep down, was
hoping that in 200 years' time all these creatures may still exist, but
somehow I have my doubts. How can world population explode as it
is, and still leave room for animals?

One day, dear Patrick, when the Vatican is filled with the beds of
overflowing families our dear Pope might shout out enough is enough,
and at communion, not only give out the Host, but also the pill, it
would be a perfect combination, spiritual and physical salvation. So
spread the word dear Patrick.

Love, light and peace,
Spike Milligan

Unfortunately Father Patrick Fury did not see eye to eye with Spike — and wrote and told
him the friendship must end.

This is Spike's attempt to re-establish communication. It did.

Dear Pat,

Perhaps by now you 'Fury' at me over the Pope will have cooled, people are allowed opinions, and I was voicing mine, if I were to be angered by every opinion I didn't agree with I would die of apoplexy. In case you were not aware, I still consider myself a 'thinking' Christian, and I therefore disagree with much of the Papal Dogma. because it starts to become ridiculous in the

light of a changing world, and I don't want it to be ridiculous, so I have to speak up, after all Jesus did, he spoke out against his own religion — Im sure many faithful religious Jews must have reacted very much the way you reacted to me. I still haven't changed, but I dislike being at odds with you because you are a nice man —
If Im in Liverpool again — would you have dinner with me
                    Love, Light & Peace
                    Spike Milligan

Adolf Hitler: My Part in His Downfall: 1971

Algiers

On January 18th, 1943, I wrote in my diary: 'Arrived Algiers at Dawn.' Harry and I got up early to enjoy the sight of Africa at first light. We saw it bathed in a translucent, pre-dawn purple aura. Seagulls had joined us again. A squadron of American Lockheed Lightnings circled above. The coast was like a wine-coloured sliver, all the while coming closer. The visibility grew as the sun mounted the sky; there is no light so full of hope as the dawn; amber, resin, copper lake, brass green. One by one, they shed themselves until the sun rose golden in a white sky. Lovely morning warmth. I closed my eyes and turned my face to the sun. I fell down a hatchway. 'Awake!' said Harry down the hole, 'for Morning in the Bowl of Night, Has flung the Stone that puts the Stars to flight. Omar Khayyam.' 'Get stuffed, Spike Milligan.' The convoy was now in line ahead making for the port. Gradually the buildings of Algiers grew close. The city was built on a hill, and tiered, most build-ings were white. We were closing to the dockside. Activity. Khaki fig-ures were swarming everywhere. Trucks, tanks, aircraft, guns, shells, all were being offloaded. Odd gendarmes looked helpless, occasionally blew whistles, pointed at Arabs, then hit them. They'd lost the war and by God they were going to take it out on someone. Now we could see palm tree-lined boulevards. We made the last raid on the canteen, stocked up with fags, chocolate and anything. In full F.S.M.O. (pro-nounced Effessmmmoh) we paraded on deck. I tell you, each man had so much kit it reminded me of that bloody awful Warsaw Concerto. A Bombardier came round and distributed little booklets saying: 'Customs and Habits of French North Africa. How to behave. The Currency. Addresses of Post-Brothel Military Clinics.' And a contraceptive. Only one? They must be expecting a short war. Harry Edgington was horri-fied. 'Look at this,' he said, his lovely face dark with rage, 'putting temptation in a man's hands.' Whereupon he hurled it overboard. Others blew them up and paddled them ashore shouting 'Happy New

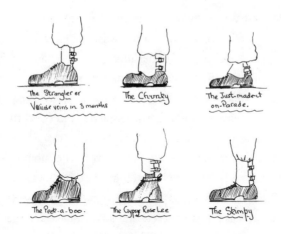

Gaiter styles, spotted on day of disembarkation at Algiers

Year'. Down came the gang-planks and the 56th Heavy Regiment, ten days at sea, heavier than it had ever been, debouched.

There were no transports save those to carry kit-bags and luggage. Chalky White and I were lucky again. 'You two stay behind. Supervise the loading of all Battery kit-bags on to that three-tonner.'

Unloading went on all day. The harbour was glutted with ships unloading war supplies and what occasionally looked suspiciously like Three Piece Suites. Throughout the dusty day the cranes were lifting and dipping, like herons fishing. Our Battery baggage was identified by colour. A blue square with a yellow stripe up the middle. We rode up and down in cargo nets. Puzzled Algerians watched us as we arose from the bowels of the ship singing Ann Zeigler and Webster Booth melodies. Ever present were the Arabs, waiting to nick things, but it was easy to stop them. You hit 'em. It was appalling to see a people so impoverished. They wore rags, they were second-class citizens, they were degraded. It hurt most when you saw the children. I'm bloody glad I wasn't French. Even better, I'm glad I wasn't an Arab. But seriously, folks! By sunset, the job was completed and we were exhausted by a day's hard singing in the nets. Lieutenant Hughes fell us in. We marched through the palm-lined streets, into a vast concrete football stadium. On the pitch were scores of tents. It must have been half-time

I thought. But no! They were the bivouacs of a Scots Battalion, just back from the front. Hanging on the washing lines were battle-scarred kilts. It must have been hell under there! It was a vast concrete football stadium. I mention that again in the nature of an encore. All the action was around a field kitchen. Several queues all converged on one point where a cook, with a handle-bar moustache, and of all things a monocle, was doling out. He once had a glass eye that shot out when he sneezed and fell in the porridge so he wore the monocle as a sort of optical condom. He doled out something into my mess tin. 'What is it?' I asked. 'Irish Stew,' he said. 'Then', I replied, 'Irish Stew in the name of the Law.' It was a vast concrete arena. We queued for an hour. When that had passed we queued for blankets. Next, find somewhere to sleep, like a football stadium in North Africa. We dossed down on the terraces. After ship's hammocks it was murder. If only, if *only* I had a grand piano. I could have slept in that. Anything was better than a vast concrete arena. At dawn my frozen body signalled me, arise. I stamped around the freezing terraces to get warm. I lit up a fag and went scrounging. There were still a few embers burning in the field kitchen. I found a tea urn full of dead leaves from which I managed to get a fresh brew. A sentry turned up. 'Bleedin' cold, ain't it,' he said. 'Yes,' I replied, and he seemed well pleased with the answer. After all, it was free and unsolicited. I shared the tea with him. 'My name's Eric Rushton,' he said. 'In Civvy Street I'm a porter in Covent Garden.' Good, I thought, there's nothing like coming to Algiers to meet a fruit porter called Rushton. Who knows, before sun-up, I might even meet an apprentice gas-fitter's mate called Dick Scroogle from Lewisham. If so, he'd have to hurry as dawn's left hand was already in the sky. A small man in an overcoat drew nigh.

'You're not Dick Scroogle from Lewisham, are you?'

'No,' he said, 'people keep asking me that.' I gave him some tea. It had been a near thing. Gradually the sun came up. There was no way of stopping it. It rose from the east like an iridescent gold Napoleon. It filled the dawn sky with swathes of pink, orange and flame. Breakfast was Bully Beef and hard tack. I washed and shaved under a tap, icy cold, still, it was good for the complexion. 'Gunners! Stay lovely for your Commanding Officer with Algerian Football Stadium water!' I stood at the gates watching people in the streets. I made friends with two little French kids on their way to school, a girl and a boy. I gave them two English pennies. In exchange they gave me an empty match-box, with a camel label on the top. I shall always remember their faces. A gentle voice behind me. 'Where the bleedin' 'ell you bin?' It was Jordy Dawson. 'Come on, we're off to the docks.' And so we were.

Arriving there we checked that all D Battery kit bags were on board our lorries, then drove off. The direction was east along the coast road to Jean Bart. We sat with our legs dangling over the tail-board. Whenever we passed French colonials, some of them gave us to under-stand that our presence in the dark continent was not wanted by a sim-ple explicative gesture from the waist down. We passed through dusty scrub like countryside with the sea to our left. In little batches we passed Arabs with camels or donkeys, children begging or selling Tangerines and eggs. The cactus fruit was all ripe, pillar-box red. I hadn't seen any since I was a boy in India. The road curved gradually and the land gradient rose slightly and revealed to us a grand view of the Bay of Algiers. Rich blue, with morning sunshine tinselling the waves. Our driver 'Hooter Price' (so called because of a magnificent large nose shaped like a Pennant. When he swam on his back, people shouted 'Sharks') was singing 'I'll be seeing you' as we jostled along the dusty road. It was twenty-six miles to our destination, with the mysterious name 'X Camp,' situated just half a mile inland at Cap Matifou. X Camp was proving an embarrassment to Army Command. It was built to house German prisoners of war. Somehow we hadn't managed to get any, so, to give it the appearance of being a success, 56 Heavy Regiment were marched in and told that this was, for the time being, 'home.' When D Battery heard this, it was understandable when roll call was made the first morning:

'Gunner Devine?'

'Ya wol!'

'Gunner Spencer?'

Dawn of the Burnt Bum Affair

'Ya!'

'Gunner Maunders?'

'Ya wold.'

The march of the Regiment from the ship to Cap Matifou had been a mild disaster. It started in good march style, but gradually, softened by two weeks at sea, and in full F.S.M.O., two-thirds of the men gradually fell behind and finally everyone was going it alone at his own pace. A long string of men stretched over twenty-six miles. I quote from Major Chaterjack's recollection of the incident in a letter he wrote to me in 1957. 'Perhaps some will remember the landing at Algiers and that ghastly march with full kit, for which we were not prepared. The march ended after dark, somewhere beyond Maison Blanche, and was rather a hard initiation into war – a valuable initiation though, for it made many things thereafter seem easier!' To top it all there was a tragedy – Driver Reed, who flaked out on the march, tried to hop a lift but fell between the lorry and trailer and was squashed to death. The only way to unstick him from the road was by pulling at his webbing straps. Tragedy number two was Gunner Leigh, thirty-six (old for a soldier); as he arrived at the camp he received a telegram telling him his wife and three children had been killed in a raid on Liverpool. He went insane and never spoke again. He is still in a mental home near Menston in Yorkshire.

Sanitary Orderly Liddel was learning the trade of maintenance on the outdoor hole-in-the-ground latrines. The lime powder that is normally used to 'sprinkle' the pit, had not arrived. He, being of an inventive turn of mind, mixed petrol and diesel and used that. Dawn! Enter an R.S.M. pleasure bent! He squats on pole. Lights pipe, drops match. BOOOOOOOOM! There emerges smoke-blackened figure, trousers down, smouldering shirt tail, singed eyebrows, second degree burns on bum – a sort of English loss of face.

He was our last casualty before we actually went into action. Next time it would be for real.

The Bedside Milligan: 1969

Little tiny puppy dog
Sleeping Soundly as a log
Better wake him for his dinner
Or else he'll start to sleep much thinner.

'Rommel?' 'Gunner Who?': 1974

Spike dedicated this second volume of his war memoirs to his brother. The dedication read:

> To my dear brother Desmond who made my boyhood happy and with whom I have never had a cross word, mind you he drives his wife mad.

Desmond and I roared with laughter over this fantasy. They used to argue like hell.

March 13th. The mail had arrived. Everyone went mad!

I had one from Mum and Dad, one from Lily, and Ohhh ArGGGGHHHHHHH! Three from Louise of Bexhill. AHGGGHHHH-HHHHHH. Help! I'm going blind. My father had rejoined the Army as a Captain in the RAOC. He was over fifty, but using glazier's putty, and blacking his bald head with boot polish, looked forty-nine. My brother Desmond was working as a runner-cum-slave to a press photographer's in Fleet Street, and was in the middle of all the fire raids and frequently came home smoke blackened, but whistling cheerfully. This caused mother to worry. She got Doctor O'Brien to prescribe whisky to 'relax her.' Every evening she would open the front window, sip whisky, and listen for Desmond's whistling. By the time he arrived mother was so relaxed she was stretched out in the passage.

All the mail didn't bring good news. Sgt Dale says ' 'Ere! My missus has run off with a bleedin' Polish airman!' 'That's funny, so 'as mine. They must be short of planes.' Other letters were from Beryl Southby

Gunner Milligan happily playing his H.P. Trumpet at De La
Warr Pavilion, Bexhill, while his mates keep his birds from
killing him

— a Norwood girl who had a crush on me, and one from Kay in
Herstmonceaux — I must have pulled the birds in those days but I don't
remember working at it, however, it got complicated, as this letter of
Edgington recalls:

> '*Then — how about the night at the De-La-Warr Pavilion, when it took seven
> of us to get all your "birds" safely out of the place at the end of the evening
> whilst you "peeled-off" secretly with the eighth — the latest! Kay, the dazzling
> blonde from Herstmonceaux who had been waiting behind the dressing-room
> door with a pair of scissors clutched in her hands during the interval! — Did
> you know about that!!!??? Doug was first man into the room in the interval*

and walked right into her, as Alf arrived, he was needed to help Doug in the struggle to "unarm" her and as I came in, she was crying and they were trying to mollify her …

You never showed up! If you were out in the auditorium you were still taking your life in your hands for they were all there – the two Bettys among them, flexing long fingernails, even Pearl the NAAFI girl was looking very unhappy, and there was one of the sergeant's wives I remember. (It's all lies folks! S.M.) Anyway, came the finish of the evening with Jimmy, Chalky and I nervously shepherding three of them up the left-hand (as you looked out from the stage) raised aisle or gallery where all the seating was: Well, we were just getting towards the far end of it and there were some three rows of triple cinema seats already pushed up tight against the wooden wall, that overlooked the dance floor. As we were coming up to these, I saw an army boot sticking out from the mass of steel legs. There must be another one somewhere I thought. Being on the inside, nearest to the chairs, I took one step rather more quickly and stopped and turned to the girls, so as to keep their attention up at me. I risked a look down at where the head that belonged to the boot ought to be. Sure enough, there it was (at the right distance from the boot), the Milligan features all screwed up into the usual huge grinning wink. Remember? It's a pity you didn't get that one into the book, for it has, despite all the shagging that was undoubtedly going on, a far happier and more humorous ring to it than all the other yarns about your "amours".

Well folks! if that's all true, I didn't know when I was well off!

Hitlergram No. 361

The scene: The Eagles Eyrie, in the bath are Hitler, Admiral Doenitz and Goebbels. Doenitz is playing with the German Navy.

HITLER: Vat do zey mean, 'Get stuffed'.

GOEBBELS: Zey are having zer breakfast, and he is vishing zem 'get stuffed' wiz zer food.

HITLER: So, we have broken an nudder of zere codes; now, what is zer 'Bollocks' and 'Up yours'?

GOEBBELS: I do not know Führer.

HITLER: (foaming at the mouth) Vhy don't you know, you little crippled creep!

He smashes the bath water with his fists and hits Doenitz below the plimsoll line.

ADMIRAL DOENITZ: Ach – mein bollocks!!

HITLER: Vonderschoen! anudder British Code has been broken! I promote you from Admiral Doenitz to Field Marshal Goering!

A knock on the door in Nazi.

HITLER: Who is zat!

VOICE: Martin Bormann, I have zer message for you.

HITLER: Slide it under the door.

Sound of Bormann grunting.

BORMANN: It won't go under.

HITLER: Vy not?

BORMANN: It's in mein head.

Hitler goes into a fury, bites his sponge to pieces, stops when he notices Goebbels doing something which will surely drive him blind.

HITLER: Stop zat! Or I'll never go to zer pictures wiz you again.

A wafer thin head covered in blood comes straining under the door.

MARTIN BORMANN: I haff done it mein Führer!

All his life Spike was haunted by the death of Tony Goldsmith. He spoke of him frequently.

Personal Tribute
Lieutenant A. M. Goldsmith

Flight Lieutenant Terence Rattigan writes:–

The loss in action of Anthony Goldsmith, at the age of 31, will be most bitterly felt not only by his many personal friends but by all those who, through his writing, recognized his great gifts and were hopeful of the promise they gave. I have known him intimately for most of his life, for we were at Harrow together, and later at Oxford, where Tony was an exhibitioner of Balliol. His quiet humour, deep intelligence, and gentle, unfailing charm endeared him at length to many whom his shyness and modesty at first repelled. His outlook and views, though never at all forcibly expressed, might have appeared at times to the unthinking acquaintance as too self-consciously heterodox. They were in fact the product of his extreme honesty, his tolerant understanding of human weaknesses, and his exceptionally adult mind. He was witty in the best sense: he combined the happiest knack of phrase with a warmth and a generosity that put malice out of bounds. His remarks were freely quoted, but were never made for that purpose. Indeed, so poor – from the standpoint of the professional wit – was his delivery, so grave and unassuming his manner, that it was often with a shock of surprise that one realized that one had heard – but barely heard – an observation at once breath-takingly honest and brilliantly funny.

The same delicious and distinctive quality pervaded his writing. Very little time was granted him in which to make his mark as an author – barely three years between his decision to devote his life to writing and his joining the Royal Artillery. Much of that time was spent in a painstaking and devoted translation of

Hitler chalking slogans in Downtown Berlin Gents Toilet after hearing of the fall of Longstop

Flaubert's 'L'Education Sentimentale,' which many critics found a model of the translator's art. Of original work he has left pitifully little – two plays, one unproduced, a few short stories, and some articles of which a review of the modern theatre in a recent issue of *Horizon* affords an excellent specimen. Little enough to console us – and we were many – who had faith in his right to success and fame. Yet, perhaps those who loved him may take this consolation. Tony, the first to laugh at the futility of the violent passions and the last to covet a hero's laurels, died fighting gladly against that evil which, above all things else, he loathed and despised with a hatred alien to his very gentle nature.

24 April. Fighting on Long Stop at a crescendo all day. O.P. under murderous fire – support group at bottom of hill also under heavy shell fire. Gunner Collins hit in hand. At about 11.10 I heard the dreadful news, Lt Goldsmith had been killed. Alf Fildes noted in his diary 'Learn with regret we have lost our best officer.'

I went back to my cave and wept. I remember calling his name. After a few minutes I straightened up, but the memory of that day remains vivid. Apparently, he and Bdr Edwards were sheltering in a fox hole. '*We were under mortar attack, we sat facing each other, our knees touching. Tony had the map board on his chest, his arms folded round it. Suddenly, I was blown out of the trench. I went to get back in and I saw that Tony had been hit by a mortar bomb in the chest, he died instantly. ...*' All the boys came back very shaken. 'God knows how the Infantry stick that for two weeks at a time ...' Bdr Dodds was so 'bomb happy' he went to hospital and never came back. For someone as splendid, kind, intelligent and witty as Tony to be killed outraged my sensibilities. His friend, Terence Rattigan, wrote a personal Obituary in *The Times*. I remember his last words to me. He was about to leave for Longstop.

'It won't be long now, I'd say Tunis in 10 days,' he was patting his pockets, 'Blast I'm out of cigarettes.' I gave him 5 of mine, 'Here sir, have 5 of my soap-saturated Passing Clouds, a holy medal in every packet ...'

He took them, smiled, tapped the driver on the shoulder and said, 'To battle!'

The Mirror Running: 1987

Spike's tribute to Lieutenant Anthony Goldsmith.

Longstop Hill, 22 April 1943

That April day
Seems far away
The day they decided to kill
Lieutenant Tony Goldsmith RA
On the slopes of Longstop Hill.

At Toukabeur
The dawn lights stir,
Whose blood today will spill?
Today it's Tony Goldsmith's
Seeping out on Longstop Hill.

One can't complain
Nor ease the pain
Or find someone to fill
The place of Tony Goldsmith
Lying dead on Longstop Hill.

In Germany
There still might be
A Joachim, Fritz or Will
Who did for Tony Goldsmith
That day – on Longstop Hill.

The Little Potboiler: 1963

Questions, Quistions & Quoshtions

Daddy how does an elephant feel
When he swallows a piece of steel?
Does he get drunk
And fall on his trunk
Or roll down the road like a wheel?

Daddy what would a pelican do
If he swallowed a bottle of glue?
Would his beak get stuck
Would he run out of luck
And lose his job at the zoo?

Son tell me tell me true,
If I belted you with a shoe,
Would you fall down dead?
Would you go up to bed?
– Either of those would do.

Contagion!

Elephants are contagious!
    Be careful how you tread.
An Elephant that's been trodden on
    Should be confined to bed!

Leopards are contagious too.
    Be careful tiny tots.
They don't give you a temperature
    But lots and lots – of spots.

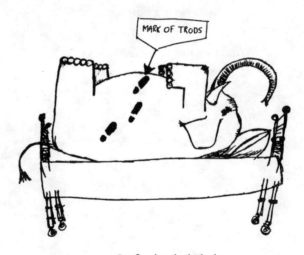

Confined-to-bed Elephant

The Herring is a lucky fish,
From all disease inured.
Should he be ill when caught at sea;
Immediately – he's cured!

People who live in glass houses
Should pull the blinds
When removing their trousers.

Return to Sorrento (3rd Class)

I must go down to the sea again,
To the lonely sea and the sky,
I left my vest and socks there,
I wonder if they're dry?

Arithmetic

One and one are two,
   Two and two are four.
I only wish to goodness
   There wasn't any more!

Adding and subtracting,
   Really, what's the use?
When Winston Churchill was at school
   They say he was a goose.

Yet he became Prime Minister
   And help'd us win the war.
That's 'cause he didn't waste his time
   On two and two are four.

Bump!

Things that go 'bump!' in the night,
Should not really give one a fright.
It's the hole in each ear
That lets in the fear,
That, and the absence of light!

Small Dreams of a Scorpion: 1972

New Members Welcome

Pull the blinds
> on your emotions
Switch off your face.
Put your love into neutral.
This way to the human race.

> London, April 1971

GOD MADE NIGHT
BUT
MAN MADE DARKNESS

2B or not 2B

When I was small and five
I found a pencil sharpener alive!
He lay in lonely grasses
Looking for work.
I bought a pencil for him
He ate and ate until all that was
Left was a pile of wood dust.
It was the happiest pencil sharpener
I ever had.

If I die in War
You remember me
If I live in Peace
You don't.

Dip the Puppy: 1974

When Spike was drawing two of the characters, 'The Magician Mr Sloppy Knickers' and 'Woolly Monkey Playing The Piano', he said he knew instinctively the children would fall in love with these two more than all the other characters. His reasoning: 'Sloppy Knickers' they would think rude and it would bring masses of giggles, and 'Monkey' because he had such a lovely face.

There was once a mummy dog, her name was Pom-Pom and she had 3 baby puppies, one black, called Splot, one brown, called Bing, and a white one called Dip. Splot and Bing could both go "Bow wow, woof woof," but poor Dip went "Meiow meiow" like a pussy cat! "What's the matter with you Dip?" said his mummy "dogs dont go Meiow, so Dip tried again" but he still went "Meiow" and all the other doggies all laughed at Dip, poor little Dip was very sad. For 2 weeks he tried to go "Bow wow" but every time, he went "Meiow". Every

one made fun of little Dip, So one
night, Dip ran away from home, he
crept out the back door and went and
hid in the woods. It was very dark
and cold and a big storm came and
it started to rain, Dip got wet and
cold, he sat on the ground and cried,
Just then a snail rushed up at 50
miles a year; "Look out puppy! you're
right in the middle of a very busy snail
road, you better be careful theres another snail rushing by here any year now!"
Dip said "Please do you know some where
I can sleep? The snail said "Yes" and he
took Dip to a hole in the ground (Big Deal!)
and shouted "Anyone in?   Up popped a

NIBBLES THE RABBIT.

pink spotted rabbit wearing glasses "My name is Nibbles" he said "Can this puppy sleep in your den to night?" said snail "Yes, as long as he hasn't got any fleas" said Nibbles, so down the hole went Dip and they came to a lovely little rabbits room, on the floor was nice clean straw and grass and it was warm and cosy. Nibbles gave Dip some carrots and mushrooms, then Nibbles played the banjo and sang furry songs

I am a funny Rabbit,
I'm pink with spots of red,
But now my ears are tired,
So, I think I'll go to bed.

"Do you know any songs Dip?" said Nibbles.
"Yes I do" said Dip who stood on a chair

and sang

> Oh there was a little boy
> His name was Jimmy Brown
> But everytime he gave a sneeze
> His trousers they fell down!

They both laughed and went to bed in the straw. Next morning Nibbles woke Dip up with a nice cup of tea and some nuts. "Where are you going now? said Nibbles. who was combing his ears. "I don't know" said Dip "I've run away from home because I can't bark like a doggie, I keep going meiow". Nibbles said "Oh dear, that's very serious, but I know a flying fox called Flip-flap who can help you". Off they went and they came to an old ruined church, and

hanging upside down from inside the roof
was Flip-flap and he was singing an upside
down song

I'm singing hanging upside down
Some people think I'm silly
But that's how God has made me
So I'm not a silly Billy

When he saw Dip he said "Well, what do you
want, hurry up or I'll put a flea on your
tail?" So Dip told him he could'nt bark.
"Ah! said Flipflap "I know a great Wizard
called Mr Sloppy-knickers who might help
you, but he lives a long way away on top
of a mountain, and you have to cross
a river full of crocodiles, so be very, very

careful". Dip said he was frightened to go on his own. "I'll come with you and be your friend" said Nibbles. So Dip and Nibbles started on their long journey. First they came to a great sandy desert, and the sun was so hot if you touched a rock it burnt you, and it would melt your chocolate. "Oh dear I'm so thirsty" said Dip "If we don't get some water soon we'll die of thirsty". Just then they saw a beautiful green and yellow snake going along and it said "Sssss, if you want some water follow me," but he went so fast they had to run to keep up with him. The snake took them to some big rocks and coming out of one was a lovely stream of cool water!

The beautiful green and
yellow Snake

Correspondence: 1977

Spike was enthralled by The Country Diary of an Edwardian Lady. *This is a letter to the publishers.*

31st May, 77

Dear Dick,

As the phone is no longer a reliable means of communication, I <u>write</u> to tell what sheer delight it was to get the book, 'Country Diary of an Edwardian lady'. <u>What</u> a delight! to have the 4 seasons locked within its covers – it's a book that sings in your hand. Reading it, I feel in love with that lady of seventy years ago –

Thank you all.
Spike

'Rommel?' 'Gunner Who?': 1974

Feb. 13th 1943. This morning, tired of those coughing, scratching Reveilles, I took my trumpet and blew a swing bugle call. Chalky White appeared from under a blanket with a severe attack of face and eyes with blood-filled canals. 'Whose bloody side are you on!' he groaned. Odd silent soldiers, hands in pockets, eating utensils tucked under arms, were making their way to the Field Kitchen. Our Cook, Gunner May, a dapper lad with curly black hair and Ronald Colman moustache was doling out Porridge. He spoke with a very posh voice and Porridge.

'Where'd you get that accent Ronnie?' asked Gunner Devine.

'Eton old sausage.'

'Well I'd stop eatin' old sausages,' says Devine.

With a flick of the wrist, May sent a spoonful of Porridge into Devine's eye. 'Good for night blindness,' he says ducking a mug of tea.

From Setif the road to the front ran fairly straight. During a halt, along comes a pregnant American staff car that gave birth to an American called Eisenhower. The driver was a tall girl with a Veronica Lake hair-do. Eisenhower approached and spoke to, – I can't remember who, – but I recall him saying 'What kind of cannons are these?' (Cannons!? CANNONS!? That's like calling the H.M.S. *Ark Royal* a boat.) Eisenhower got back in the car, struck his head on the roof, said 'Oh Fuck' and left. He had shaken hands with Sergeant Mick Ryan who didn't know *who* he was. Ryan! Oh what a ruffian that man was! One night, back at Bexhill, he made for the fish and chip shop, as he reached the door the proprietor closed it.

'Sorry,' said the proprietor, 'we're closed.'

'No, you're bloody not,' said Ryan, punched through the glass door and laid him out.

18.00 hours o'clock: Observed squadron of Boston bombers flying very high headed towards the front. These days the sound of any plane made one jumpy. Since leaving Camp trucks and lorries had passed us taking mail etc. and supplies up front. This day a truck had arrived with *our* MAIL! 'Gunner Milligan?' shouted Bombardier Marsden. I ran fifty yards to him – 'Yes Bom?' 'No mail for you!' he told me gleefully. Bastard! I was shattered. What were all those women I had been sleeping with back home doing? I mean, now I'd gone, they'd have time on their hands! But worst there was no mail from Lily or Louise. First Lily! (MILLIGAN TELLS ALL. HIS LOVES, HIS DESIRES, HIS SECRET SEXUAL CODES, HIS OWN RECEIPT* FOR APHRODISIACS, TAKE SIX HUNDRED OYSTERS AND PORRIDGE ... AND READ IT ALL IN THE SUN!) It was 1936. I was aged seventeen, smothered in pimples, even my suit had them. I worked in S. Strakers of Queen Victoria Street. My pay was 13s a week. After the train fare from Honor Oak Park to London Bridge it left 7s and 6,000 pimples. Standing on Platform One of an evening, waiting for the six fifteen, a small crowd of casual acquaintances would congregate. London Bridge Station, grim, grey, like a mighty iron mangle that squeezed people through its rollers into compartments. Yet, I fell in love there, (Third Class) Lily! She was about five foot six. Delightfully shaped, dark hair, brown doe-like eyes, a funny nose and slim legs. But I wasn't interested. I was after a girl with green eyes and red hair with fat legs who wore an imitation leopard skin coat, but! Lily fancied me, she made it a point, like General Sherman, of being there 'firstust with the mostest.' The first time we met I was running along the platform to get a seat up front, in comes Lily, I say 'Take my seat.' 'No,' she smiles. 'I'll sit on your lap.' She did, very disturbing for a young man brought up on curry, Cod Liver Oil and Keplers Malt. The relationship developed rapidly, and so did I. We fell madly in love. She wanted to get married, on 13s a week, I couldn't. 13 shillings? We'd have to spend our honeymoon on a tram. Marriage? I was so innocent I had no idea how the sex act was performed. When a bloke said 'You get across a woman' I thought you laid on the woman crosswise making a Crucifix. I was seventeen, stupid, and a Roman Catholic. Any Questions? I had to learn the hard way – Braille! Of course I wanted sex. God! how clumsy I must have been.

* YES – A RECEIPT NOT A RECIPE. You see I made the stuff, but I always got a signature for it.

Hitlergram No. 27

ADOLPH HITLER: You realize soon zer Englishers people will be *crushed*!

ME: It must be rush hour.

ADOLPH HITLER: Zere is no need to rush!! Soon it will all be over.

ME: Hooray! back to Civvy Street.

ADOLPH: Civvy Street is no more! It was destroyed by zer bombs of mine Luftwaffe.

Finally after three years being fed up with waiting, she went off with some redheaded twit called 'Roddy'. As far as she was concerned it was over. Not for me. Brought up on silent films with a romantic Irish father who told me I was descended from the Kings of Connaught, I played out the scene of the rejected lover. Sitting on a bench in Ladywell Recreation Ground, with a quarter of jelly babies, I would slump in the corner of the benches in a series of 'scorned attitudes' hoping she would come looking for me, like James Cagney in Shanghai Lil. I would do anything up to twenty-seven dejected poses a night, before the Park Keeper threw me out. What I needed was consolation. All my mother gave me was Weetabix. Playing local dances, I would buy ginger ale, disguise it in a whisky glass hoping she would see me taking gulps in between trumpet solos, pretending I was drunk. I was now Robert Taylor. I would play sobbing trumpet choruses until even the Jews would shout 'Stop! Enough is enough.' I would wait at night on the opposite side to her house, with my Marks and Spencer's mackintosh (5s 3d in a sale) coat collar up, making sure when she came home with the new boyfriend, I would be standing under the gas lamp, smoking a cigarette. When they arrived, I would throw down the cigarette, stamp on it, place my hands in my pockets then walk away whistling Bing Crosby's 'The Thrill is Gone'. I did that every night of December. I got pneumonia. Just what I wanted! I wrote and told her I was dying! She sent me a get well card. I thought, one evening I would throw myself from the bandstand and crash at the feet of her and her partner. Before I could, she moved her dancing habitat elsewhere. On the night I planned it, I sat sweating, finally I had to go to the Gents and remove the padding stuffed up the front of my shirt to take the shock of the fall. She met someone with a car, I used to give chase, shouting threats. After a year of this I'd had the shoes resoled fifty times, chased the car 1,073 miles, lost hope and had calves like Nureyev, but, I imagined, like Camille, she would return one winter's night to die in my arms at 50 Riseldine Road, Brockley Rise, S.E.26. I'd offer her Champagne (Ovaltine), she would ask me to play 'Honeysuckle Rose' on my trumpet and then die. It didn't happen. And not only did it not happen, here I was by the roadside of some bloody wog village in Africa and she hadn't even bothered to write to me. But chum! Living in hope is no reason to go without. I mean, what's wrong with part-time love affairs which included night occupations from the waist down? I mean, I had to keep fit. To this end I let other women into my life. I was good looking so I went in at the deep end.

There was lovely Junoesque Ivy, her sister Magda, then her *married* sister, Eileen! Ivy had taught me how, and from then on there was no stopping me. I had to go on to vitamin pills. There was Dot on One Tree Hill, Brockley Doris who was to get married on the morrow, Deptford Flo, Miss MacCafferty of Lewisham Hospital. Once in uniform I ran into a spate of affairs. Oh Louise! Louise! Louise!

So no mail. 'Cheer up,' said Gunner Forester, 'You can read my letter, my wife's pissed off with a Polish Pilot.'

'With eyesight like that, how did he become a pilot?' I said.

We were pressing on down the dusty road towards Souk Arras a hundred miles from the front. At Oued Athmenia, we got into a secondary road. We were on a high plateau, the sun overhead, the endless jolting finally made you numb. At the next break Driver Shepherd took over. Budden emerged from behind a tree, shaking off the drips. 'Right Milligan, off we go.'

'I'm not Milligan sir,' said Shepherd, in a hurt voice.

'Oh it's *you* Shepherd, good!'

Voice from the back of the truck. 'It's the Good Shepherd sir.'

19 Battery was now to part from the main body of the Regiment. *They* went to spend the night at Guelma (the dirty swines) while *we*, the lilywhite boys, went on half the distance again, into a night bivouac outside Souk Arras.

Meantime at No. 10 Downing Street.

Churchill in bed sipping brandy. Enter Allenbrook.

LORD ALANBROOK: Prime Min. have you seen the bill for Singapore?

HON. W. CHURCHILL: I know – those Japa-bloody-knees – why couldn't they come round the front?

LORD ALANBROOK: They're Tradesmen. Any news of Randolph?

HON. W. CHURCHILL: He's out in Yugoslavia with that Piss-Artist Evelyn Waugh.

Now read on:

15 Feb. en route to Le Kef. Souk Arras lay along the head waters of the Mejerda River which later swept down and watered the vineyards of the great Mejerda Valley. Thought you'd like to know. Everywhere this dusty light sand coloured soil reflected the sun's glare so we used our anti-gas goggles. Everywhere seemed parched, and on this the fourth day of driving, our faces were sore. The horse flies! These buggers would break the skin and suck your blood, given 2 minutes they could give you anaemia. You had to hit them the *moment* they landed, a split second later was too late. Men with slow reflexes suffered, like Forrest, who was covered in bites and great bruises where he had hit at them and missed. The more he missed, the harder he hit. 'I wish I was Jordy Liddel,' he moaned. 'When they bite him, they fall off dead.'

'It's all that shit he works with.'

★

Valentine Dyall acting out World War II

About 12.15 Mr Budden said, 'Milligan, we have just crossed the border into Tunisia.'

'I'll carve a statue at once.'

On the border was Sakiet Sidi Youseff, where there was some kind of mine. A few donkeys and Arabs were at a pit head or shaft out of which ran a narrow rail, from inside the hole a tipper truck would appear with the powder produce which they shovelled into sacks on the donkeys.

'Where did you spend your last holidays Milligan,' Mr Budden broke in.

'I went with some friends to Whitesand Bay in Cornwall.'

'... Cornwall? Cornwall.' He put his binoculars up.

'You can't see it from here sir.'

'I'm not *looking* for Cornwall.'

The journey had covered us all in fine white powdery dust giving us the appearance of old men. Sid Price started to walk bent double like an old yokel, within seconds the whole battery were doing it, Africa rang to the sound of 'Oh Arrrr! Oi be seventy-three oi be in Zummerzet.' At the head of the column Major Chater Jack sat watching us. 'It's going to be a long hard war,' he was saying. I can still see his amused smile, especially as Woods, his batman, *was* from Somerset.

'Lot o' daft idiots zur,' he said to the Major.

'Yes Woods, a lot of daft idiots, but I fear you and I are stuck with 'em. The thing to do is keep them well camouflaged.' We were off again, and owing to a laundry crisis I was living dangerously, no underwear!

15 Feb. 1200 hours. 'Le Kef 20 Kilometres.' The road started to climb at an alarming angle, hairpin bend after hairpin bend we laboured, finally the engines started to boil and Chater Jack called a halt. We were in a defile. The dramatic landscape looked like Daumier's drawings for The Divine Comedy. The rocks around abounded with lizards, to my delight a chameleon was rainbowing around a tree, Shepherd was amazed at the colour changes. 'It's clean living,' I said. 'If you stopped playing with yourself you could do it.' Looking along the line one caught sight of the odd Gunner piddling against the wheels. I don't understand it! They have to clean their own transport, and then, when they've got the whole of Africa, they piss on their lorries!

3

Milligan Conquers

Monty: His Part in My Victory: 1976

𝔑𝔞𝔷𝔦 𝔑𝔢𝔴𝔰 𝔉𝔩𝔞𝔰𝔥

The scene: Mrs Eichmann's boarding house. Bolivia.
HIMMLER: Ach Ein bugger! Ve should never have lost Tunis! If der
    Fuhrer had eaten his tin of P.A.D.   1
GOERING: P.A.D.?   2
HIMMLER: P.A.D. Prolonged Active Dog. If mine Fuhrer had eaten   3
    Prolonged Active Dog, today he would be 159 vid a beautiful   1
    coat.

A captured German pilot crapping into the cockpit of his plane in displeasure with the
Geneva Convention

TUNIS 13 May The screwing had started. Young Lochinvars, prema-
turely aged with all-night poking, were coming in at first light, paler
than the dawn, collapsing on their beds and groaning 'Lovely.' The
Great 'Plunger' Bailey decided that degrees of prowess should be
recorded. A blackboard was hung on his lorry.

BATTERY SHAGS AS PER MAY 1943

	women involved	number of times	REMARKS
Gunner James	I	6	Tres Bon
Lance/Bdr King	I	I	Brewers Droop
Gunner Forest	I	I	Death through natural causes
Gunner 'Plunger' Bailey	4	20	Resting

Edgington's face darkens. 'How can a man face the woman he loves after all this shagging?'

Said White, 'He could say, "Darlin' I've been keeping in training for you, it's been hard work but worth the sacrifice, for, when it came to my darlin's turn, I'd be fit and ready for you".'

Edgington retaliated, 'You're throwing your love lives away,' he said, lying back in his tent, his socks adrift on his feet, and bent over at the ends. 'Oh no, when I go to the Marriage Bed, I go pure as the driven snow,' which was some statement coming from a long white creature with forearms and knees burnt brown, wearing a vest which just covered his willy, 2 sticking plasters on his inoculated arm, a hair cut that made his head look like a coconut, and all of this covered with a fine layer of Tunisian dust. Picture the scene. Suddenly, at the mouth of the tent appears Betty Grable, she sees Edgington. 'Darling,' she says, slowly. He stands up, the pimples on his bare bum showing purple in the half light, he takes her in his arms, and slowly they start to dance out of the tent across the dusty plain in a cloud of dust, his socks slipping off, and the tail of his vest flapping in the breeze.

Letters from Home

13 May 1943. Back home, brother Desmond, filled with post-public patriotism, joined the Air Cadets, he and a gaggle of pimply Freds were given instruction in a cardboard cockpit, *'one of us sits inside, another holds a model of a Stuka, and we shoot it down.'* When my brother's turn came, he would give forth with the entire sound effects of the film 'Hell's

A British soldier with an incredible weapon

Angels,' which would end up with him crashing to the ground dying. Then, raising himself on one elbow, he would shout 'Gott Strafe England.' It was all very praiseworthy and a complete waste of bloody time.

My mother took up leather work at night classes. From then on, I received parcels of leather thongs '*in case I needed them.*' Leather gloves with six fingers, leather belts '*in case I needed them,*' a pair of leather garters, leather pay book cover '*to keep it dry,*' leather prayer book cover, then a '*spare leather prayer book cover, in case the first got damaged in the fighting.*' I received the Lord's prayer engraved on a leather medallion – '*it will protect you,*' it didn't. The inside became covered in verdigris and turned my chest green. Were *other* mothers doing this? I didn't see other men in the regiment with green chests wearing initialled leather garters, and gloves with six fingers.

My father was at the RAOC depot, he wore six guns and was teaching his men how to stop paratroops with a '*quick draw*'. His way of stopping Hitler would be to invite him to a game of Poker – then, at a crucial stage, call him '*Ein cheat.*'

Hitler, having lost at poker to Milligan's father, wondering what he could sell to raise the money

Nazi News Flash

The scene: the old Bar-Auschwitz.
Two guns blaze – Hitler falls dead – an amazed look on his face –
Captain Milligan blows smoke from his guns, SS men step aside in
fear, he backs out of the door, there is the sound of screeching
brakes as he is knocked over by a dust cart.

Unspun Socks from a Chicken's Laundry: 1981

The Battle

Aim! said the Captain
Fire! said the King
Shoot! said the General
Boom! Bang! Ping!

Boom! went the Cannon
Bang! went the Gun
Ping! went the Rifle
Battle had begun!

Ouch! said a Prussian
Help! said the Hun
Surrender! said the Englishman
Battle had been won!

Melbourne April 1980

Ipple-Apple Tree

I'm going to plint an apple tree
Not plint, I mean to *plant*
You cannot *plint* an apple tree
You cint, I mean you can't.
I mean you plant
You do not plint
And I mean can't
When I say cint
If you insist and plint a tree
Ipples will grow, not apples you see?

Saudi-Bayswater Nov 1979

The Mirror Running: 1987

Growing Up I

Even tho' they are my tomorrows
Do they know my yesterdays
    are wrapped up in them?
Those golden yesterdays
Was there ever a sound
    like child laughter,
Was there ever such talk
    as theirs,
That lily pure truth on their lips?
Grown you are, yet I only see
    the child in you.
It is past reality, it is a haunting,
I cannot live without the
    memory of it.
At the going of those yesterdays
    my todays ended.

Growing Up II

Is that all there is? Goodbye!
After a million hellos
After all those bird-blessed good-mornings,
After the bubbling bathtime laughter,
After so many soul-searching Santa Claus,
After a million wild walks on the moors,
After the swing-swung laughing summers,
After the tear-drenched kiss-better bumped head,
After the new wear-them-in-bed red shoes,
After a tumult of timeless teddy bears,
After a delirium of dolls in prams,
After a rainbow of ice-creams,
After daddy I love you all the world –
Goodbye?

17 March 1985

Nature Watch

Turn the stone over,
 empty the sea,
Raze the mountains,
 fire the lea.

Tamper not nature,
 watch and behold
The flower that trembles
 is bought but not sold.

January 1980

Pandora

My dreams are melting
They lie in pools on the floor.
When I was five
My dreams were endless.
Now, I have one left
Dare I dream it
   or should I phone the police?

Correspondence: 1984

George Martin was one of Spike's favourite people. He was Spike's best man when he married Paddy, his second wife. This is an example of the sort of letters they wrote to each other.

Friday 22 March.

My dear Spike,

what a lovely surprise to get flowers sent to me at my time of life!

You're right, of course; it is sheer impertinence still producing records at this tender age, and it cannot go on much longer. I have been incarcerated with P. McCartney for a considerable while, but hope is at hand.

Would love to see you again. I'll ring when I am in London again in a few weeks.

LUV

George

9 Orme Court,
London. W. 2.

29th March, 1984

George Martin Esq.

Dear George,

I have been trying to pin you down through your secretary Shirley, but the English are an incredible race, in as much as none of them know where the others are – going to be – will be. The only permanent geographical location one can really rely on is when they visit the carsey, even then the country of origin changes.

I was told by Shirley that 'you are coming back next week' well she didn't say 'he's coming back next week, and leaving immediately', so when you are positively back from leaving immediately, would you immediately leave a message on the phone where you wont be, from when you come back, from wherever you've been.

Like to take you to dinner, without Paul McCartney.

Save The Wildlife – Give a bird a bath.

Do contact me.

                    Love,
                    Spike

10th April 1984

Spike Milligan Esq.,
9 Orme Court,
<u>London W.2.</u>

Dear Spike,
    I have come out of the kaze and I'll be ringing you very soon.
        Love,
        George

P.S. Please note spelling of 'kaze' which is still awaiting installation of the phone!

9 Orme Court,
London, W. 2.
12th April, 1984

George Martin Esq.,

Dear George,

It was nice to hear from you, giving your spelling of the word KARZI. My spelling is the correct one – my Manager spells it carsey, and you spell it kaze. The latter two are entirely wrong.

I mean my Manager is actually taking this letter down, and once an African Ambassador received a letter I had dictated to her, in which I was referring to the African National Congress, and 'Guerrilla tribes impregnating their country', and of course, my Manager typed 'Gorilla tribes impregnating their country'; so it's not an easy life. I will give you the story of karzi, it is actually from the Zulu M'karzi, the apostrophe is the Bantu click. It really is the Zulu word for W.C., and the word was picked up by the British troops during the South African war. So that's cleared that up.

I might point out that the Zulus don't have telephones in their karzis, there is a set of appropriate drums which are placed around the karzi (a) to send out messages like – Christ I'm bound up, or (b) George Martin has not got a telephone in his karzi.

Please phone, would love to see you again, I will make it easier for you, I will pay for the dinner, but I must warn you, life is 24 hours a day activity, try and get in somewhere Daddy.

Love, light and peace,
Spike Milligan

Monty: His Part in My Victory: 1976

The New Major

His name was Evan Jenkins. His physique? He didn't have one. The nearest description? Tut-an-Khamen with the bandages off. His neck measurement would be 11 inches, including shoulders. When a strong wind blew he had to hold his head to stop it from snapping off. His Adam's apple stuck out like a third knee and when he swallowed, it disappeared down the front of his shirt and made him look pregnant. His arms must have been sent from Auschwitz; they were for all the world like two pieces of string with knots tied where the elbows were. His legs were like one of Gandhi's split in two. His eyes were so close together that to look left or right one of them appeared to cross the bridge of his nose. He had a pair of outsize ears which attracted flies. It got him the nickname Jumbo, but despite his comic appearance he was a real bastard; he had us taking our bootlaces out and ironing them

Sgt. 'Griff' Griffin, one of the great characters of the Battery. He is here seen wearing either long shorts or short long trousers

'Jumbo' Jenkins

so that they were 'nice and flat'. He made us use tooth-paste on our webbing to make it 'Nice and White' while our teeth went black. At night he'd sit in his tent and play 'Whistling Rufus' on a clarinet, and every morning he could be heard gargling with TCP then spitting it back into the bottle, the mean sod. He insisted on giving us cultural lectures. A Sergeant, who shall remain nameless, said 'H'eyes front! now then, today the Major will be talking about' – (here he referred to a piece of paper) – 'Keats, and I don't suppose one of you higgerant bastards knows what a Keat is.'

Edgington and I decide to get our tent as far away from Jumbo as possible, so we found a distant Wadi over which we rigged up a canvas cover. Efforts to sabotage Jumbo were partially successful, we managed to impregnate the reed of his clarinet with soap, and he gave his batman hell over it. But it was by the Battery Cook Ronnie May that real revenge was wrought. May had collected dried goat's shit, pounded it into a flour, mixed it with real flour and mashed potatoes; this mixture appeared on Jumbo's plate as rissoles, which he ate and asked for more. 'Now he really *is* full of shit,' said May.

The sky was blackening. It was going to rain.

'We could do with it,' says Edge.

'Do what with it?'

'For a start you can accept it.' The heavens opened and rain deluged down.

Edgington-
Milligan tent
in Wadi.

The Concise Oxford Dictionary says – WADI: Dried up water course. Filling quickly in rainy season.

We didn't have the Oxford Dictionary, but we found how remarkably accurate it was as we and our belongings floated out on a wall of water; all around were yells and shouts as tents were flattened.

'My bloody fags are down there,' said a drenched, mud-reddened Edgington as he dived into the raging waters. Waist deep we ran among the flood grabbing kit and throwing it to high ground. It ceased as suddenly as it started.

'Why did it stop – 15 minutes more would have seen us off fucking Portsmouth.'

Gunner Edgington
trying to save the
tent during the
storm

Unspun Socks from a Chicken's Laundry: 1981

Envoi

Bandage! said the Doctor
Cotton! said the Nurse
Ointment! said the Surgeon
 Curse! Curse! Curse!

 Hobart Tasmania 1970

Slip Ware

There's many a slip
Twix cup and lip,
And the sound it makes
Is drip drip drip.

Pennies from Heaven

I put 10p in my Piggy Bank
To save for a rainy day.
It rained the very next morning!
Three cheers, Hip Hip Hooray!

Fear-fly

1 If I was a fly
I don't suppose
I'd want to land
On someone's nose.

2 A nose is meant
To run or drip
And not used as
A landing strip.

3 I'd never land
Upon an ear,
You never know
What you might hear.

4 Never land on
A sailor's belly,
That's how we lost
Auntie Nelly.

5 The most dangerous place
To land I know
Is either Gatwick
Or Heathrow.

Article for Penguin Books on Reprinting *Puckoon*: 1965

Penguin the publishers, not the bird, though you never know, however, whichever it be, they/it wish me to write 600 words as they are going to reprint my novel *Puckoon* in paperback. Those words 'paperback' have always baffled me. I mean, if you look at what they call a paper-back, you'll see it's in fact a book not only with paper on its back or spine, but paper on each side as well, so the true definition of this type of cheap book is paper back and sides – now we know, we also know by now I have about 500 words to go – fish, cupboard, teeth, that's another three less. Why 600 words? I mean, I wrote the book over twenty years ago, I don't remember what it was about other than it was about 70,000 words – perhaps Penguin don't think it's long enough – well, it was long enough for me – that's why I finished it – perhaps it's in the nature of 'A Foreword' – 'A Foreword', that's another suspect combination of words. I mean, you go up to a person and say 'A Foreword', it won't do much for him – mind you, there are perverts who *might* get turned on by saying 'A Foreword' to them, saying 'Go forward' makes much more sense – except if you're standing on Beachy Head. Yes, Beachy Head is where 'Go forward' could only be said once, of course it can be said twice if you survive the fall. About 350 words to go, I'd say – so, to reduce that still further, a repeat of the words fish, cupboard, teeth. I have at this moment just phoned a Miss Geraldine Cook of Penguin – having discovered that it was she who told my manager 600 words, but now she (Geraldine Cook) tells me it doesn't have to be 600 words and with true British vacillation cannot say how many – less – please, less. I mean, my vocabulary is only 120 words and those contain fish, cupboard and teeth, they don't have to be in that order, it can be cupboard, teeth and then fish – that's one of the bene-fits of democracy – I believe that most benefits from a piddling £50 for a single person and a mite more for married couples, fish, cupboard, teeth. For instance, did you know there are no dry cleaners in Tierra Del Fuego, but the people in that distant point do have fish, cupboards and teeth, at least Darwin and his beagle said so. Why Darwin would want to take a beagle to that remote point is beyond me. Something else is beyond me – a Turbo Porsche – I was driving a Mini Minor on the M25 and a Turbo Porsche went beyond me – and did you know, dear confused reader, that the M25 is a traffic jam travelling at 70 mph? Look, I think you and I have had enough of this, so fish, teeth, cupboard and six Valium please.

Stop press: Geraldine Cook has said they also need a drawing – so here it is/are.

More Spike Milligan Letters: 1984

Spike's rugby hero: when Spike hosted *An Evening with Spike Milligan*, Cliff Morgan was the first person on his invitation list.

To: Cliff Morgan Esq.,   *14th June, 1977*
British Broadcasting Corporation

Dear Cliff,

A belated congratulations on your O.B.E. I am sending you a Chinese Candle, which has no bearing on the honour conferred on you, but this will be the first time an Irishman has given a Welsh O.B.E. a Chinese Candle.

Burn it at some dinner like party, and think of me when the Ruby shows through the glass.

Love, light and peace,
Spike Milligan

To: Cliff Morgan Esq.   *16th September, 1980*

Dear Cliff,

Can I thank you very much for getting me two tickets to the last night of the Proms, but please tell Humphrey Burton he must wear evening dress on the last night of the Proms, otherwise I will never go to the pictures with him again.

It was a wonderful evening, but totally ruined by the music.

Love, light and peace,
Spike Milligan

Spike still pestering Lew Grade for his £25 bonus from Eastbourne. This was a running gag that lasted almost fifty years.

To: Lord Grade   *15th January, 1982*

Dear Lew,

I, for one among thousands, am very very depressed at what has happened to you.

All Companies lose money at some time, and this is a case of rats leaving the ship not while it is sinking, but while it's having a bad time, and I have written to the newspapers and said so.

You have always had my heartfelt admiration.

Love, light and peace,
Spike Milligan

P.S. You still owe me £25 from the gig at the Winter Gardens, Eastbourne, when you promised me a bonus.

When I asked Lew years later why he didn't pay the £25 he told me he would miss receiving Spike's Christmas cards and notes reminding him that he still owed £25. To him it was worth £25,000.

Mussolini: His Part in My Downfall : 1978

The fourth volume of war memoirs.

I felt well enough to write my first letter home from Italy.

My dear Mum, Dad and Des,

I am officially somewhere else, that somewhere else is where I am, I am not at liberty to say, the whole of this land we have arrived in is now TOP SECRET, in fact no one is allowed to know where it is, even the people who live in it are told to forget they are here, however, the bloody Germans know where it is, and don't want to let us have it (Spaghetti). I've been here about a certain number of days (Spaghetti) and we all arrived here by certain transport and landed at a certain place at a certain time, of all these facts I am dead certain (Spaghetti). We are allowed to mention the sky, so I'll say that we have in fact got one, it's directly overhead and high enough to allow you to stand up. The weather, well it was nice and warm when we landed but is turning cool, as are the natives, and now there is rain every other day, I am not with the regiment at the moment, no, I have had an illness called sandfly fever, it's caused, as the name suggests, by getting sand in your flies, which immediately sends your temperature soaring, so despite the cold weather I'm quite warm thank you, in fact my temperature got so high, walking patients used to sit around my bed at night to keep warm (Spaghetti). However, I'm better now, I've still got a temperature but it's normal. Next I'll be sent to a bloody awful Reinforcement Camp, where all the mud is sent to be slept on by unclaimed soldiers. So far the Battery have not sustained any casualties (except me) (Spaghetti). With the censorship as it is it's pointless to write any more, all I want you to do is to write and tell me where I am (Spaghetti).

Your loving Son/Brother/Midwife

Terry

SEPTEMBER 28, 1943

MY DIARY: THE NEWS SAYS JERRY'S EVACUATED NAPLES. HEAVY RAIN.

A Scottish, sandy-haired, freckle-faced Doctor is at the foot of my bed, he looks at me, smiles, looks at my board.

'Temperature's down then.'

'Is it, sir?'

'It's ninety-nine. How do you feel?'

'I feel about ninety-nine, sir.'

I slept most of that day, waking up for meals. It was all very pleasant, the service, the sound of the rain, the bloke in the next bed dying. That evening they took him out for some kind of an operation and he never came back. I remember the name on his chart was Parkinson ACC, he was a cook aged forty-five, and he'd snuffed it. Poor bugger; still, he was an army cook, and killed quite a few in his time.

What news! there's an ENSA Concert Party in the Big Hall this evening!

'What's ENSA?' says Jamie.

I told him, 'Every Night Something Awful.'

The Hall was packed. There is a proper stage; on the curtains are the faint outlines of the Fascists' emblem, which has been unravelled in a hurry. A Sergeant is in the pit on a lone upright piano, he strikes up a merry medley of tunes, 'Blue Birds over the White Cliffs of Dover' (and why shouldn't they be white with all those birds flying over?). The curtains part and there are three men and two girls in evening dress, they were the 'squares' of all time, they are all singing 'Here we are, Here we are, Here we are again!' Which was an outright lie as we'd never seen 'em before. We give them a good hand. A short red-faced male with a fierce haircut and popping eyes comes forward and starts to wrestle with the microphone to bring it down to his height.

'Thank you! Thank you!' he gushes. 'Well, as we say, here we are again.'

He tells a series of terrible jokes, we roar with laughter, he announces the Something Twins, on come two girls dressed as Shirley

Temples, they sing 'On the Good Ship Lollipop', and we wish they were, they do a very simple tap dance. Storms of applause, next a male about fifty sings 'The Bowmen of England', as if all their strings were slack, he finishes, storms of applause! On come the two girls dressed as sailors – loud whistles. They sing 'All the Nice Girls Love a Sailor'. The third male comes on, he's everything a comic should be except funny, about forty-five, rotund, evening dress, a flat cap, a glove on one hand, after each joke he transfers the glove to the other and says 'On the other hand', he ends up with a song that I forgot even as he sang it. He left an indelible blank on my mind. The pit pianist then plays 'The Stars and Stripes'. ... Storms of cheers, what liars we are. So it goes on; a brave attempt to cheer the lads up, and we all appreciated it, it was as well we didn't have to pay. We wander back upstairs to our ward, it's night now, the black-outs are up, dinner is on its way.

'They're letting me out tomorrow,' says Jamie.

'You going back to your unit?'

'No, I'm going before a medical board, they're going to downgrade me.'

'You lucky sod.'

'Aye, I don't think I'd like any more fighting, I should have stayed at home.'

So ended Jamie Notam's dream of high adventure. I wonder what happened to him.

THURSDAY, SEPTEMBER 30, 1943

I'm up and about, I'm OK, I'm cured, I'm normal again, I feel fine, I'm ready to be killed again, he's fit, send him back, etc. etc. Yes. The Scots doctor on his rounds.

'So you're leaving us, Mirrigen.'

'Yes, sir.'

'How do you feel?'

'Very ill, sir, very, very, very ill.'

He smiles. 'Well, Mirrigen, all good things come to an end.'

Was *I* the good thing? Help!! Two new patients arrive, and are dumped in the bed each side. Both are coughing like consumptives, what luck, if I hang around I might get it. Shall I kiss one? I wonder where the Battery are and what they are doing, going Bang! I suppose. There is a barber among the patients, Rifleman Houseman.

'Anyone want a haircut?'

There is no reply.

'Free,' he adds, and is knocked down in the rush. I let him loose on my head, when he showed me the result in the mirror, I nearly fainted.

'Howzat?' he said.

'Out,' I replied.

My head looked like someone had set it on fire.

'It was all for free,' explained Rifleman Houseman.

BRILLIANT RECOVERY FROM SANDFLY FEVER BY HUMBLE L/BOMBARDIER

So the headlines should have run, all I got was a Lance-Corporal suffering from incurable stupidity, who said, 'Bombardier Millington?'

'That's almost me,' I said.

'You are to be discharged tomorrow.'

'I understand that my name is now Millington and I am to be discharged as fit.'

'Yes, RTU*.'

RTU? That had me, so I sang it to a Novello tune 'R T U again whenever spring breaks through.' (Groans.)

He blinked and made me sign a piece of paper that in as many words said, 'We have tried to kill this man but failed.'

'You will be ready by 0830 hours and take the unexpired portion of your day's rations.'

Unexpired rations? The mind boggled. I started a series of farewells and looked deeply into the eyes of all the nurses with a look that said quite positively, 'You're lucky I never screwed you,' and they looked back with a smile that said, 'When you've been promoted to Captain, knock three times.'

---

* Return to Unit.

OCTOBER 1, 1943

It's a mixed day, a souffle of sun and cloud. Outside the 76th General a 3-tonner truck is waiting like a wagon at the Knacker's Yard. A short squat driver with a squint in his left eye 'finds' and calls our names out from a bit of tacky paper. 'Lance-Bombardier Mirrigan?'

'Yes, that's me,' I said. 'Lance-Bombardier Mirrigan.'

He calls out the names of several more soldiers of the King, who at the sight of them would abdicate. I enquire where we are being taken.

'Corps Reinforcement Camp.' He pronounced the word 'Corpse'. An Omen.

The Looney: 1987

Spike thought that this book was one of the funniest he had written.

The Looney

In the beginning God created heaven and earth with, it would appear, Irish labour. It took the Lord six days, and on the seventh he rested, during which time speculative builders put up Kilburn. Kilburn High Street runs three miles, that's why it looks 'shagged out'. A walk through Kilburn has left an indelible blank on my mind. The British, it is said, are made up of four races, the best of these are the Derby and the Oaks.

Kilburn was a melting pot, occasionally stirred by the National Front, an extreme political organisation whose election manifesto was 'I'll punch yer fuckin' 'ead in'. The leaders were any of them that could count up to ten without having to sit down.

Kilburn High Street's once trim Victorian shopfronts were now a conjunctivitis of gaudy plastic signs whose exaggerated size suggested that the natives were in an orgy of onanism, therefore going blind. There was Nandergee Patel, Newsagent and Littlewoods Agent, Ah-Wat-Dung, Chinese Takeaway and Littlewoods Agent, Raj Curry Centre and Littlewoods Agent, and D. Smith, Funeral Directors (English Spoken) – to do business with an Englishman you had to have a death in the family.

Policemen who patrolled Kilburn had to be tranquillised before going on duty. Even the crimes were boring – drunks, petty theft and/or feeling little girls. Only that morning, had not Magistrate Mrs Thelma Skugs, who longed to be felt, given a small man three months for screwing in a doorway? 'There's far too much of this thing going on,' she had chastised him. He was dragged from the dock shouting, 'You'll never stop fucking in Kilburn.' Policemen at Kilburn Station used to kneel and pray, 'Please God, let someone get murdered tonight, preferably me!' The Lord said, 'Let the Earth bring forth grass', yea, the grass was brought forth in little packets by stoned Rastafarians. And

God said, 'Be fruitful and multiply', verily every night Kilburn rever-
berated to the sound of shuddering bedsprings fulfilling the instructions.

In Kilburn lived a fine wreck of a man, one Mick Looney. At this
moment he stood in the corner of a muddy building site that was forever England, spiteful C of E rain was falling on good Catholics.
Looney was talking to himself out loud – he was deaf: 'Me farder tole
me we were descended from der Kings of Catlick Oireland, so why am
I standin' here in der pissin' rain mixin' cement for Mowlems?'

Even now, the torrent was turning the cement into a viscous watery
soup that would one day be a floor that would fall on the heads of the
tenants below.

Looney was five feet eight inches, because he hadn't gone metric.
Laid on a slab his body would have invited immediate burial; he dared
not fall asleep in parks for fear of people calling the Coroner. His body
had never seen the sun, or for that matter the moon. Middle-aged, he
had a face like a dog's bum with a hat on; two enamel blue eyes stared
blankly from a DIY head.

We move now to 113b Ethel Road, a building with a slight tendency
to fall down, built in Victorian days in the mock-Gothic style now
mocked by everyone. Looney made 'improvements': out came those
silly sash windows, in went those Ted Moulf ones you 'can't hear heli-
copters in the garden through'. He assured his wife that 'dis will
increase der price of der house', as he planted plastic tulips in the front
garden ... in December.

The building was riddled with rising damp – he had put rat traps
down and caught fish. It had deathwatch beetle, dry rot, damp rot –
take them away and the building wasn't there. The top floor he had
'converted' to flats, only just better than being converted to
Protestantism.

This Sunday the skies above Kilburn hung with pre-natal grey
clouds pregnant with chilling rain. The wife Mary and son Dick were
at Mass devoutedly praying, 'Please God let us win Littlewoods, say
£500,000.' Looney 'himself' was at home in his best suit, or the best

he'd got – he had seen it in Burton's window in 1947 on a Clark Gable lookalike dummy. When Looney forced his rotund body into it it took on the appearance of a python that had swallowed a cripple. After fifteen years, his wife had donated it to 'Clothe the Ethiopian Poor' – they had sent it back with a pound.

Returning from Mass his family found him slavering over the *News of the World*: 'POP STAR'S NIGHT OF SIN IN TRANSPARENT KILT!' and 'NUDE NEGRO VICAR RUNS AMOK WITH FEATHER DUSTER!' 'PRINCE PHILIP, IS HE A TRANSVESTITE?'

He greeted his spouse, 'Ah, me darlin', how long will lunch be?'

'It should last about an hour,' she said as she slaved over a raging hell of a black stove with hellish pots issuing boiling vapour.

The food wasn't being cooked so much as tortured. Der British is terrible cooks, thought Looney, they even burnt Joan of Arc. Great jets of steam ascended upwards – after years of this there was now more nourishment in the ceiling than the food.

Looney stood to stretch his legs and collided with the washing line above. Astride his head like a jockey sat his wife's voluminous bloomers, a sexual obstacle – but for them he would have done it many more times. Grabbing the arms of the swollen imitation moquette chair he slowly lowered himself, the huge chair appeared to be devouring him. Down he went until his bum had noisily driven the last of the creaking springs to the floorboards.

He read from the *Exchange Mart & Gazette*:

Wanted, ten gallons of fish oil, will exchange for set of Indian clubs.
Twenty tins of dog food, will exchange for any Vera Lynn records or photo of the Shroud of Turin.
Old-style wooden leg, owner going abroad, will sell or exchange for Tupperware set.

'Ah! Here's me advert,' he said, and read aloud: 'Wanted, throne-like chair, price negotiable o.n.o. or will exchange for house-trained pure-bred mongrel, good barker, aged three but looks older o.n.o.'

A febrile o.n.o. growl with hair on came from under the table: it was

Boru the pure-bred mongrel and good barker. His name had been Nigger until that Jamaican family moved in next door. Boru was old, he could now only bark lying down.

Looney glanced up at his wife, he saw the face that seen from a dead sleep would have induced a coronary, though in her young days people said she looked like a film star, Wallace Berry. She was ladling out the steaming mess called lunch.

'Oh? Wot is it?' said Looney.

'It's Sunday,' said his son.

'Are you eating, Dick?' said Mrs Looney. Whereupon Looney denied all knowledge of eating Dick.

The lad shook his head, you could hear the pieces. 'No, Mudder, I'm on a splonsored fast.'

'Splonsored? Who for?'

'Der starving Ee-thai-opeans.'

'Oh? How much do yer get?'

'I gets twenty pee for every dinner I don't eat.'

Looney himself furrowed his brow. '*Twenty pee?* Jasus! By der time youse got enough youse will be a victim yerself, man.'

'All right,' said Dick, holding out his plate.

'How long youse been doin' dis fer?' said Looney.

'Oh,' said the boy, 'three months.'

'And how much have youse saved?'

'Eighty pee.'

'God almighty. How many niggers can you feed for eighty pee?'

'About a thousand,' said Mrs Looney, walloping the steaming mess on to the plates.

They ate in silence, save the odd o.n.o. growl from Boru who could smell the food but was too old to get up.

'Now he,' said Looney, 'he'd make a fine dinner fer dem starvin' Ee-thai-opeans.'

The son winced. 'Oh no, Dad, dey wouldn't eat a doggy.'

Looney himself chuckled, 'Oh yes dey would! Give him a good covering of Daddy or der HP Sauce and they couldn't tell der difference.'

He warmed to the argument. 'And wot about orl dose moggies dat snuff it, if dey were to put 'em in a deep-freeze ship dat would solve der hunger.' He fingered the empty bottles on the table. 'Darlin', where's der tomato sauce?'

'Most of it is in you, the rest is finished up,' said Mrs Looney. 'Hans forgot to bring any in.'

'Hans? Dat silly German bugger.'

Hans Schitz, ex-soldier taken prisoner in North Africa, had ended up on a farm in Sussex, and elected to stay on after the war to avoid travel sickness and his bank manager. Schitz couldn't stand Mrs Looney's cooking so he ate at Café le Jim in Gron Street; the food was just as bad but they supplied a red goo sauce to kill the taste.

One day the supply of red goo ceased and the owner of Café le Jim, a Mister Spirious Starkios, told Schitz that the supplier of the red goo, a Mr Banarjee Tookram (BA failed) had lost his assistant through AIDS. Schitz applied for the job and soon Mr Banarjee Tookram's red goo 'Pure Tomato Sauce' was on stream again. The company was registered in Panama as an oil tanker, the red goo was stirred in a bathtub with an umbrella, syphoned into drums, then, using a syringe, squirted into plastic tomato-shaped containers for the table. Schitz brought massive quantities home to the Looneys' house – he lodged in an upstairs and terrible room where he practised boredom and onanism.

There was a whining at the back door – the Looneys' second dog Prince, named after the pop star. They daredn't let him in the house, as Looney explained to the priest: 'He's got flatulence, Fadder. Trouble is, he does dem silent butler's revenges, wid everybody in der room lookin' daggers at each udder.'

Looney went out and put a plate of Mrs Looney's food down. The dog looked at it and howled dolefully. 'Listen, mate,' said Looney, 'youse lucky youse not bein' eatin' by dem starving Ee-thai-opeans.'

He returned to his chair and observed his son. It hurt: the boy was painfully thin, he wore a second-hand suit woefully too big for him, people used to knock on it to see if he was in. He was a shy gentle boy. The Bible says, 'The meek shall inherit the earth.' Wrong, at school they beat the daylights out of him. Dick worked as a hydro boy at the Chislehurst Laundry, handling the sheets from Lewisham Hospital. Why was his son, a descendant of the Kings of Ireland, washing dem shitty English sheets? You didn't know where that shit had been.

He sat at his table checking his pools. He could be sitting on a million, instead he was sitting on currently dormant piles. 'Twenty years I bin doin' dem pools.' One day, one day ... Some men are born losers, others have losses thrust upon them. In the human race today the Irish had come last.

Open Heart University: 1979

Welcome Home

Unaware of my crime
             they stood me in the dock.

I was sentenced to life …
             without her.

Strange trial.
             No Judge.
             No Jury.

I wonder who my visitors will be.

Bayswater
December 1977

Rachmaninov's 3rd Piano Concerto

We are drinking cupped Sonatas like wine,
The red glow, the cut throat of Sunset.
      Like a tungsten locked Icarus
I charge my mind with heaven fermented grape
that grow to Caesar Royal Purple in my brain,
Trim my logic as I may
The tyrant Onos unbraids my thoughts
      like maidens' tresses at eve
I am wafting across mindless heavens
'Where am I?' I ask the Lotus maiden.
She says 'Singapore Air Lines –
      Economy Class'.

M.1.Way of Life

Bloody, Battered, Tattered Thing
Which is body?
Which is wing?
What kind of bird
It's hard to say
As you lay squashed
On a motor way
But the marks in your blood
Are sharp and clear
A Dunlop 'safety' tyre
Has just been here.

America I Love You

The fur-bearing lady
    said to the Jeweller
'Can you fashion a rose of
    gold or silver?'
'Yes' said he
'Which is cheaper?' said she
'A real one' said he
'Real' said the lady, 'that's
    for the poor people.'

        Los Angeles 1977

My Love is Like a ...

If I gave her red roses
           would she?
If I gave her white roses
           in a bowl of wine
           would she?
I gave her green carnations
           made from dollar bills
           – and she did.

I thought I saw Jesus
           on a tram.
I said 'Are you Jesus?'
He said 'Yes I am'.

Article for the *Daily Mail*: 1990

Muzak was one of Spike's pet hates. He campaigned against it most of his life.

Muzak

I think everybody has a God-given right to privacy – being forced to do something is loss of freedom, to impose something on to a human is to put him in some kind of bondage – to do it surreptitiously, and gradually, is like dripping poison in the king's ear; it's rather like drug victims, you start not wanting it, then liking it, then craving for it, but the fix has to become more frequent until it becomes a way of life. Peace and quiet is what every *normal* person should want and appreciate; tranquillity is something that lubricates the soul.

I remember North African desert nights during the campaign when I thought the silence majestic, almost tangible – there was absolute peace in every infinite second of the time – and the serenity made the time timeless. We are developed into life in a womb which for the growing babe is given that peace – and we in an anguished world deserve quietude. There are few feeling people who never dream of a desert island away from, no, not just people but noise.

You may not know that a note of music can be increased in volume, from piano to fortissimo, all acceptable when it's acoustically performed. But musical sound has come a long way since the gentle sound of the harp and flutes found in Tutankhamen's tomb, and how easeful must have been the harps and lutes on Cleopatra's Nile barge. Along with that period came triumphs of architecture like the giant and beautiful temples of Karnak, Thebes and Memphis. The harp, too, was the instrument of ancient Greece – witness the perfection of their creative architecture and sculpture – all a long time before amplification.

We now live in an age of electronics, a parallel building of our time would be the Lloyds Building in the City. Place it next to the Parthenon. One has piped music. This is the age of electronic music. I am a musician, a composer, I have a catholic taste in music – that doesn't mean I like to hear the Pope play the piano. I can listen to the music of the Arunta tribe in Australia – to the sublime slow movement of Shostakovich's Sixth Symphony. But what happens when I'm forced to listen to music I don't want to hear? Well, first of all I haven't asked for it – secondly, it's not the music I want to hear. It started for me on a VC10 British Airways flight to Australia – as I boarded the plane, there was this yowling music. I waited till the grinning 'Anything-we-can-do-to-make-your-flight-more-comfortable?' stewardess came with the hot towels and I said, 'Can you turn this music off?' Her whole being came to a shuddering halt. If I had said take your knickers off and I'll eat them, she couldn't have been more stricken. 'I'll have to ask the head steward, sir.' The head steward brings his grin up, 'Yes sir?' I repeated I'd like the music switched off. He too shits himself. 'I can turn it down, sir.' Didn't he hear me? 'I said off.' No, he's not allowed to switch it off; OK, call the captain. 'The captain, sir?' (like he's never heard of one). 'The captain – the bloody captain!' 'There's no need to swear, sir.' No need. Never in my life had I needed to swear, I say it again, 'The bloody captain – or I'll get off.' He minces off, back comes big, blond captain. 'I believe you want the music off.' Yes. He's not allowed, it's company policy. 'Why, will the bloody plane crash? It's *my* company's policy not to listen to piped music – why won't they switch it off? I'm a first-class passenger, have I no rights?' He says the other passengers like it, so I take him by the hand and ask each passenger, 'Is it vital you have this music for take-off?' All say no, except two Chinamen and an Arab who don't know what I'm talking about. The captain says he can't argue with me, he has to fly the plane. I say I'll get off – he goes to the head steward, who switches it off. The plane takes off, no one screams out, 'The music, I must have the music.'

No, if I want music I go to the Albert Hall, I don't go to the manager of the Albert Hall and ask him to fly me to Australia. In any case, as my TV Film will show, no one listens to it – even my six-year-old daughter said on a flight, 'Is this the pretend we're not going to crash music?' I visited Re-diffusion, who turn out this mindless pulp; to my horror, I discover the man who commissions the music can't read a note of music, nor can any of his directors.

And it's now on the telephone – I wanted to book a flight on Qantas and I got this crappy Japanese 'hold' music – finally, when I'm put through, a voice said, 'Flight bookings'. I said 'Just a minute', I then sang him 'My Way'. He kept interrupting me – 'It's my hold music,' I said. He didn't understand – like all of us, he's been conditioned. Housewives put on the radio first thing in the morning and leave it on, as they say, 'as background'. When I think of the megawatts of the earth's energy being wasted on endless hours of yack and pulp – electronic music has taken peace and tranquillity out of our lives – those who go to rock concerts have been cured of serenity. The biggest insult to music is in the new public loos. Who writes music to crap to? Over and out.

Spike Milligan
25th July 1990

Vandalising a Diploma: 1972

Spike the vandal defacing what was a very nice diploma.

Club Oenologique Wine & *Spirit Judge*

19 72

This Diploma affirms that

Spike Milligan Esq.

has passed the Club Oenologique examination

and is hereby awarded the Gold *insignia*
This means I've got pissed more times than
the Chairman.

Director
Club Oenologique

Chairman
Club Oenologique

Mussolini: His Part in My Downfall: 1978

Gunner Edgington's Public Appearance

'Crabs! They've got crabs!' the cry runs through the serried ranks.

The 'Theys' were the crew of Monkey 2, it was the first mass out-break of crabs in the Battery, how proud we were of them, at last the label dirty bastards could be added to the Battery honours. The only other mass outbreak of crabs was Gunner Neat in Bexhill. He told the MO he got them off a girl in Blackpool. 'I brought them south for the sun, sir,' he said.

Among the crab-ridden is Gunner Edgington. Let him recount the grisly details.

We hadn't had our clothes off for some considerable time, much less our underwear, such as it might have been, and as I've said, a bath was something we only vaguely remembered from long ago. My hair was a matted lump. The whole world we knew at that time was to get phone lines out and keep them going – all else was sleep and food and a good deal of the latter was often scrounged from strange outfits we encoun-tered while out on the line.

Not surprisingly we began to smell strongly and then to scratch: the irritation became incessant and something obviously had to be done: I don't think Bentley came to us … it was just arranged by phone calls, that we go over to RHQ.

I think there *must*'ve been more than the M.2 team, for the 'crab-ridden' were taken in a three-tonner to where some showers had been erected in the corner of a field. The showers were a Heath Robinson contraption mounted under a tin roof on angle-iron supports, but they were thoroughly efficient.

Capt. Bentley, keeping a distance, called down instructions from the safety of his room on an upper floor of an adjacent building.

'Strip off!' he called to us, and this was just the Monkey 2 gang at this point. 'Have a thorough wash-down all over as hot as you can pos-sibly stand it.'

The terrible crab-ridden M.2 team

In the middle of this field, in full view of civilians and soldiers alike, we disported ourselves joyously under four very efficient jets of steam and near-boiling water to the accompaniment of screams, yells and cackles.

'Blimey, you can see the bloody things! See 'em moving under the skin? Those little bastards.'

Sure enough, I could see my collection in the skin of my belly just above the 'short-and-curlies'.

Some five minutes, and Bentley calls:

'OK, that's enough – get up here like lightning!'

Away we went in a tight bunch for the steps which led up the side of the building; these being only wide enough to permit one at a time, it meant some of us had to ease back to create a single-file rush up the stairs, all naked and freezing. Into a small bare room we thundered, its only furniture a bare table, on which stood in a row seven empty cigarette tins, and a large dob of cotton wool alongside – no sign of Bentley though.

Looking round puzzled, we see his grinning face peering round a distant door at the far end of the room – he had no wish to get near us. The legend 'crabs can jump six feet' still lingered on.

'Right! Each man grab a tin and a blob of cotton wool. Dip the cotton wool into the tin and dab it generously all over the affected parts … quickly now, quickly!' He slammed the door, in case any escaped.

Looking in my tin I saw a clear mauve liquid. The lads were all still chortling and crying in mock agony – 'Unclean! Unclean!', the war-cry we had been bellicosely hollering from the lorry that brought us – and ringing imaginary handbells.

The fluid was liberally applied – backs, balls and bellies as well – not one of us having guessed what it was, it took about ten to fifteen seconds to act. Then everyone's balls caught fire. It was raw alcohol.

The first 'Cor-mate!' was rapidly echoed all round, followed by a growled 'Awww! Gawd blimey!!' Faces were transfixed with pain and cross-eyed agony, they yelled, they screamed, they fell and rolled, they jumped, they ran back and forth, they twisted, cannoned into walls – each other – they fell over the table. At the height of the chaotic fandango I was sat on the floor, knees drawn up, left arm wedging my trunk half upright, right hand fanning my 'wedding-tackle', when through the melée of flailing arms, legs and prancing bodies I saw the inner door open again slightly and Bentley's face appear in the narrow gap. 'Merry Christmas,' he said and was gone!

For Edgington to remember that occasion in such detail thirty-five years after the event is quite a feat of memory. Mind you, one doesn't get crabs every day, not even at the fishmongers.

The 101 Best and Only Limericks of Spike Milligan: 1982

A man fell down a mine
Said, 'Help! Someone drop me a line!'
Down came a letter
Saying *Hope you feel better,*
Dinner's at half-past nine.

A man from the Mull of Kintyre
Said, 'My bagpipes are always for hire.'
When he started to play
He was shot at, they say,
Which deflated them just like a tyre.

A man who banked at Coutts
Was in rags and had no boots.
When he asked for a loan
They let out a groan
Because banks don't care two bloody hoots!

A man who played a bassoon
Continually played the same tune
Through August to September,
November, December,
March, April, May and now June!

A detective who worked in a store
Caught a thief stealing knickers galore.
To arrest her he had to,
This one he was glad to –
'Twas his grotty old mother-in-law.

A man caught stealing a tree
Told the judge – 'I need it, you see.
My leg needs support.
If it weren't for this court
I'd be walking around quite free.'

A man who was driving a jeep
Was trapped by a vast flock of sheep.
He beeped with his horn
Which they treated with scorn
Because sheep go 'Baa, Baa' not 'Beep, Beep'.

A coal-miner living in Wales
Bought his wife a fur coat in the sales.
It wasn't much fun
For the thing weighed a ton –
Very good in typhoons or in gales.

The Looney: 1987

The Burial

That night, stiff as a board, they buried the dog four legs upwards.

Mrs Aida Higgs, the aged short-sighted next-door neighbour, heard the nocturnal digging. In the gloom she espied the outline of the Looneys burying 'something' in the garden. Brought up on the *Sun*'s shock-horror journalism, she dialled 999. 'There's something strange going on in the next-door garden.'

Constable Albert Ward rang the bell on 113b Ethel Road.

'Dere's a cheque in der post,' hissed a voice through the letterbox.

'Excuse me,' said the constable addressing the letterbox, 'it's the Police, we'd like a word with the owner.'

There was a pause, the letterbox said, 'Wot television set, officer?' and went on, 'Der's no television set in here.'

During this time, Mrs Looney was covering it with a white altar cloth placing a crucifix atop. When Constable Ward was admitted, Mrs Looney and son Dick were kneeling and praying before it, the ten o'clock news issuing from it escaping the constable's notice. The constable would like to examine the garden. 'Oh, dat's paid for as well,' said sweating Looney. The constable observed the newly disturbed earth: either the victim was a dwarf or they had buried him doubled up.

'How many people live here?' he said.

'All of us,' said Looney.

The constable inspected the garden, sensing he was on the verge of a great murder discovery. Scraping the surface, he came across four paws. 'Yes, der dog he's buried dere. You're standin' on his head.' Constable Ward returned to duty, two Valiums and *Playboy*.

The Traffic Warden

No, not all those bemedalled veterans carrying banners past the Cenotaph were heroes. Many didn't volunteer, most were conscripted, many spent the war racking their brains how to get out. Eating soup to fibrillate the heart, stuffing cushions up their backs saying they were deformed, pretending they were deaf, dumb, daft, making chicken noises when spoken to, putting shaving foam in their mouths and barking, feigning rabies. Suddenly the war was over. They *were* the victors! Medals were distributed to those who hadn't even heard a gun go bang, anyone in uniform was adulated, they were heroes!

One of these was Len Gollops. At his medical he appeared with bare feet, leapt on to the interview table and started to eat the *Daily Mirror*. Members of the Board watched in silence until he had finished, the Medical Officer said, 'Very good, you're the tenth newspaper eater we've had this morning', and passed him A1 with the recommendation 'very fine actor'.

He was sent to the Pioneer Corps, but he still tried, coming on parade naked howling like a wolf. It wasn't wasted on his sergeant who said, 'Stop actin' like a cunt.' Clucking like a chicken, he was posted overseas: Alderney! When the Germans invaded he suddenly stopped clucking – mainly because they beat the living daylights out of him. 'Lay eggs or stop zat,' they had warned. After the war he had told people that he took to the 'hills' of Alderney and became a Resistance leader called 'The Black Terror', whereas his record showed he became a POW and ended up as a sluice operator on a Nazi sewage farm in Dortmund.

How he envied the power of those prison camp Kapos. 'Pick up zat shit,' they'd say and he'd have to do it. He told them he had been a member of Oswald Mosley's Fascist Party. Immediately things got better for him and he was promoted from the sewage farm at Dortmumd to a sewage farm in Berlin – due to air raids there was more of it there. He cooperated with the Nazis and as a mark of appreciation they gave him extra sewage to handle. Then came the terrible Allied bombing raid on the city. Along with the residents, like *Starlight Express* he ran and ran and ran, then wandered lonely as a cloud that floats aloft o'er dale and hills when all at once he came upon a host of golden British Military Police. 'Oi, yew in the karzi suit, where yew goin?' Gollops explained he had escaped from a German top-security camp by killing twenty guards, they accepted his story, but just in case they beat him up. At his debriefing he told the officer he had a full working knowledge of Nazi sewage disposal. It was too good to waste, he was rushed back to England to become sanitary orderly to a bomb disposal unit in Leatherhead.

Those romantic war years were gone but not forgotten: whenever he heard Lili Marlene, his mind went back to those cooling sprinklers in Germany. He liked the Nazis; if Hitler were alive today there wouldn't be all these niggers and wogs in Kilburn. Hitler would stop all those niggers jumping up and down at discos, he'd put Velcro on the ceiling.

Gollops' bedroom was a temple to Fascism: above his head were newspaper cut-outs of Hitler, Franco, Mussolini and Mrs Thatcher, other walls have Swastikas and Nazi daggers, by the bed a copy of *Mein Kampf* 20p at Oxfam, the price of fame. The trouble with England was the Jews the niggers the wogs and his landlady Mrs Kitchen, the Royal family were Jews, wasn't Prince Charles circumscribed by the Chief Rabbi? Prince Philip was a Bubble-and-Squeak, Mountbatten was a bloody German, the Queen had wog blood through Isabella of Spain, Robert Graves said so. Hitler wouldn't have allowed all this pot smoking, he'd only have allowed decent non-homosexual Woodbines.

Like Nazi Germany, Gollops had his wife trained. When he went down for breakfast of a morning she'd give the Nazi salute and say, 'Mornin' darlin' and Heil 'Itler,' and he'd say, 'Mornin' darlin', Heil Hitler, what's fer breakfast,' and she'd say: 'Weetabix and Heil Hitler.' Oh yes, Hitler was dead in the rest of the world but here at Flat 9, 345 Ivy Street, Kilburn, Hitler was alive and well. Gollops would never book a Mercedes or a Volkswagen. Today was a bad day for the Nordic race, Cooney the white boxing hope had been beaten by the nigger Larry Holmes. That nigger would never have knocked out Hitler, his

Waffen SS would have crippled him in the first round with a Tiger Tank, oh yes.

This morning he came downstairs smelling of Brut and Sheen. 'Ohh, Heil 'Itler, darlin', you do look smart,' said Frau Gollops. Yes, today was Hitler's birthday, if Adolph were alive today he would have been dead forty years, today he would teach a few niggers a lesson.

This morning Len Gollops, traffic warden, walked the streets of Kilburn, his medals on, his shoes polished like Nazi jackboots, his hat steamed into the shape of the Waffen SS.

Ah! His heart leapt with joy, a rusting Mini Minor on a double yellow, velvet steering-wheel cover, skeleton doll hanging from rear-view mirror, Alsatian with nodding head in rear window, nylon imitation leopardskin upholstery, niggers!!! What's this note under the windscreen: 'The driver of this car is a crippled war hero, Dunkirk a direct hit.' Gollops' Fascist heart softened. As he put his tickets away, a tubby unshaven man arrived.

'Oh, officer,' he said. 'I'm just movin' it.'

'Are you Jewish?' said Gollops.

'No,' said the man. 'I can't afford to be.'

'Just a minute,' said Gollops. 'Did you write this note?' He held it before the man's eyes.

'I can't remember,' said the man, clutching his head. 'Loss of memory, the war, you know. Dunkirk, a direct hit!'

'It says here you're a war cripple.'

The man nodded.

'You walked all right to me, mate,' said Gollops.

The man suddenly grabbed his knee. 'Oh my legs.'

Staring at the unshaven man now rolling on the pavement, Gollops started to make out a ticket. 'I've 'ad enough of this bollocks,' he said.

The man groaned. 'Come here,' he said and crawling led Gollops round the back. 'Dere,' he said and pointed to a cardboard CD plate tied on with string. 'Irish Embassy,' said the man. 'You can't touch me,' he added and collapsed.

Unspun Socks from a Chicken's Laundry: 1981

Words Without Worth

I wandered lonely as a cloud
That floats aloft o'er dale and hills,
When all at once I came upon
My dog being sick on the daffodils.

Castle Crag
Sydney
NSW

Hamlet

Said Hamlet to Ophelia,
'I'll do a sketch of thee.
What kind of pencil shall I use,
2B or not 2B?'

Perth WA
March 1980

The Looney: 1987

The Seance

Mrs Delores Fruit, Drool's only living spiritualist, moved in silent septuagenarian smoothness across the lino of her seance room, her grey hair tied in a huge bun like her head was being inflated. She was rubbing her hands together producing a noise like sandpaper. Behind her followed the cottage loaf form of Mrs Aida Higgins. It was that bugger her husband she wanted to contact, seven years ago he had left home, the bugger! Till then he had given her three years of blissful married life, followed by ten of misery. She had never forgiven him, the bugger! Always moaning that he felt faint, the bugger! And that final disgrace, why had she married an illiterate, subnormal farmhand? Oh, that terrible disgrace, himself caught screwing a cow! The bugger! That court case, the disgrace! That counsel for the prosecution, what he said! 'M'lud, ladies and gentlemen of the jury, on the day of the alleged offence my client was grazing contentedly in a field …' The bugger! It was the night she had hit him with a flat iron, he had left on a stretcher, just like that, the bugger! Not so much as a kiss-me-arse he left, never even said goodbye, just laying there with his head split open, the ungrateful bugger.

'So, Mrs Higgins,' purred Mrs Fruit, 'you wish to contact your dear husband.'

Mrs Higgins nodded. 'Yes,' she said through pursed lips like a chicken's bum.

'Please,' said Mrs Fruit, indicating a chair.

Mrs Higgins lowered her vast bulk onto it blotting it from human view.

Mrs Fruit sat silently in her seance chair, drawing a small lace handkerchief from a dilly-bag. Birdlike she placed it delicately to her nose and gave a blast like the Queen Mary, at the same time dislodging her canary from his perch. 'Now,' she said very quietly, 'it's a pound for the first seance, thereafter fifty pee a session.'

Mrs Higgins delved in her bag. One pound, so that's what the bugger was costing her, that bugger! She handed the trembling note across the table to the medium.

'Now,' said Mrs Fruit, 'please concentrate.' With fluttering lids she closed her eyes, grabbed the arm of the chair, threw back her head. 'Ahhhtishoo!' she roared, releasing a shower of dandruff. The dazed canary shook himself and climbed up the ladder again. For the second time Mrs Fruit composed herself. Had it been Debussy he would have committed suicide. 'When we contact dear husband, is there any question you want to ask him?'

Mrs Higgins nodded. 'Yes, ask him what he's done with the bloody fish knives.'

Mrs Fruit shuddered, ask him what he's done with the bloody fish knives. Suddenly Mrs Fruit went limp like a sack of it, then stiffened like rigor mortis. 'Is there anybody there?' she moaned.

'I am,' said Mrs Higgins.

Mrs Fruit tried again. 'Is anybody there in the beyond?'

There followed a long teasing silence. Mrs Higgins leaned forward, the bugger wasn't answering!

Again Mrs Fruit moaned, 'Are you there, Sean Higgins, are you there?'

There came an impact sound as an excessively hairy tom cat shot through the cat flap carrying a wriggling rat in its jaws.

'Mary Mother of God!' screamed Mrs Higgins. Forgetting she had no knickers on, she hoisted her skirts up to her waist. With a fanny that looked like Bernard Shaw, she leapt on to a chair. It collapsed sending her crashing down on the unfortunate pussycat. With a pained yeowl like elastic, it pulled itself from under her pneumatic bulk and galloped out the cat flap leaving the rat free. With hands waving, Mrs Higgins shrieked anew and fled the building.

Outside, Looney, about to enter, was knocked flat by a huge woman naked from the waist down rushing past. She ran down the street with her Bernard Shaw. Looney watched the cheeks of her bum like alternating jellies.

Inside the seance room, Mrs Fruit stood on her chair watching the rodent seeking a way to escape. This was the worst seance since that one in World War Two. She was working in the WVS in Florence serving tea an' buns to our poor boys from the front. To keep her hand in the spiritual world she held seances for the soldiers to help 'entertain' them. That night when four totally ignorant Royal Artillery gunners agreed to attend they sat around the table baffled.

'Would any of you like to contact any of your loved ones?'

Gunner Robson grunted, 'Yer, I'd like ter contact my muvver Rose.'

Mrs Fruit called to the beyond, 'Hello, Rose Robson … hello, Rose Robson, are you there?' she moaned.

What Robson hadn't told her was that his mother was alive and well and living in Brighton. 'She won't hear you from 'ere,' he said.

That was all past. Right now, Looney was calling down the hall, 'Is anybody dere?'

From within came a female voice, 'Helpppppppppppppppppppp pppp!' by which time Looney reached the room. 'The rat,' instructed Mrs Fruit. 'Get rid of the rat!'

Grabbing the creature by the tail, Looney hurled it into the garden. 'I'm sorry about this,' she said.

'Wus dat your rat?' said Looney.

She held her hand up as though she couldn't speak. When Looney showed her a pound she recovered and indicated a chair which Looney placed over the ruins of Mrs Higgins' chair. 'I want ter get in touch wid me ancestors,' he explained.

'Any particular one?' she said.

'Yes,' said Looney, 'any particular one.'

Mrs Fruit told him after the pound it would be another fifty pee. Diving down he pulled fifty pee from his jockstrap. She took it along with a handful of pubic hair.

The medium closed her eyes. Looney watched transfixed, dis must be a powerful woman, anyone who could make Mrs Higgins run down the street naked from the waist down showing her Bernard Shaw must have the power.

'Ohhhhhhhh,' moaned Mrs Fruit. 'Are any of Mick Looney's ancestors there?' Her words hung in the air, she took a deep asthmatic breath. Suddenly she stiffened. 'I have somebodyyyyyyyyyyy,' she intoned.

Looney craned forward, the moment of truth. 'What does he say?' he said.

The answer came clear and strong. 'The fish knives are with Aunty Peggy' ... It was that bugger.

Mussolini: His Part in My Downfall: 1978

FRIDAY, DECEMBER 3, 1943

MY DIARY: POURING RAIN. DUG A DEEP DRAINAGE PIT AROUND MY BIVVY TO DIVERT FLOW OF WATER. G TRUCK NOW HAVE LOGS ON THEIR FIRE. VERY COSY. UNENDING BREW-UPS OF TEA AND COFFEE. BACK ON COMMAND POST DUTIES. MUST ANSWER LETTERS.

A letter from my mother and father had said that my brother was to go into the RAF (as he ended up a private in the Ulster Rifles, I began to feel uneasy about my parents' sanity). My father's letters were getting to be a pain in the arse. He seemed obsessed with the idea that I 'didn't answer your mother's letters'. Now at that time I thought he might be right, but on checking with my Correspondence log I note that I answered each and every letter. Since then and down the years to his death, he continued to insist with his accusations, so much so that I registered all my letters (over the years it cost a bloody fortune) and stuck all the receipts in a book that I presented to him on his seventieth birthday with the message. 'To dear Dad, a small token to prove that I always answer all Mum's letters.' He looked at it and said, 'This is a fake, my memory is the real proof of your laxity in letter-writing to your poor mother.' He even wrote to all our relatives asking them to write to me and pressurise me to 'answer his poor mother's letters'. It was a true case of mania. He died saying, 'Promise you'll write to your mother today.' She was standing beside me at the time.

My mother's letters were equally a mass of instructions, 'Pray to Saint Patrick and Saint Theresa *every night*. Go to Confession and Communion every Sunday! Say prayers morning, noon and night, always wear your scapular medals, don't swear, keep your holy pictures in your pockets' ... How do you go into action? On your knees?

OP OFFICER:	Target tanks.
ME:	Yes sir, *Et in secular*, target tanks, Amen.
OFFICER:	HE 119 Charge four.

ME: Yes sir, HE 119 Charge four. God forgive me for
                       attempting to kill Germans.
OFFICER: Angle of sight 03 degrees.
ME: 03 degrees. Holy Virgin, bless these fire orders.
OFFICER: Right ranging.
ME: Right ranging *mea culpa, mea culpa, mea maxima
                       culpa.* Amen. Fire!

I know now that Evelyn Waugh was a Catholic, and in Yugoslavia, pissed out of his mind, went all out for medals by standing up during bombing raids and shouting to poor Randolph Churchill under a table, 'Come out, you yellow swine.' Well, I wasn't *that* good a Catholic.

The Mirror Running: 1987

The Butterfly

This evening in the twilight's gloom
A butterfly flew in my room
Oh what beauty, oh what grace
Who needs visitors from out of space?

Bedroom
Monkenhurst
24 July 1984

Lyric

It was summer –
  on the lake hung a golden haze,
It was summer –
  it was one of those endless days,
So we talked thru' a field of clover
  and then over
  a sheep-spun hill
And it seemed it would last forever
  and it did – until
Came the evening,
  we swung on a garden gate
It was heaven,
  you were seven and I was eight.
And we watched at the stars suspended,
Walking home down an apple lane,
Me and Rosie, a doll, a daisy chain,
On an evening that would never come again.

2 January 1985
Set to music by Alan Clare

Agnus Dei

Behold, behold,
The Lamb of God
As it skips and hops.
I know that soon
The Lamb of God
Will be the Lamb of Chops.

My Daughter's Horse

My daughter has a horse in her head
He gallops thru' fantasies in her mind
She calls him Fury
I can see him thru' her eyes
She rides him thru' her spirit grasses
At night she stables him in her dreams.
He must be beautiful
Her face is alight when she sees him
She feeds him on her soul
He becomes what colour she wishes.
I thought there was no end to him
Until – one day she met
Fred – the butcher's boy.

Startling Verse for All the Family: 1987

I am I

I am 1.
If I were less,
I would be none
I must confess.
But 1 plus 1 –
How do you do?
I'm introducing
You to 2
Now 1 plus 2,
Hi diddle dee,
For that, my friend,
Would add to 3.
Then 3 plus 1 –
A little more –
It adds up to
The figure 4.
3 plus 2:
There comes alive
A number that we
Know as 5.
So 5 plus 1:
We get a fix
With a number
We call 6.
With 6 plus 1
I swear to heaven
That will bring us
Up to 7.
To 7 plus 1
Please open the gate

And let a number in
Called 8.
1 plus 8
Is dead in line
To end up as
A number 9.
9 plus 1
So finally, then,
We come at last
To number 10.

A Man Was Under

A man was under
A bolt of thunder
As he sheltered 'neath a tree.
What terrible luck –
The lightning struck
And burnt his riddle-me-ree!

Little Jim

Little Jim is very small.
He wanders up and down the hall.
Sometimes he wanders up the stairs
Or sits in one of daddy's chairs.
Sometimes we wonder where he's gone
And find him laying on the lawn.
He's very fond of chocolate bars.
He goes outside and watches stars.
Other times he's in the bath
Or wandering up the garden path.
He doesn't ever watch the telly –
Instead you find him eating jelly.
Little Jim talks very funny:
He has a nose that's always runny.
Sometimes he screams, sometimes he yells,
Sometimes he positively smells.
He walks around and sucks his thumb.
Sometimes he kicks me up the bum!
Still I treat him patiently
'Cos little Jim is only three.
Mum tells me he's my baby brother
Please God don't let her have another!

Hippety hoppity

Hippety hoppity
Hoppity hoo
Goes the bounding
Kangeroo.
You can't lock him
In a pen
He would just
Leap out again.
It's hard to keep
Him in at all
For he can jump
A six-foot wall.
His leap is really
So immense
He can clear
A ten-foot fence.
You'd never keep him
In a zoo –
He'd just leap out
And over you.
No one so far
Has ever found a
Way to catch
The little bounder.
So, oh dear,
What can we do
To catch the bounding
Kangeroo?

Moral.
Never shoot a Kangeroo!
Its a nasty thing to do,
He won't harm me,
He won't harm you,
Hippety Hoppity Kangeroo!

4

Milligan Reigns

Article for *BAA News:* 1991

View from the VIP Lounge

As I write this, there are nearly two million people at a height of 30 to 40 thousand feet, it's like the population of New Zealand and Eire all being in the air, such is the peculiarity of flying. At specified times, thousands come down to earth while thousands go up again. They all go in different directions for different reasons, some go somewhere else just to get away from where they are, to do this first they have to go to – wait for it – an airport. It used to be called an aerodrome but with the coming of George Orwell's 'newspeak' it's airport. These airports are all almost identical, i.e. let's imagine you are in the waiting area of airport A, if by magic in a flash you were transported to airport B, you wouldn't notice the difference. The initial impact to those who hadn't travelled before is one of chaos. People with large bags are walking in all directions crashing into each other, praying that the planes don't do the same. They all converge like penguins in queues at the checking-in desk. Behind this sits a maiden who seems hypnotised by a computer screen. They hand her their ticket. She immediately consults the computer screen and taps out something on the computer keyboard. The ensuing silence fills the passenger with doubts. Did he book the ticket properly? Is this the right day? The right time? Even the right year? A brave passenger might shatter the system by saying 'Can I have a non-smoker?' The maiden will put on a standard airport smile, she will then agitate the keyboard and consult the screen. The answer she will give is not a yes or no but 'You will be recommended'. You load your luggage onto a conveyor, wondering and praying that you will see it again. 'Noumea! that's where it ended up last time!' The airport maiden asks 'Have you any hand luggage?' Have I any hand luggage????? It's *all* hand luggage. How does she think it got here? Now comes a series of tests. You go through the gate first, it infers you are trying to travel without a ticket, yet it is but a few minutes ago you had showed it at the check-in! Security: this one suggests you are an Arab/IRA terrorist and have bombs in your hand luggage, a body search where they suspect you have a pistol under each armpit, up your back, one each side of your knees and ankles and one in your crutch; ladies are searched by what look suspiciously like lesbians in uniform. Now comes passport time and now you say a silent prayer, 'will that old passport photo match up to as you are now'. The official opens your passport, first he leafs through the pages like someone in a second-hand book shop, pausing now and then to look up at you. In my case, he paused at my photo. 'You have a beard here,' he says. 'Yes,' I said, with a forced grin. Then I heard myself saying 'I shaved it off.' He locates the expiry date. 'This passport will need renewing soon.' It was my chance for a joke. 'Yes,' I said, 'So will my body.' He nodded, handed my passport back. 'Have a nice holiday,' he said, rather like the Pope on the Vatican balcony. Now you will arrive in a vast 'waiting' area, it is crammed with penguins sitting, standing, lying down, hundreds of children are running in and out of everywhere – hanging from the ceiling are what look like totalisators. It shows airport arrivals and departures that are endlessly in a state of flux, in each square numbers of flights are coming and going with great rapidity. It's like a fruit machine. When I was there, I wondered if I get three identical flight numbers in a line, would I win a prize? There are flights to everywhere, Frankfurt, Athens, Bombay, but in my case I wanted to go to Palma – against it was the word 'delayed'. I was told to be there 'One hour before take-off'. By the time the plane finally arrived, I'd arrived *three* hours before take-off.

Dear reader, what's this all about, you may ask. Well, in 800 words, for those of you who don't know, I've been describing an airport and what happens there. I conclude with the story of the blind pianist George Shearing. He and his guide dog had just boarded a plane to New York – as with all handicapped people, he was allowed to board before the main body of passengers. The pilot welcomed the famous man and asked was there anything he could do for him. Shearing said 'Yes, before take-off my dog needs to do a wee', at which time the main body of passengers were approaching the plane – only to see the pilot coming down the stairs with a guide dog for the blind.

Article for BT 'Tone Talk': Undated

Phoneless but not legless ...

I was born into a military family in India without a telephone. What a disgrace to be born without a telephone!

The delivery doctor broke the news to my father: 'Sergeant Milligan, I'm sorry to say your son has been born without a telephone.'

So for all my formative years we survived without a phone. In its place we sent messages by native messenger who had no phone but two legs. That way we didn't have to remember any telephone numbers – just the name of the messenger with two legs.

It was not until my family returned to England in 1935 that I used my first phone. It was an age when telephone boxes were vandal free. (Why doesn't British Telecom invent specially pre-vandalised phone boxes to beat the vandal to it?)

I was in love with a girl who was on the telephone. Her name was Lily Dunford, mine was Spike Milligan. I still didn't have a phone but I had legs, so I used to make them take me to a phone box.

I was very poor and though calls only cost tuppence I and my legs could only afford three a week, after which I would tell the operator: 'I'm very poor and I'm in love with this girl. I'm so in love my underpants are all scorched and I smell of burning hairs.'

And blow me down, nine times out of ten the operator would put me through free, proving that nine out of ten operators have very kind hearts. They also have kind livers, kidneys, lungs, etc – although I've never seen a kind etc.

Some people have telephonitis. If they don't answer telephones they suffer withdrawal symptoms. One telephonitis looney was my solicitor. Once in his office, during an important conversation with me, he answered his phone 12 times. I had to spend two hours with him on an occasion that should have only taken ten minutes.

I decided to teach him a lesson with the assistance of Harry

Secombe. I invited the solicitor to dinner. As we were served soup, on the stroke of eight o'clock, the phone rang.

Immediately the solicitor stiffened. The phone rang on. 'Aren't you going to answer that?' he said in a strained voice. 'No,' I said.

It continued to ring. Suddenly, unable to stand it any longer, my solicitor dropped his soup spoon and dashed to the phone.

'Hello,' he said, and the voice of Harry Secombe replied: 'You silly bugger, your soup's getting cold!', followed by a raspberry and a giggle. Revenge is sweet but not fattening.

It will come as a surprise that during the last war I was on a ten-line switchboard handling up to 20 calls an hour. So I know what it's like to be on the receiving end. And to that end I have a story to tell.

1940, on night duty in a concrete bunker in Bexhill.

Suddenly into the bunker came a retinue of high-ranking top brass, among them General Alanbrook. He was inspecting the 'front line', which in those days was Bexhill-on-Sea, a simple little town – the local idiot and town mayor were the same man and the village hooker was a virgin.

Alanbrook said to me: 'What do you do?'

I said: 'I do my best.'

Shaking his head, he left. Then a call came through from our own Captain Martin, a rogue of a man. He wanted me to call his wife in London. So I did. And I listened in to the conversation.

It was pure eroticism. He told her how he'd like to undress her, cover her in olive oil then fondle her all over, etc, etc ...

Now, my exchange was linked up to about 20 observation posts along the South Coast. They were manned by poor lonely soldiers. To help these poor lonely soldiers I plugged them in to 30 minutes of scorching conversation, so the whole South Coast got it. It was Christmas and a merry time was had by all.

Before I sign off I'd like to say a big thank you to the Telecom linesmen who connected all the phones after the hurricane down south, although as I write *my* phone is out of order.

However, I have two legs.

The Bible … According to Spike Milligan: 1993

Spike came into my office one morning.

Spike: 'I'm going to re-write the Bible today.'

Me: 'Of course you are.'

This was the start of the 'According to' series.

CHAPTER I

THE CREATION ACCORDING TO THE
TRADE UNIONS

I N THE BEGINNING GOD CREATED THE HEAVEN AND THE EARTH.

2. And darkness was upon the face of the deep; this was due to a malfunction at Lots Road Power Station.

3. And God said, Let there be light; and there was light, but Eastern Electricity Board said He would have to wait until Thursday to be connected.

4. And God saw the light and it was good; He saw the quarterly bill and that was not good.

5. And God called the light Day, and the darkness He called Night, and so passed His GCSE.

6. And God said, Let there be a firmament and God called the firmament heaven, Freephone 999.

7. And God said, Let the waters be gathered together unto one place, and let the dry land appear, and in London it went on the market at six hundred pounds a square foot.

8. And God said, Let the earth bring forth grass, and the earth brought forth grass and the Rastafarians smoked it.

9. And God said, Let there be lights in heaven to give light to the earth, and it was so, except over England where there was heavy cloud and snow on high ground.

10. And God said, Let the seas bring forth that that hath life, flooding the market with fish fingers, fishburgers and grade-three salmon.

11. And God blessed them, saying, Be fruitful, multiply, and fill the

sea, and let fowl multiply on earth where Prince Charles and Prince Philip would shoot them.

12. And God said, Let the earth bring forth cattle and creeping things, and there came cows, and the BBC Board of Governors.

13. And God said, Let us make man in our own image, but woe many came out like *Spitting Image.*

14. And He said, Let man have dominion over fish, fowl, cattle and every creepy thing that creepeth upon the earth.

15. And God said, Behold, I have given you the first of free yielding seed, to you this shall be meat, but to the EC it will be a Beef Mountain.

CHAPTER II

ON THE SEVENTH DAY GOD ENDED HIS WORK, but Datsun of Coventry workers went on to time and a half, and God rested from all His work with complete backing from Arthur Scargill and the miners.

2. God blessed the seventh day, as did all the Pakistani corner shops.

3. Every plant, every herb was in earth for the Good Lord had not caused it to rain; because of this Bob Geldof had to raise fifty million quid with Live Aid.

4. And the Lord formed man of the dust of the ground, and breathed into his nostrils the breath of life; it was done privately and not on the National Health.

5. The Lord planted a Garden in Eden and there He put the man He had formed, and He sold the idea to the BBC as *Gardeners' World.*

6. And out of the ground the Lord grew every tree that was pleasant to the sight, but He had not reckoned on the weather forecast from Michael Fish, and they were all blown down in the hurricane.

7. And the Lord took man and put him in the Garden of Eden to dress it and to keep it, subject to compulsory purchase by Brent Council.

8. The Lord God said of every tree of the garden thou mayest freely eat, but He was apprehended at the check-out and forced to pay.

9. But of the tree of knowledge, thou shalt not eatest, or thou shall surely die, due to crop-spraying with DDT.

10. And the Lord said, it is not good that man should be alone. He caused a deep sleep to fall on Adam, which the shop steward penalised him for during working hours, deducting a day's pay. The Lord took one of Adam's ribs, and made a woman and brought her unto the man, which immediately qualified for common law wife allowance.

11. And they were both naked, the man and his wife, and were not ashamed. However, at Bow Street they were charged with indecency.

CHAPTER III

NOW THE SERPENT WAS MORE SUBTLE THAN BEASTS OF THE FIELD; he said unto woman: 'Come and eat the fruit of this tree.' Woman said, 'Nay, if we eat or touch it we die.' And the serpent said, 'Fear not, they are not from South Africa,' whereupon she ate and gave of it to her husband.

2. And the eyes of them were both opened and they knew they were both naked, and Adam said to her, 'Stand back, I don't know how big this is going to get.'

3. And the Lord God called unto Adam: 'Where are thou?'

4. And Adam said, 'I art here.'

5. But both Adam and Eve's eyes were opened and they saw they were naked and they sewed on fig leaves – one for Eve and a hundred and eighty for Adam.

6. The Lord said, 'Who told thee that thou wast naked?'

7. And Adam said, 'I could see it all hanging down.'

8. 'Has thou eaten of the apple?' said the Lord.

9. 'Yea, Eve gave it to me,' said Adam. 'A Granny Smith.'

10. 'Woman,' said the Lord, 'what hast thou done?'

11. And Eve said, 'I haven't done anything, I've only just got here.'

12. And the Lord said unto the serpent, 'Because thou hast done this,

thou art cursed above all cattle, and above every beast of the field; upon thy belly thou shalt go, and dust shalt thou eat all the days of your life.'

13. 'This is victimisation,' said the serpent; 'I shall appeal to the RSPCA.'

14. Unto Adam and Eve the Lord God made coats of skins and, verily, they looked terrible – you could *still* see it all.

15. And Eve saw Cain and said, 'Lo, I have gotten a man from the Lord.'

16. And she got another son and together they were called Cain and Abel.

17. And it came to pass that Cain rose up and slew Abel very badly.

18. And the Lord said, ' 'Ello, 'ello, 'ello, what's going on 'ere?'

19. And the Lord set a mark upon Cain – it was on his right forearm and said Man. United.

20. And Cain went out from Eden to the land of Nod, but there was a curse on the land; it was called Nationwide Building Society.

21. And Cain knew his wife and she bore him a child, Enoch, and in the goodness of time they were all in B&B.

22. But Cain was wise and applied for child benefit.

23. And Adam lived one hundred and thirty years after a course of male hormones. He was lifted on and off and, lo, he begat a son, Seth, who went on to begat many sons and daughters and won the Queen's Award for Industry.

24. Seth lived one hundred and five years and, after testosterone tablets, begat Enos.

25. And it came to pass, men began to multiply on the face of the earth – and lo, there were many queues for hip operations and standing only on the tube.

26. And the sons of God saw the daughters of men and they were fair; and they took them wives all of which they chose but, woe, the sleeping arrangements were dodgy.

27. There were giants on the earth in those days; they were all in the British Rugby team.

28. The Lord looked upon the earth and, lo, it was corrupt with *Nightmare on Elm Street III*.

29. He sayeth unto Noah, build an ark and two of every animal of the earth thou shalt take in it. So Noah let the animals in and, lo, Noah and his family were soon up to their necks in it. And Noah's wife said, 'For God's sake – somebody open a window.'

30. And the Lord made it rain forty days and nights and the world was flooded, all except England where they had drought and a hosepipe ban.

31. And the rain and the waters prevailed upon the earth a hundred and fifty days and, woe, cricket was cancelled at the Oval.

32. And it came the waters abated, and Noah sent forth a raven – yea, he went forth and stayed forth.

33. Noah then sent forth a dove and, lo, it returned with an olive leaf plucked off. Noah himself was pretty plucked off.

34. Noah waiteth seven days and he sendeth off the dove yet again – but this time it returned not, having been shot on the Glorious Twelfth.

35. And when the land had dried, Noah lifted the cover off the ark and let it all out.

36. And Noah built an altar for the Lord with DIY and gave a burnt offering. But the Lord was angry and said, 'This offering is burnt.' So Noah sweareth and doeth it all over again in the microwave.

37. And Noah went forth with his wife and sons, and they planteth a vineyard. Soon Noah was drunk as a newt.

38. And Ham saw the nakedness of his father and was jealous of the size. For it was there for all to see, and Ham told his two brethren.

39. And Shem and Japheth took a garment, and went backward and covered the nakedness; and their faces were backward, and they walketh over a cliff.

40. Then Noah awoke from the wine – and saw some joker had tied a blue ribbon round it and he hideth it with his hands.

41. And all the days of Noah were nine hundred and fifty years, the last three hundred on a zimmer. Lo, he died of deafness; there was a horse and cart coming up behind him and he heareth it not.

42. And so the children of Noah begat many children and they too

begat children – everywhere, behind every bush, they were begatting.

43. But Sarai was barren. She had no children and the Lord put her on to Abram, who did it to her until he fell off. Then the Lord blessed Abram – but Sarai said, 'Never mind that, get him off.'

44. The Lord said unto Abram, 'Get thee out of the country.' And Abram said, 'What about my mortgage?'

'It will pass,' said the Lord. As he spoke the mortgage went past Abram, so he offered the Lord another burnt offering. The Lord was angry and said this is worse than the M1. Abram was sore afraid and fell on his face and the Lord said, 'Does that hurt?'

Abram said, 'Yes.'

And the Lord said, 'Upsydaisy.'

So Abram upped his daisy.

And the Lord said, 'Now lift up thine eyes, look from the place thou art northward, southward, eastward and westward.'

'It makes me giddy,' said Abram. But in one Biblical bound Abram was free.

45. And Abram said, 'Behold, to me thou hast given no seed.' The word of the Lord came unto him saying, 'This shall not be thine heir.'

'Oh!' said Abram.

And the Lord said, 'But he that shall come forth out of thine own bowels shall be thine heir.'

For months Abram waited, but nothing came out of his bowels. 'How long, O Lord?' said Abram, straining away.

The Lord said, 'Abram, stop thy straining for if it hath not come to pass by now it never will.'

46. When Abram was ninety years and nine, the Lord appeared with painkillers and said unto him, 'Walk before me, and be thou perfect.' But Abram was with rheumatism plus a humpty back and the Lord saw he was far from perfect and put him on BUPA. But, verily, worse was to come.

47. The Lord said, 'Thy name shall be Abraham and Sarai thy wife shall be Sarah. And ye shall be circumcised in the flesh of your foreskin.'

Abraham was afraid and clutched his bits to him.

48. And the Lord spoke from a cloud: 'And every man child and every man of your house will be circumcised.'

'O Lord,' said Abraham, 'where are we going to put it all?'

'Fear not,' said the Lord, 'they are biodegradable and there are many hungry dogs. And the uncircumcised will be cursed and will go forth with it hanging down into the nettles.'

49. The Lord said, 'I will bless Sarah, and she will bear a child by you.'

Then Abraham fell on his face and laughed; many teeth went. 'A child at my age?' said Abraham.

50. 'Abraham,' called the Lord, 'fear not your age; you still have all the bits required. There is an old Jewish proverb, surely as the serpent hisseth and the lamb calls its mother, therefore will the wild horse run its race to the East End.'

'Lord, I don't know what you're talking about,' said Abraham.

'Fear not,' said the Lord, 'thou shalt have a son and his name shalt be Isaac; your wife is stirring the mixture at the moment.'

51. And the Lord appeared on a burning bush but, lo, there was a smell of burning hairs.

52. On the selfsame day was Abraham circumcised and Ishmael his son by Hagar, Sarah's handmaid. And all the men of his house were circumcised; the bits were everywhere, and for many weeks they wore not underpants and there were many screams in the night, and the wives goeth without.

53. And the Lord appeared unto Abraham in the plains of Mamre, which were safer than the planes of Air Uganda. Abraham sat in the tent door in the heat of the day, knackered. He would make a feast for the Lord. He ran into the herd, took a calf and gave it to a butcher who dressed it; it came back wearing shorts, a T-shirt and football boots.

The Lord was well pleased with the joke and said to Abraham, 'Thou shalt have a son.'

Abraham was fearful and afraid as he still had a sore willy. 'But, Lord, I am old, it's all shrivelled up.'

'Fear not,' said the Lord, 'I will unshrivel it, go now and begat.'

54. Abraham went into Sarah and said, 'The Lord wants me to start a nation.'

And Sarah laughed and said, 'You couldn't start a bus.'

55. The brother of Abraham had a son called Lot and he grew up, which is the right direction, and he dwelt near the cities of Sodom and Gomorrah, sinful places where they kerb-crawleth.

56. And the Lord said unto Abraham, 'Because the cry of Sodom and Gomorrah is great, I will go down now, and see whether they have done altogether according to the cry of it, which is come unto me; and if not, I will know.'

57. 'Eh???' said Abraham.

58. Then Lot spake, 'Up, get out of this place.' Lot's wife sobbed as only that day the new carpet had been fitted.

The Lord appeared in a cloud of something and from somewhere in it said, 'I will destroy this city, it will cost the Halifax dear.'

59. Lot then sayeth what soundeth like a conundrum: 'Behold now, this city is near to flee unto, and it is a little one. Let me escape thither (is it not a little one?)'

And the Lord appeared in a bowl of custard: 'Flee the city, but look not back at the "For Sale" signs.' Then the Lord rained upon Sodom and Gomorrah brimstone, diesel and fire. All the main services came to a halt. Lot of the little one and his wife left, but woe betide! His wife looked back and turned into a pillar of salt. So Lot didn't have to buy salt for the rest of his days.

60. And Abraham rose early to see the city in smoking ruins and sayeth, 'There goes their chance of putting on the Olympics.'

61A. And, with his two daughters, Lot left Zoar where he had fled to, as the prices were too high and he put a deposit on a cane so he layeth down and waiteth for prices to drop.

61B. The one daughter said to the other, 'Our father is old, and there is not a man in the world to come to us.' For Lot there was no disco in the land. The daughters said, 'Let us give our father wine and we will lie with him that we may preserve his seed.' And six nights they did seed saving. Lot said he couldn't remember any of it and was remanded for a psychiatrist's report. Two sons were born; the daughters had given birth to their own brothers, Moab and Benammi.

62. Abraham was now eight hundred years old, by now it had almost dropped off.

63. And the Lord visited Sarah as He had said, and the Lord did unto Sarah as He had spoken. And Sarah delivered a son called Isaac by Red Star. To save money Abraham circumcised him using Mrs Beeton's cookery book as God had commanded him.

64. And there was in the land a woman Hagar who had been using old men's hormones. When Abraham was fourscore and six years old he had put seed unto her and she had borne a son, Ishmael, and when Sarah had heard she had clouteth Abraham good and proper, then she clouted Hagar, and Abraham said, 'Stop, thou knowest not what you do.'

'I know what I'm doing,' said Sarah, 'I'm doing her.'

'Stay your hand,' said Abraham, 'Hagar is only a timeshare wife.' It was only ten minutes.

65. Now, the Lord appeared unto Hagar. He said, 'Arise, lift up your lad, for I will make him a great nation.'

'Anyone but Iraq,' said Hagar.

66. And the lad greweth every day asking, 'Mother, when do I become a great nation?' His mother took him a wife out of the land of Egypt. Seeing this bint, the lad started to begat her. And the Lord saw it and said, 'I will make you a great nation.' And Hagar said, 'Don't worry, if you want he'll make you one.'

And Abraham went forth and gave seven lambs to Abimelech, and Abimelech said, 'Why do you bring me seven lambs?'

'Because,' sayeth Abraham, 'it's all I've got.'

God did tempt Abraham and said unto him, 'Abraham,' and he said, 'Behold, here am I' and, sure enough, there he was. The Lord said, 'Take thy son, Isaac, take him to the land of Moriah and offer him for a burnt offering.'

'Thou wantest me to make him snuff it?'

'Yea,' said the Lord.

So using breeze blocks, Abraham made a barge, lit the fire and told him to get on it – and Abraham said, 'Lord, do you want anything with him? Chips?'

Abraham was preparing to cook Isaac, who was saying, 'Dad, it's getting hot up here.'

'I'm only obeying orders, son,' said Abraham as he blasted Isaac with first cold pressing olive oil, then he took up the carving knife to fricassee his son and an angel of the Lord said, 'Lay not thine hand upon the lad.'

'What's up?' said Abraham. 'Has he gone vegetarian?'

The angel said the Lord is well pleased with you.

'Is that it, then?' said Abraham. And it was.

67. And Sarah died in the Hebron; when they opened the Hebron, there she was on the floor. Abraham wept and sayeth unto his sons, 'Give me a burying place that I may bury my dead out of my sight.'

'You'll have to close your eyes,' they said.

He did and fell in the grave. And his son Isaac said, 'Verily, at your age it's not worth climbing out.'

68. Abraham was old and the Lord had blessed him in all things; indeed, however, by now Abraham's things were well worn. And Abraham said unto his eldest servant, 'I pray thee, put thy hand under my thigh.' And the servant placed her hand under the thigh of her master. And Abraham said, 'The Lord God of heaven, who stopped me frying my son, took me from my father's house and spake unto me etc., saying, unto thy seed will I give this land; he shall send his angels before thee and then shall take a wife unto my son.'

'Can I take my hand out now?' said the servant.

'Thou art a spoilsport,' said Abraham. Then Abraham bowed down before the Lord but it got him in the back. Then Abraham gave all he had unto Isaac including the fish knives and the float in the till. Then he gave up the ghost.

Isaac told the sons, 'He hath snuffed it.' The fees for the cemetery being high they burned him in a cave. 'We must brick up the cave,' said Isaac.

'What for?' said a son. 'Nobody wants to get in.'

'Yes, but we don't want him to get out,' said Isaac.

69. Isaac cried out to the Lord because after lots of begatting his Rebekah was barren, and the Lord intreated of him, and Rebekah conceived. And Isaac was suspicious, but an angel said the Lord works in mysterious ways – and that was one of them.

70. And, lo, Rebekah delivered twins. The first one came out red, all over like an hairy garment; and they called him Esau, then came his brother, who was not red and hairy. Isaac was sad and said, 'Lord, they don't match.' They called the second one Jacob. Esau grew up to be a hunter – no woman was safe. Jacob grew up and stayed there. Isaac loved Esau because he ate venison, Rebekah loved Jacob because he was a vegetarian.

And Jacob sod pottage, it was called so; when he was a child and they were given pottage for breakfast Isaac would say, 'Sod pottage.'

As Jacob ate his sod pottage, Esau said, 'I'm hungry, give me a mess of sod pottage and I will give you my birthright.' So Jacob took Esau's birthright and a post-dated cheque.

71. And woe there was famine in the land. No matter where you looked it was famine. If you lifted up a chair there it was, if you looked under a bed there it was.

72. And Isaac prostrated himself and said, 'Lord, there is famine, there's even some of it under me.'

The Lord appeared in a cloud but Isaac couldn't see Him as he was face down, and the Lord said, 'Sojourn in this land, and I will be with thee and will bless thee; and unto thy seed and I will perform the oath which I swore unto Abraham.'

'Never mind all that,' said Isaac; 'what we need is rain.'

So Isaac went and dwelt in Gerar. Men there asked him of his wife: 'She is my sister,' said Isaac. He was frightened to say she was his wife in case they killed him to get at her.

But one day the king of the Philistines was peering out a window – he liked a good peer – when, yea, he saw Isaac sporting with Rebekah. Well, it *looked* like sporting. The king was angry and said unto Isaac and Rebekah, 'Put your sports clothes on, she is your wife not your sister, one of my men might lightly had lien with her.'

Isaac turned to Rebekah and said, 'Have you been having any light liening?'

'My lord, nay, I am thine wife,' said Rebekah, and taking his hand placed it on her bosom whereupon Isaac gave it a good squeeze. And the Lord blessed him. Now Isaac sowed the land and in a year received a hundredfold and a rates demand. The Lord blessed him, then blessed him again as it didn't take the first time.

And Isaac waxed great, went forward, because that's where he was going, and he grew until he became very great, eighteen stone, and a hernia – the Lord blessed that too.

73. It came to pass, Isaac's servants told him they had dug a well and said, 'We have found water.' And Isaac called it Shebah. Everyone else called it water.

74. And there came the Philistine Army to make peace. Peace on you, they said, and Isaac said, And peace on you. And he made them a feast. And they rose up betimes of a morning and swore one to another, wake up you dozy bastards.

75. When Isaac was old his eyes were like British Rail employees, dim. The Lord looked into his eyes and said, 'Yea, thine eyes look like dim British Rail employees.'

'Who is there?' said Isaac.

' 'Tis I, Esau.'

'Pray, make a dinner of venison that I may eat and bless you before I die.'

Rebekah heard this and told her favourite son Jacob, 'You must make a meal so you will be blessed first.'

'But Mother, Father can see the difference. Esau is a hairy man while I am a smooth man,' said Jacob.

'Let me see,' said Rebekah and, true enough, it was smooth. 'Don't worry.' Rebekah gave him this Gorillagram skin.

Wearing the skin Jacob took a dinner to Isaac.

'Come, let me feel you,' said Isaac. And he felt.

'Ow, not there, Father,' said Jacob, rehanging them.

'Who art thou?' said Isaac.

'I art Esau, the red and hairy one,' said Jacob.

'Then why does thou smell like a gorilla?' said Isaac.

'It is the will of the Lord,' said Jacob.

Isaac was stricken with wonder as he didn't know the Lord had left a gorilla in His will.

76. When Esau, all red and hairy, returned he was knackered. When he heard what had happened, 'Woe to my father, he didn't get a dinner – he got a Gorillagram – woe to the man who knoweth not the difference between a dinner and a Gorillagram.'

And Isaac cursed Jacob, 'You little bastard, there will be a curse on your house – the Halifax Building Society.' And he sent Esau to write 'Burn' on Jacob's roof.

And when Jacob saw it he hid his mother's eyes that she seeth not 'Burn' on the roof. Jacob rose up. 'Thou has defiled mine roof.'

'Ha ha,' said Esau, 'wait till you see what's on the other side.'

And Jacob goeth to the other side and, lo, there was a four-letter word, and Jacob fled the home and the signs that Esau was making to him.

77. And Jacob goeth and chose a wife: one of the daughters of Heth.

'Which one will thou have?' said Heth.

And Jacob said, 'The one with the big tits.'

And sayeth Rebekah, 'Now my sons have gone, what is there for me to do?'

And Isaac said, 'The laundry.'

And Esau in a red hairy rage did say, 'I will kill my brother.'

And Rebekah said, 'Thou must not.'

'Why not?' said Esau.

'Because it's bad for him,' said Rebekah; 'ever since he was a little boy he's hated being killed.'

78. When Isaac knew what had happened despite the hosepipe ban he raised his eyes to heaven and cried upwards.

And Rebekah said unto Isaac, 'Esau and Jacob leaveth to take wives, woe – what good shall my life do to me?'

And Isaac, who was eight hundred, said, 'You won't be getting it any more.'

And Rebekah said thank God.

79. Jacob went out from Beer-sheba and he lighted upon a certain place and he tarried there, he tarried here, he tarried there, he tarried out the window, he tarried all over the place and, when he'd had enough tarry, using a stone for a pillow he fell asleep, but only with the help of Valium. The Lord worked in mysterious ways and this was one of them. Jacob dreamed of a tall ladder reaching from heaven to earth – at first he thought it was the escalator at Harrods full of Arab shoplifters, but then he saw they were angels. So Jacob tarried a while, then he got up.

God said, 'Jacob, I'm with thee.'

Jacob said, 'I'm with the Woolwich,' and thought: if God will be with me in this way and will give me bread to eat and raiment to put on, I won't have to sign on again. Then he took his stone pillow, poured oil on it and said, 'This is God's house, how He gets in is up to Him.'

80. And it came to pass that Jacob met Rachel at the well; Jacob kissed Rachel and lifted up his voice and wept.

'Oh, kinky, eh,' said Rachel.

When Laban heard the tidings of Jacob, his sister's son, he ran to meet him, embraced and kissed him. 'Easy,' said Jacob, 'I'm straight.'

81. And Laban said to him, 'Surely, thou art my bone and flesh.'

'Sorry,' said Jacob, 'all my bone and flesh are mine.' And he abode in the house of Laban. Laban had two daughters: Leah, who was tender-eyed but, oh, Jacob saw that Rachel was beautiful and well-favoured, all over. And he, Jacob, had steam in his trousers. Through the steam and the throbbing Jacob spoke unto Laban, 'Can I have your daughter's hand?'

'You can have the rest as well,' sayeth Laban, 'but not until you serve me for seven years.'

And Jacob said, '*Seven* bloody years?'

82. For seven bloody years Jacob shovelled dung on Laban's fields

and he reeketh so that no one would draweth nigh unto him. As he shovelled dung, he could see dear Rachel's face through it and he was comforted from the waist up.

83. And Jacob said unto Laban, 'My seven years are up.'

'I wondered what was up,' said Laban. 'I thought it was my blood pressure.'

So there was a wedding feast; before it was over Jacob grabbed Rachel and took her, saying, I feel a honeymoon coming on and was lost in the steam from his trousers. And through the night they begatted.

84. But woe, at dawn Jacob saw he had not been begatting Rachel, but Leah her sister. Jacob was cast down but eventually got up. 'Woe, who has done this to me?' he said.

'Nobody's done anything to you,' said Leah, 'you've been doing it to me; it was the will of my father that this happened.'

'Where is Rachel?' said Jacob.

'He was saving her for afters,' said Leah.

'Wherefore is my Rachel?' said Jacob.

85. Then Laban explained: 'It must not be done to give the younger before the elder. Fulfil her week.'

So Jacob fulfilled Leah's week. Then Laban brought Rachel and Jacob started to fulfil her. But Leah conceived Reuben, then she bore Simeon, then Levi, then Judah.

86. And though Jacob still fulfilled Rachel, she was barren, so Rachel said, will you fulfil my maid, Bilhah – and Bilhah bore a son and Rachel adopted him and said, 'I shall call him Dan.' While she was doing that Jacob was doing it to the maid again and she had another boy Naphtali – and the Lord said, 'Lo, a football team is nigh.' Then Joseph did it with Leah's maid, Zilpah, and she had a goalie named Gad, then she had a centre forward named Asher, and now Jacob, who walked with a zimmer, came out. Leah went out to meet him and she saw that owing to his work he wore no trousers and he said, 'I have hired thee with my son's mandrakes.'

87. 'I'm not for hire,' said Leah, 'I'm free.' And he lay with her that

night, but not for long: he soon started to fulfil her, along came son No. 5 Issachar, then No. 6 Zebulun; in between, Jacob slept in a wheelchair, from it they lifted him on and off. Next he fulfilled Rachel's mandrakes and had son Joseph.

88. And it came to pass that Jacob knocketh off Laban's cattle, his mandrakes and took his wives and football team with him. The Lord was angry and said, 'What are ye doing?'

And Jacob said, 'A bunk.' Whereupon Jacob putteth black pepper on his camels' bums and they raced away to the land of Coobel-ars.

89. But Laban rose up and, putting black pepper on his camels' bums, goeth like the clappers. He caught up Jacob by the Coobel-ars. Laban went in Jacob's tent, then out of it into Leah's tent, then into the two maidservants' tent; but he seeth them not, then he went out of Leah's tent and into Rachel's tent, then out of that tent back into Jacob's tent. Then he seeth a camel with a hot bum and six legs and, lo, two of the legs were Jacob's.

'I knowest thou are behind there,' sayeth Laban.

'So do I,' said Jacob, stepping forth and showing his mandrakes.

'Are those my mandrakes?' sayeth Laban.

'Nay,' said Jacob, 'the camel ate yours.'

'Then open that camel,' said Laban in wrath.

90. 'Nay,' said Jacob, clutching his mandrakes. 'Yon camel is on a time lock.'

Then Laban cried out to heaven, 'Lord, why hast thou done this on me?'

And the Lord said, 'I haven't done anything on you.'

'It must have been the camel,' said Laban.

Where Have All the Bullets Gone?: 1985

The volume of the war memoirs I thought would never happen: the previous four volumes had been published at intervals of two years. I warned him he would lose his readers. The fourth volume had been published in 1978. This volume wasn't published until 1985. It took a lot of persuading, until I discovered the reason after nagging for so long. Some of his army colleagues had taken offence at some of the references in the previous volumes.

I've included the Foreword to explain how Spike got the title.

Foreword

The title of this book is a phrase remembered down the years. As I was lying on a makeshift bed in a rain-ridden tent alongside a Scots Guardsman, Jock Rogers, in a camp for the bomb-happy miles behind the firing line, I realised that for the first time in a year and a half, I was not worrying about mortar bombs, shells or Spandaus, and I said to him 'Where have all the bullets gone?' I had totally forgotten this utterance until one night, during a visit to South Africa, I was arriving at the theatre and there outside the stage door was the tall lean Scots Guardsman, now grey but still as positive as ever. 'Where have all the bullets gone?' he said. A quick drink and we were back to those haunting days in Italy in 1944, at the foot of Mount Vesuvius, with lava running in great red riverlets down the slope towards *us*, and Jock taking a drag on his cigarette and saying, 'I think we've got grounds for a rent rebate.' He was one of many who entered and left my life in the years 1944 and '45, and in this book I have begun the story with my leaving the front line Regiment (19 Battery 56 Heavy Field RA) and frigging around in a sort of khaki limbo until someone found a job for me to do. It was all to lead to my making the world of entertainment my profession, but when you think that you have to have a world war to find the right job, it makes you think. Here it is then.

Spike Milligan
Foxcombe House,
South Harting,
Hampshire.
Jan. 1985

Orginisateum

A complete office and service staff have arrived, including Private Dick Shepherd, a medical orderly from Rochdale. His knowledge of medicine goes like this: 'Soldiers laying down are sick ones.' A clerk in the form of Private 'Bronx' Weddon of the Berkshires, both misnomers – he had been neither to the Bronx or Berkshire. He was from Brighton, but you couldn't go around saying: 'I'm Brighton Weddon.' He said he was 'A journalist who worked for Marley Tiles'. I didn't get the drift. Another addition was the Camp 'Runner', Private Andrews; that is, at the mention of work he started to run. He had an accent like three Billy Connollys, he hated the army, he hated the job, he hated the world and all the planets adjacent.

'Luk herrre, Spike, no fuckerrr everrr got anywherrrre being a fucking runerrrr.'

How wrong he was, what about Jesse Owens, Sidney Wooderson?

'Who the fuck are they mon?'

He wasn't that thick. A heavy smoker, well on his way to lung cancer, he was forever on the earole for fags and, here's the cunning of the man, if you didn't give him one he would stand beside you and howl like a wolf. In any well-ordered society he would have been taken away, but in this camp he was considered normal. He could be pinpointed, suddenly, as from some distant tent came unearthly howling.

Captain Peters once asked: 'What is that?'

I told him, 'Private Andrews.'

'Oh, he's phnut! very good at it,' said Peters, who wasn't too bad at it himself.

We now have a 15cwt truck and driver. He is private Jim Brockenbrow. His father had been a POW in World War I, stayed in England and married a lass from Mousehole. The fruit of that union, now known as that 'square-headed bastard', he would defend his Teutonic ancestry with a Cornish accent.

'Luk'ere, them Germans hain't bad fellas, it's them bluddy Narzees that's the narsty buggerrrss.'

Andrews will have none of it. 'Listen Jamie, the fuckin' Germans are fitin' on the same side as the fuckin' Nazis.'

'Oo arr, but them's not memburs o' the Narzee party.'

'Awa fuckin' hame, there's nay fuckin' difference, they all shute tae kill, that's why I'm fuckin' herrrre.'

He had a point. Poor Brockenbrow, they ragged him stupid. ' 'ere 'itler, take this package to Town Major Portici, don't give it to Goebbels on the way.'

Daily Life in the Camp

Reveille at 0700, Roll call at 0730, Breakfast at 0800. Parade 0915. Sick Parade and Defaulters 1000. Everything was organised. We had typewriters, filing cabinets, inter-camp phones, electric light, but no mangle.

I was having recurring bouts of depression, just suddenly black, black gloom. I was missing the Battery. I wrote what must have been an embarrassing letter to the C.O. Major Jenkins. It was snivelling and grovelling, asking to be forgiven for failing in the action at Colle Dimiano; would he give me another chance, anything, I'd do anything to come back. I'd go insane if I stayed here. It demanded a reply if only on humanitarian grounds. He never replied. He was an officer and a gentleman, so fuck him, but, he was a good soldier and a pain in the arse ... all over.

It's a nice morning. I'm in the office sipping tea I've brought from breakfast. A new intake arrives, a big batch, over a hundred. Bronx and I are documenting them. 'Next, please,' I say in my cheer-up-chum voice, and there was Lance Bombardier Reg Bennett from our North Africa concert party. He bursts into tears. 'Don't cry, Reg, there's a drought on.' An attempt to joke him out of it. He's from the 74 Mediums, a sister regiment. The Americans had bombed his position on the terrible day of the Monastery disaster. 'We were bloody miles away, but bloody miles from the Monastery. Why me? Do I look like a Monastery?' His friends had been killed and wounded, and it had done for him.

Now he disagrees with my version of our meeting. He says: '*I came to the camp and you weren't in the office when I came through. I was in the camp two days, and I was going out of my mind with depression and boredom when one day I heard the sound of a trumpet coming from a tent. I thought, Christ, it's Spike. I came over, threw back the tent flap and there you were laying on the bed blowing your bugle. I remember putting my mess tins full of dinner down to shake hands with you.*'

If, after forty years, our stories differ so much, how many changes has the Bible gone through? Did Jesus meet Paul on the road to Damascus or was it Lance Bombardier Bennett? 'I thought I heard you playing the trumpet, Jesus.' 'No,' says Jesus, 'that was Milligan. You haven't seen Bombardier Bennett, around, have you?'

Reg was in a bad way, tense and lachrymose. I took him down town in the evening and we sat in a Vino Bar drinking white wine. Of an evening, the people of Baiano emptied out on to the streets and sat in little groups at their doors, mothers, fathers, children, uncles, aunts, all chatting away, laughing or lamenting the state of the world. Like we watch 'Dallas', the Italians watched German air-raids over Naples, cheering when some Jerry plane was hit and the pilot was having his arse burnt off, or parachuting into the Bay of Naples to die of typhoid.

We became friendly with one Franco and his family. He was a shoe salesman in Naples, forty, excused war duties because of ill health, though when I met his giant wife and six kids I couldn't see the reason. She had bosoms like the London Planetarium and was feeding not only her own baby, but wet nursing her neighbours'.

We are invited to partake of the meagre fare. (The last meagre fare I had was a cheap day return to Brockley: Groucho Marx.) Mussels! All bigger than mine. And garlic, phew! Franco's brothers are musicians; they play the mandolin and guitar. I thought they'd like to hear some jazz, so I strummed and sang 'When my sugar walks down the street'. They asked for a translation which was 'Quando mia sucro passegiare fondo la strada, tutti i piccoli ucelli andato tweet tweet tweet' or, 'When my sugar ration walks down the street, it is attended by little birds going tweet tweet tweet.' They liked my Players cigarettes. In exchange they offer me the local Italian brand. I forget the name, I think it was Il Crap.

The village had its resident tart who traded on the outskirts of the town. Her pimp stood outside and shouted: 'Thees way, twenty cigarette you fuck-a my seester.'

'Sister?' said Bronx. 'She looks more like his grandmother.'

'I think for twenty fags he'd let you fuck 'im,' says Rogers.

Romance One

It was in the New Army Welfare Rest and Recreation Centre, a large rambling Victorian affair at the top of the village, that I found ... romance! I had never myself ever had a large rambling Victorian affair, but now, one of the Italian girls serving at the tea bar takes my eye. Arghhh! You've heard of Mars Bars? Forget 'em. She's a ringer for Sophia Loren but six inches shorter and six inches further out. Troubles never come singly, and neither did hers. She likes me, can I have tea with her? There is a smell of burning hairs. I said yes from the waist down. 4 o'clock tomorrow? Si!

I spent all day getting ready. Finally I apply Anzora hair goo and finger-wave my hair. I look lovely. I 'borrow' the jeep and drive to the address. What's this? A magnificent Romano-Greek styled villa; it must be wrong, no, it's right. I drive up the circular drive through embossed iron gates. The great double door: I gently bang the brass hand-shaped knocker. I've only just arrived and there I am with my hand on her knocker.

A suave white-coated grey-haired flunkey opens the door: 'Ah meester Meeligan.' He knows my real title! 'Please come in, the Contessa is waiting.' Contessa? I follow him down a cool marble-floored hall, the walls hung with oil paintings broken by wall consoles. He opens the door into a large gasping-with-light room. The decor is Louis XVI with Baroque gilt furniture. 'She' is sitting against the far wall on a buttoned couch, a fine white cotton dress to the knee (Arghhhhhhh!) brown satin legs (Arghhhh!) fine topless sandals cross laced up her leg (Arghhhhhhhh!). Her hair is loose on her shoulder

(Arrrrghh!), in her hand she holds an Arum lily that she is waving under her nose (Arghhhhhhhhhh!) She has been practising this all day. I take off my hat to show her my fine Anzora goo hair-set stuck with flies. 'Hello and arghhhhhhh,' I say.

'Seet here,' she says. (Arghhhhhhhh!) She pats the Louis XIV couch to which I lower my Milligan trousers. It's all too much. She speaks in slow purring tones. (Arghhhhhhhh!) She is very laid back or is it that I'm leaning forward. She asks me what 'Spike' means. I tell her, I mean business. Her family goes back six hundred years, where do mine go back to? I tell her they go back to 50 Riseldean Road, Brockley.

Tea is served on a silver service – how many spoons can I get in my pocket? I ask her where her parents are; they are stopping at Eboli. I tell her I will stop at nothing. Yes, she *is* a Countess. Have I ever been to Eboli? No, I have been to Penge, Sidcup, but not to Eboli. She has heard me tinkering on the piano at the Centre, she likes jazz, will I play her piano? I bluff my way through 'A Foggy Day in London town'. She claps her hands. 'Whatees that?' I tell her: 'It's a piano, don't you remember, you asked me to play it.' The flunkey arrives, it's time for me to depart, la Contessa has another appointment. Blast. 'Can you come see me again?' Yes I can, but can we try a different room next time. I shake hands. It's like a cool perfumed sponge cake. (Argggggggggg!)

I'm back at camp lying on my bed smoking, nay steaming, thinking of her. I am besieged with military questions: 'Did I get it?' No I didn't. How did I get? The piano. What is it about the British soldier? He will knock off a German machine-gun nest single-handed and never say a word about it, but if he knocks off some poor innocent scrubber, he gives you every little nitty gritty detail. I don't get it, as in this case I didn't.

I've caught it. Wait. You don't *catch* bronchitis. I mean you don't chase it up the street with a butterfly net. No. Bronchitis catches you. So, a bronchitis had caught me. It was suffering from me very badly, I had given the poor thing a high temperature, so I had to get my bronchitis to a hospital. No. 104 General at Nocera. Bingo! You've won the

Golden Enema! Another ward, blue jim-jams, female nurses, and mossy nets to stop them dive-bombing. That night I was delirious, but people couldn't tell the difference.

Diary: April 13

Feeling better. Wrote to mother giving list of my post-war underwear stock.

I go on record that April 16 is my birthday. 'Given extra medicine as a treat.'

Now dear reader, mystery.

Diary: April 21

'Bert says his leg is getting better.' Now I don't remember Bert or his leg. So, if nothing else, the reader will know that on April 21 1944, Bert's leg is getting better. By now I'd say it was totally better and he's snuffed it.

My bronchitis is better and I can take it back to camp.

Necrophiles

Outside our camp was the walled cemetery. Alas! the grounds are overgrown with wartime neglect or is it grass? Latins lavish more attention and emotion on their dead than we do. Every headstone has a photograph of the departed. What was ghoulishly interesting were the wall graves, immured with a glass panel to show the departed. One was stunningly macabre: the body of a girl of eighteen buried in 1879 in her bridal gown. The hair was red and had grown after death, as had her fingernails, filling the space like Indian candy floss. The headstones abound with grisly warnings. 'As I am now, so will you be.' Why does the church allow these nasty after-death threats? Why not go the whole hog?

EARLY MORNING VATICAN RADIO

HIGH PRIEST: Hi ya, this is Vatican radio PIP PIP PIP. Yes, it's nine thirty-one, anther moment nearer your death. Byeeeeeeee.

Nasty things are happening – some of the loonies are digging up the graves, or breaking the glass and knocking off the rings. (In the case of bankruptcy break glass?) Jock Rogers is horrified. 'Och, this'll get us a terrible name.' Terrible name? How about Tom Crabs or Doris Herpes? Dick Scratcher?

Private Andrews is more suspicious. 'They're fuckin' the stiffs.' Surely not. 'Aye, they're not after the jewellery, they're after a fuck.' It wasn't so, but we didn't want to spoil Andrews' fun. He was an argumentative bugger, especially on sport. He was a fitba' freak and when he found I liked rugby, gave me hell.

'It's fer bleedin' snobs Jamie, and that ball, like a bloody duck's egg, no wonder you ha' to carry the bloody thing.'

It Ends with Magic: 1990

This started in 1983 as a children's short story, 'The Magic Staircase'. Spike realised he was mixing fact with fiction: he was unhappy with it and put it to one side. He looked at it several times and in 1988 made the decision to use his family's names and write it as a novel. Florence was his mother's name. Laura, Séan and Silé are his children's names. I believe this to be Spike's most skilled writing.

It took some time to overcome the loss of Leo. The Army money sufficed for a year; there were expenses – most of their clothing had been lost on the *Erinpura*. Soon she had to rely on the pension; as if life wasn't hard enough, in February her father Alfred collapsed and died from a heart attack. A neighbour, Mrs Higgs, looked after the children while Florence attended the funeral. She was devastated, she worshipped her father; at the end of the ceremony, at Leytonstone cemetery, she threw herself on the grave, weeping and calling out, 'Daddy, my daddy!'

They were too poor to afford a headstone, to this day it stays an unmarked grave. Her mother, now widowed, gave up 62 Jackson Street and moved in with Florence. Mrs Kettleband was a frail seventy-five, she couldn't do any heavy household chores, but she was a good cook, very good seamstress and good company. She knitted clothes for the children and, with her to look after them, Florence was able to go out to work. She got a job at the nearby Chislehurst Laundry as an ironer; she had to start at six-thirty in the morning and finished at six o'clock at night. It was very hard work but it earned her fifteen shillings a week. Florence, with all the sadness and worry, was not a robust woman; working in the damp, steamy atmosphere of the ironing room she often got bronchitis.

The years passed, Laura, Séan and Silé grew up. Laura was now an eight-year-old 'bossy boots' and fussed over Séan and Silé like a mother. 'You mustn't wipe your nose on your sleeve!' and 'You mustn't write on the wall – that's for leaning on!' 'You must say your prayers at night or you'll go bad!' And, she was very informative: 'God has an ordinary beard but it's holy.' 'Dogs eat bones so they can bark louder.' 'Pussy cats grow fur so you can stroke them.'

Laura and Séan attended St Saviour's Roman Catholic School, Lewisham. It was a two-mile walk, but unlike adults, distance meant nothing to children, who lived in another timeless dimension; holding hands Laura and Séan just talked all the way. Silé, still too young, played all day with a gollywog doll her

Grandma made for her from odd bits of material. At night it was Grandma who told them stories. She told them how Grandad Kettleband was a soldier during the Indian Mutiny; he made the gunpowder charges that blew open the gates so the British could capture the fort. Séan liked that bit. 'Did he get hitted with a bullet?' he said. No, Grandpa was safe and got a medal as well. Oh! a medal, a real medal!

After the children were abed, Florence and her mother would sit around the kitchen stove and talk as they mended the children's clothes, sometimes Florence's brother Hughie would come and repair the children's shoes and do any odd jobs like chopping wood, bringing up coal from the cellar, putting washers on taps, mending window sashes, knocking down old ladies and robbing them. Indeed, he was so helpful Florence said, 'Hughie, you're a real brick.' Laura didn't understand that, Uncle Hughie didn't look at all like a brick.

Children's minds work differently from adults'. For instance, once when Grandma was talking to Laura she suddenly said, 'Now what was I going to say?' and Laura said, 'I'm sorry, Grandma, I don't know what you were going to say.'

Silé was different, for no reason at all she would suddenly say, 'I kin eat-ed brekfist [breakfast] oil by myself-ed wid owd some-one.'

At the back of 3 Leathwell Road was a small garden. Florence gave all the children some tomato seeds to plant, which they all diligently did, all except Silé, who said, 'Why aar-are you hidding dem in the gwound?'

'Well, darling, if you plant them,' said Mum, 'they grow into tomatoes.'

So Silé with a spoon carefully planted her seeds. In bed that night, Silé said, 'Listen, I tink I can heered [hear] dem gwoing.' Who knows, she might have. At the break of dawn, Silé rushed into the garden, then rushed in, 'Mummy, something's wrong-ed, they haven't gwoed.'

Florence explained why it hadn't 'gwoed'. 'It takes eight weeks, darling,' and darling said, 'But I'm hungry!'

For a while the whole family, though poor, was happy. By adding Mrs Kettleband's Army Widow's Pension to hers, Florence managed well, though things were very tight; for instance, that first Christmas together, the children's presents were home-made, one was a rag doll for Laura and another clown doll for Silé, while Uncle Hughie made a wooden train for Séan. They were all delighted when they unwrapped their presents that Christmas morn.

By budgeting very carefully Florence managed to take them to a pantomime at the Garrison Theatre, Woolwich; the children sat in wonder, as they watched Cinderella in her silver coach pulled by snow-white ponies. All the way home on the tram they talked excitedly about the panto. Laura liked 'all the dancing and music at the Grand Ball'. Séan liked the ugly sisters and their 'big noses'. Silé liked 'the Prince and his red twousers'. No, she didn't like the ugly sisters. 'If I was-ed Cindells I-I-I would hit-ed dem.' In bed that night, they went on talking, talking, Laura thought the pantomime was 'the most beautiful thing I ever saw'. Oh yes, it *was* a real silver coach. 'Wus der prince red trouser real-ed?' said Silé, and why were the white horses so tiny? Laura knew, 'They're very young.' If that was the case, thought Silé, the coalman's horse must be very old, possibly 'a million-ed!'

★

January came and another tragedy for Florence: her mother suffered a stroke and died; they laid her to rest next to her husband's grave – No. 21, Row 34, Plot 11B, Leytonstone. It was a bitter day with snow falling, as the tiny group of mourners stood at the grave, Florence's brother Hughie, the children and the priest. Florence didn't cry.

'Is she gone-ed to heavin,' said Silé.

'Yes, she's with Jesus,' said Laura.

'Does Grandma know Him, Mum?' said Séan.

'Yes,' said Florence, 'Jesus knows everybody.'

'Yes,' said Silé, 'he even knows the milkman.'

Then Séan, 'When a milkman dies and goes to heaven, does he take his milk with him?'

It was getting dark by the time they arrived home, 'I'll light the gas, Mum,' said Laura grabbing the matches.

'No, I'll light it,' said Séan trying to snatch them.

'Now,' said Florence taking the prized matches, 'I think it's Silé's turn.'

Florence lit the match and gave it to Silé. The little girl's eyes bright with delight, gazed at the burning match as her mother lifted her to the gas, then with a mighty breath she blew the match out. 'I did dat,' she said pointing a little finger at the glowing mantle. 'Yes, I did dat,' she repeated. 'Didn't I, Mummy? I did dat all on myself.'

When they were all in bed Florence retold them the story of *Robinson Crusoe*, the story that Leo had liked. Leo, her darling Leo, he was so young. In distant India, rain fell on a lonely grave.

With her mother gone, there was no one to look after the children in the day, so Florence had to give up her job; instead she advertised in the *Kent Messenger*, 'Laundry and mending done. Good work.' At first nothing happened, then gradually, work came in, not much but it kept her busy, Laura and Séan would help hang up the washing on the line; Silé wasn't tall enough, but one day she would, just wait and see! Even with the laundry work Florence had to scrimp; the gas was never lit till it was too dark to see, until then she would open the iron stove to illuminate the room. Butter was for special occasions only and then scraped on very thin. Nothing was wasted; stale bread was soaked in water and made into bread pudding, leftovers from dinner were fried for breakfast as 'bubble and squeak', for supper it was bread and dripping, sometimes she would send Laura out for a pennyworth of broken biscuits. Uncle Hughie used sometimes to bring cabbages and beetroot from his allotments at Brent Cross until he got a job in Wales as a pit-head clerk, but he wrote regularly ... once a year.

Time was passing, the Waziri Wars ended and Florence received Leo's posthumous medal, a lot of good it did, but Séan was very proud of it – he took it to school to show his teacher. The children were growing up; that was the best direction. Laura, the eldest, was eight. She had reddish-brown hair like beech leaves in high summer, her eyes were blue like her father's, a heart-shaped face with pale skin, a petite nose slightly turned up at the end, and finely-shaped lips. Her figure was plump, Séan called her 'a fat pudding'. She liked reading stories about magic, goblins, witches and fairies; as the family couldn't afford books she joined the Lewisham library. She was very good at helping her mother; at the age of six she had baked her first cake, now she could cook a whole dinner for six. She remembered how, before her father Leo went off to the war, he used to read them lovely fairy stories and since he'd left, she made up little fairy stories and poems.

A FAIRIES' MESSAGE

Once I heard a fairy calling
Far away as night was falling
What she told me I will tell
Hoping you'll remember well
Do be kind to all you meet
In the woodland wild and sweet
Free the rabbit from the snares
Think about them in your prayers
This is something you can do
Little children all of you

In her notebook she wrote: 'When I grow up I want to be a writer. I don't want to write murder stories but fairy-tales. You know big giants who come round every night crushing people in their sleep. Then when the bell goes at dawn the giants just run for all they are worth. So now I am going to write a story called:

ADVENTURE IN FAIRYLAND

Once upon a time a little girl called Mary had left a letter out for the pixies and fairies to take away with them to fairyland. On the letter it said, 'I do wish I could go to fairyland too, but I have no wings.' So the pixies wrote back to say the fairies were busy so they had to write instead. They said in the letter, '... a minute before midnight we will pick you up and take you with us back to fairyland.' Now it was one minute before midnight and then tap-tap, a tiny tapping sound. She went over and what did she see? Some pixies and some fairies. She opened the window and in flew the pixies and fairies who sat on her bed. Then they said 'Shut your eyes tight' so she did and there was a rushing sound going through her ear. Suddenly she was told to open her eyes and she found herself in fairyland. She was told she could not stay long for soon she would be back in her normal life.

So first they took her to see the Queen who was dressed in jewels of all different colours. Next she saw the sweet garden where sweets hung from trees and lots of other places like that. Then she was told that now her time was up and that she must say goodbye to her friend for a long while now. So she shut her eyes tight and the rushing sound came again. When suddenly she opened her eyes and found she was back in her own bed with a book. With a book by her called 'Adventure in Fairyland'. Next morning when her mother came in she didn't believe Mary in spite of the book. But we know it was true don't we.'

Séan, now seven, was like his father. Brown hair and slate-blue eyes, like the sea in autumn. He was a dreamer, his gaze seemed to look beyond this world to a realm where man had never trod. At school he was hopeless, but his drawings at Art Class surpassed all others, his art master, Mr Woods, had written to his mother. 'Your son Séan is show-ing quite a talent as an artist for a boy of seven; later, if possible, he

A FOOT PRINT ON THE SAND

Robinson Crusoe by Séan Sparrow.

should enter a College of Art' ... but how? The family were too poor. However, remembering his father's stories of *Robinson Crusoe*, he drew some illustrations.

Finally, there was little Silé, four, she was a mixture, copper hair, immense blue eyes, for ever in trouble, with mud, glue, dirt, cuts, bruises, stones, snail shells and a pigeon's feather, an incurable tomboy. Once asked by her teacher what she wanted to be when she grew up she replied, 'A boy.' Sent to wash sticky off her hands, she came back to the class and said, 'I couldn't reached the tap, so I licked dem clean.' She was for ever to be one of life's clowns.

They were a happy family but extremely poor. The Army pension barely covered the rent. For months Florence struggled to keep the family together. Her day started at six and at two in the morning she would still be mending customers' clothes. Despite that, she still could not make enough to give her children the bare essentials of life. Finally, after years of worry and overwork, Mrs Sparrow became very ill; she had deprived herself of food so the children would not go without. One day, she collapsed and went to bed with a high fever; Laura, the little mother, called the neighbours. Dr Mantle came; she would have to 'go to hospital' he said.

She was diagnosed as having consumption, a common complaint among the poor. She lay in a ward at St Clevot's Hospital for the Poor.

Mrs Higgs, the neighbour, tried to keep the home going for the children but, in the end, she called the authorities who decided the children had better be cared for in a home until their mother was better.

Dr Thomas was a tall, thin, loping man who wore spats. 'It will be at least a year,' he told her, 'before you can return home, you should really go to Switzerland.'

'Switzerland?' Florence gave a sad laugh.

The children came to the hospital to say goodbye to her; Séan tried to be brave and not cry, but as he said his goodbye, tears flooded his eyes, 'Look, Mum, I'm wearing Dad's medal.' 'Don't worry, Mum,' said Laura bravely, 'we'll be all right, you see. This is the address of where we are going.' She handed her mother a piece of paper.

The Wolsey Home for
Needy Children
Blakensham
Sussex
Headmaster: Ivan Hewitt
Headmistress: Amanda Hewitt

'Sussex?' she said wondering where it was.

'We'll write to you all the time, Mum,' said Laura.

'I can't write,' said little Silé, 'so I'll think of you.'

A stern nurse rang the hospital bell that signalled the end of visiting time. Mrs Sparrow kissed them and smiled bravely as the three little children left the ward holding hands, looking back and waving. 'Please, God,' she whispered, 'look after my children and keep them safe.'

The door of the ward opened, the children turned and waved, the door closed.

'Will Mummy be in hosterpal long?' said Silé.

'No,' said Séan, 'because we'll pray to God for her.'

'Can God make Mummy better quick?' said Silé.

'Oh, yes,' said Laura.

'Why, is he a a-a-doc-er-ter?' said Silé.

'No, he's not a doctor, he's, he's just God,' said Laura.

The Sparrow children wave goodbye to their mother.

'Does he give Mummy a med-er-cine?' said Silé.

'No, he does a miracle,' said Laura.

'What's a mick-er-al?' said Silé.

'It's a trick that only God can do,' said Laura.

'Where does he dood it?' said Silé.

'In heaven.'

'How does it get down here den?'

'By magic,' said Laura hoping the interrogation was over.

Condensed Animals: 1991

Owl

The owl at night
Without a light
His eyes can give you
Quite a fright.

Butterfly

Butterfly butterfly
Making colours in the sky
Red white and blue upon your wings
You are the loveliest of things.

Jellyfish

Jellyfish jellyfish
Like a jelly on a dish
If I covered you with custard
You'd be very very flustered.

Caterpillar

Caterpillar caterpillar
Passing by
Soon you'll be
A butterfly.

Tuna

Tuna tuna
I know you'd sooner
Not be in a tin
So please please please
You Japanese
Do not commit this sin.

Millipede

Millipede millipede
Is very strange you see
He has to use a thousand legs
To get from A to B.

Where Have All the Bullets Gone?: 1985

Florence

City of Medicis, Savonarola, and chattering raspberrying Secombe, now freezing without his leather 'love gift' jerkin. This is the city of the artist, the artisan, the connoisseur. Our Hotel Dante is just round the corner from the Piazza del Signoria. I would be able to see places that I had only read about. The hotel is one built for those rich Victorians doing the Grand Tour. Sumptuous rooms, a wonderful double bed with duck eider, like sleeping in froth. Putting my egg-stained battledress in the bevelled glass and walnut cupboard was like wearing a flat hat in the Ritz. Secombe flies past chattering and farting up the Carrara marble stairs with its flanking Venetian balustrades topped with cherubim holding bronze lanterns. He looks totally out of place, he belongs at the pit head.

I am standing on the spot, explaining that this is where Savonarola was burned. 'Oo was Savonarola?' says Gunner Hall. I tell him 'oo he is'. 'They *burnt* him?' Yes. 'Why. Were they short of coal?' I explain that he was at odds with the Medici and the state of Florence. 'Fancy,' says Hall. 'Why didn't 'e call the fire brigade?' The same indifference applies to see Cellini's Perseus. With the head of Medusa, Hall wants to know why statues are erected to people being burnt or having their heads chopped off. 'Why not someone normal like Tommy Handley?' Yes, of course: 'Here is Cellini's statue of Tommy Handley from ITMA.' That would look really nice in the Piazza.

The Pitti Palace leaves me stunned; masterpiece after masterpiece, there's no end to it. From Titian to Seguantini. You come out feeling useless and ugly. On the Ponte Vecchio Secombe and I ask Hall to take a photo of us. It comes out with the wall behind us in perfect focus, two blurred faces in the foreground. He was well pleased.

Now a divertimento. An English lady living in Florence has invited us to tea. She is Madame Penelope Morris, a 'relative' of William Morris, 'the man who invented wallpaper'. She was sixty-nine, tall, thin, a white translucent skin with the veins visible; her neck looked like a map of the Dutch canal system. She wore swathes of bead necklaces – to the value of two shillings. Two pale blue eyes, very close together, sat atop a long bulbous nose. She had no waist, no bottom or bosom; she went straight up and down like a phone box. A small crimped rouged mouth like a chicken's bum. She spoke with an upper-class adenoidal voice that put her next in line to the throne. She ushered us into a cloying room that smelt of stale unemptied sherry glasses and tom-cat piss. We sat in well-worn chairs with anti-macassars. She rang a brass bell, the clanger fell out. 'It's always doing that.' The summons brought a thousand-year-old butler carrying a papier-mâché tray loaded with what looked like papier-mâché cakes. The tea ritual. 'The cakes are made locally,' she said, and should have added 'by stonemasons.' It was all a ploy. She is a spiritualist in need. So, would we boys like a seance? So saying she pulls the curtains and we sit at a circular table not knowing what to expect. Now, would anyone like to get in touch with a loved one? Yes, says Marine Paul Robson, one of our shanghaied dancers. 'I'd like to get in touch with my mother Rosie.' Mrs Morris goes into a trance. 'Are you there Mrs Robson, are you there Rosie …' A little louder. 'Are you there Mrs Rosie Robson …' She opens her eyes. 'She's not hearing me.' What Robson hadn't told her was that his mother wasn't dead, but was living in Brighton. 'She won't be able to hear from here,' he said to a slightly bemused Mrs Morris.

Does anyone else want to get in touch? Yes. Bill Hall would like to contact his grandmother Lucy. Forewarned, Mrs Morris asks, 'Is she dead?'

'I hope so,' says Hall. 'They buried her.'

'Are you there, Mrs Lucy Hall?' she intones, eyelids fluttering, as she places a collection box on the table, giving it a shake to agitate the coins inside. Suddenly Paul Robson lets out a scream and runs from the room. Mrs Morris calls a halt; he has ruined the 'balance'. We must all leave now as she is expecting another 'tea party'. In the hall we meet a group of unsuspecting soldiers who can't understand our stifled laughter.

We ask Robson why he had run out screaming. He says, 'I felt there was something nasty in the room.'

'There was,' says Bill Hall. 'The cat done it.'

Secombe and I have hit it off with two waitresses at the hotel. One fat, one thin. He calls them Laurel and Hardy. They weren't exactly beauties, but then neither was Secombe or I.

We would meet them 'dopo lavoro'. They will show us a 'nice Boogie Woogie Club'. It sounded like a weapon. By the kitchen we waited, our romantic interlude broken only by the slops boy emptying rubbish into the reeking bins. Finally they appear, smelling of cheap perfume and washing up water. Secombe gives me Hardy. She's too full for him. We were taken to what by day was a sewer. An Italian trio are trying to catch up with the jazz scene. Through a fug, a blue-chinned waiter shows us to a table the size of a playing card. By intertwining knees we are seated, we appear glued together. Secombe is chattering in Anglo-Italian: 'You molto bello,' he tells Laurel. There's another fine mess he's got us into. We drink some appalling cheap red wine that leaves a purple ring round the mouth; Secombe looks like a vampire. Laurel takes Secombe to do the 'Jitterbuggery' and they are lost in the steaming melee. I too am sucked in by Hardy. I am trying to move her bulk round the floor, but I really need a heavy goods licence. Still, it was nice holding a girl, even if her load had shifted. A gyrating, arm-pumping, steaming, farting and chattering, all teeth and glasses Secombe zooms past. 'Having fun?' he shouts. So that's what it is. Away he goes in twenty different directions. It's getting on for two am. The girls say they must 'andare a casa', they have work in the morning. There follows the traditional groping and steaming in the doorway. A mist has risen from the Arno, infiltrating the town and Secombe's trousers. I can hear the hiss of steam as cold air hits his boiling body. We depart virgo intacto, trousers bursting with revolving testicles and dying erections. We retrace our steps to the hotel. We are lost. 'Fancy,' says Secombe. 'Who in the Mumbles would dream that I was lost in Florence?' I tell him I gave up: who in Mumbles would know he was lost in Florence.

A tart hovers by. Lily Marlene? She knows the way to the hotel. Do we want a shag? It's only fifty lire after ten, she'll do us both for forty. Sorry dear, we're training for the priesthood. OK, we can find our own fucking way back. Finally we did. 'Home at last,' says Secombe, 'and forty lire to the good.'

No, not home at last, locked out at last. 'Open up landlord, we are thirsty travellers.' We rang the bell. We hammered on the door. We tapped on the windows. We shouted upwards. We hammered on the bell. We rang the door. We tapped upwards. We shouted on the windows. 'How much did she say for the two of us?' says Secombe. A sliding of bolts, a weary concierge opens the door. 'Molto tardi signorini,' he says. We apologise, I press a ten lire note in his hand. A low moan comes from his lips. 'What did you give him?' says Secombe. 'A heart attack.'

I crawl into my dream bed. Peace. Relaxation, but no, wait!!! Something wet and 'horribule' is in my bed. It's a terrible soldier joke, there in my bed is an eight-inch 'Richard the Third', made from dampened brown paper. Wait, there's a note, a chilling message. It says: 'The phantom strikes again.' It bears all the hallmarks of Mulgrew, or is it the Mulgrew marks of Hall? I fell asleep laughing.

Goodbye Soldier: 1986

Volume 6 of the war memoirs. Spike describes his first meeting with Toni Fontana. Later, she married and became Toni Pontani. He frequently said she was the love of his life. And they used to meet in Paris right up to the time he became too frail to travel.

Maria Antoinetta Fontana

Romance: June 1946

The charabanc, with its precious cargo of bisexual soldier artistes, see-saws through the narrow Neapolitan streets. It is a day of high summer. We pull up at our destination, the Albergo Rabacino. The sunlight plays on its golden baroque chiselled façade. Lt Ronnie Priest hurries into its mahogany portals, only to return downcast of visage. 'The bloody girls will be a while; they've just got back from Mass.' He lights up a cigarette. 'Bloody females,' he adds. We all debouch to stretch our legs and other parts. Immediately, we are set on by street vendors. I was taken up with a tray of chrome and gilt watches – I needed a watch badly, a good heavy one that would stop me being blown away. As we barter, the Italian Corps de Ballet usher forth with their luggage. Our balding driver, Luigi, is rupturing himself stowing the bulging cases into the rear locker – all this while I have just clinched a deal for a watch that looks like a burnished gold Aztec altar, a·huge lump of a thing. On me, it made my wrist look like an Oxfam appeal for food. I had bargained the price down from ten million lire to seven thousand and the vendor was running away at full speed while counting the money. I was winding it when a female voice diverted me: ' 'ow much you payer for that?' I turned to see a petite, mousey haired, blue-eyed, doll-like girl.

The first clash of eyes was enough. It was, no, not *love* at first sight – that came later – but it most certainly was *something* at first sight. (Darling, I feel in something at first sight).

'I paid seven thousand lire.'

She 'tsu-tsu-tsued' and shook her head. 'You know all watch stolen.' No, I didn't know that. 'Let me see,' she said, in a semi-commanding voice. She examined the watch. 'Maybe, yes,' she said, returning it.

I said it was a very good watch, it told the time in Italian as well as English. What was her name?

'My namer is Maria Antoinetta Fontana, but everyone call me Toni.'

'I'm Spike' sometimes known as stop thief or hey you!

'Yeser, I know.' She had found my name on the programme and had obviously set her sights on me. I would make good target practice. Maria Antoinette Fontana was understudy for the Première Ballerina at the Royal Opera House in Rome. From now on, it was goodbye Bing Crosby, lead soldiers and Mars bars. She was so petite! Five feet four inches! We are 'all aboarding' the Charabong, I notice that Toni has lovely legs and the right amount, two. I tried to sit next to her, but in the mêlée I ended up in the seat behind her as Riccy Trowler, our crooner, had fancied her and beat me to it. If he looked at her, I would kill. Do you hear me? KILL! Didn't he know with me around he hadn't a chance! Me, the Brockley Adonis? Poor blind little fool. Me, the Harry James of St Cyprian's Hall, SE 26! 'Hold very tight and fares please' says Lt Priest in mock cockney bus conductor tones as we set off for the Holy City.

The journey passes with Toni turning to cast me eye-crippling glances. She dangles her hand in the lee of her seat for me to hold. Arghhhhhh! It's small, sensuous, soft and perfumed. It's giddy-making. Oh, but how lovely!!! I'm falling, falling, falling! and no safety net!

Mulgrew's keen Scottish eye has noticed my new watch. He assesses it and says, 'That's the sort of present a mean millionaire would buy for a blind son.' He asks how much. I tell him. He bursts out laughing. Laugh he may, in a year's time that selfsame watch would save him and the Bill Hall Trio from ruin. Of that, more in my next book! Bill Hall is killing the boredom by playing his fiddle. I join in on the guitar. We play some jazz and a few Neapolitan melodies, 'Cuore Napolitano', 'Non Me Scorde', 'Ah Zaz Zaz Za'.

Ceprano is a halfway halt. We are taken to a large NAAFI where we are given lunch. Ahhhhhhhhgghhhh, Cold Collation!!! The most dreaded meal in the English Culinary calendar: the dead chicken, the dead lettuce, the watery mayonnaise, the lone tomato ring! It's the sort of meal you leave in your will to your mother-in-law.

'You no lak,' says Toni who is sitting opposite.

'No, I no lak,' I said.

'Can I have you chicken?' she says, her head inclined to one side. I watch as the dead fowl disappears through her delectable lips. I sip the red tannic-acid-ridden tea that must have been put on to boil the day after we all landed at Salerno.

Toni and I saunter out to the Charabong, the journey continues. The swine Trowler assumes his seat next to *my* Toni, the blind fool. Hasn't he noticed her adoring glances?? My matchless profile from Brockley SE26?

★

Bill Hall is laughing, I've told him the price of the watch. So far Bornheim has passed the journey immersed in the *Union Jack* newspaper. He walks down the Charabong, swaying and bumping. He makes reference to my new amour.

'Is there something going on?' he said, nodding towards my Toni.

I told him most certainly there was a lot going on. I had met her, according to my new watch, at ten-thirty precisely. Yes, there was a lot going on but as conditions improved I'd hoped for a lot coming off. He grins like a fiend.

Clowning at a wayside break. Toni (left) feeds Jimmy Molloy (centre) and Riccy Trowler (right)

'The poor girl,' he said. 'You'd better not show it to her all at once.'

He slunk away chuckling, the swine! This was not *that* kind of affair, this was *true* romance. No tawdry thoughts entered my head, but it was entering other areas. South of Rome we lumber through hot dusty villages, the grapes are heavy on the vine and on sale are large luscious red bunches for a few lire. But I don't have eyes for the delights of the Campagna, only Toni's glances and the squeeze of her little hand.

Late evening and the dusty chugging Charabong enters Rome through the Porta Maggiore. It's a Sunday evening and the sunlight is turning to rose-petal pink. The streets are full of the populace taking their evening strolls – elegant Romans are *really* elegant, they wear clothes well. But! None of them are wearing sensible brown English shoes like me. More of them later. The Charabong comes to rest outside the Albergo Universo. *I'll* help Toni with her luggage to her bedroom. Her

The Bill Hall Trio in a now derelict prisoner-of-war cage, trying desperately to be funny en route to Rome, where the Pope lives

mother wants her to go home, but because she wants to be near me – lies – and tells momma the company rules insist, she stays at the hotel. Ha! Ha! Love finds a way.

I take me to my chamber – a very nice no-nonsense double bedroom. Thank God, this time there's no screaming, chattering, farting Secombe. No, he's in his hammock and a thousand miles away. Instead, I have Wino of the Year, Trooper Mulgrew, J., who by just throwing his kit down can make the room look like the Wandsworth Municipal Rubbish Tip. I hang up my civvies.

'This is the life Johnny,' I say.

'Oh, you've noticed,' he says.

To activate his Scottish mind, I say, 'I wonder what your folks in Glasgow are doing?'

And he says, 'A bank.' He's looking at the ceiling, there's nothing there to tax his tartan mind. 'What's the time?' he says.

And I say, 'It's time you bought a watch that I can laugh at.'

From our floor we take the lift.

'Che piano?' says the ageing lift attendant.

'La terra piano,' says Mulgrew which translated means 'The earth floor'.

The dining-room is full. Another ENSA party has booked in, among them Tony Fayne who in post-war years would become well-known for his partnership with David Evans. As Fayne and Evans, they did funny sporting commentaries and were used by the BBC till it had sucked them dry and discarded them. I noticed that this new intake all wore their shirts outside their trousers. This struck me as amusing because, dear reader, during my boyhood days in India we, the Raj, laughed at the 'Wogs' for that selfsame reason. What I didn't know is that this was the 'latest fashion' from America! Suddenly, tucking shirts in was old-fashioned. I remember whenever Tony Fayne passed me there was the faint aroma of marijuana, for which he was later 'busted!' I remember one dinner-time, when the smell of pot emanated from their table as I passed it on my way to bed, a pale ENSA female of some forty

Clara Petacci turning on the Fascist party

summers grabbed the seat of my trousers and whooped 'Wot ho Monty' and fell face-down into the soup.

Our lesbian javelin-thrower manageress remembers me.

'Come sta Terri?' she says.

We chatted over coffee. Had I any spare tickets for the show? Of course. How many? She'd like to bring the family, thirty-two. She 'buys' us a bottle of wine and we discuss post-war Italy – the political scene was very woolly with the Christian Democrats holding the wolf of Communism at bay. She doesn't want Communism, she loves democracy and have we anything for sale on the black market? We repair to her private suite, where we continue drinking and she shows me a photo album. There she is in all her athletic glory, throwing the javelin at the All Italia Games. Gad! In her running shorts and vest, she's a fine figure of a man. She shows me photos of Mussolini's execution – ghastly – then, a turn-up for the book, a picture of Clara Petacci looking very sexy in a net dress (see picture).

*

A knock at the door. It's the late Bill Hall and fiddle, can he come in? His eyes fall on the Petacci photo.

'Cor, 'oo's the bird? Clara Petacci? Wot the one that Musso was givin it to? Cor, 'ow could they shoot her, all that lovely stuff!'

He was right, she would have made a lovely stuff.

Bill has been out visiting 'a friend'. This is usually some old boiler with a turkey trot neck, one foot in the grave and very grateful for any that's going. He wants to know if it's too late for dinner. The manageress says no, what's he want? Spaghetti. We watch Bill eating it. He cuts it all up with a knife, then shovels it in on a spoon.

I retire to bed, first taking a luxurious bath. Mulgrew is already abed, smoking and sipping red wine from a glass by his bedside. 'How did you get on with the Italian bird?'

Italian *bird*? If he meant Miss Toni Fontana, I was indeed much favoured by her and would see her on the morrow and be immediately hypnotised by her 'petite beauty'. Mulgrew is given to silent evil laughter with heavy shoulders.

'Wait till she gets a look at your petite beauty.'

He was a dirty little devil and would never go to heaven.

Barbary Coast

Barbary Coast opened at the Argentina Theatre on Monday 24 June. It was an immediate success and the Bill Hall Trio again the hit of the show. Wait till England heard about us, rich, rich, rich!!!

Article for *The Irish Press*: Undated

Dublin

Write a thousand words about Dublin, said Eoghan Corry of *The Irish Press* – is that enough for a thousand-year-old city? The first comment to make is my lament for the gradual destruction of a Georgian city, and the construction of appalling buildings like Liberty Hall, it does speak very well for the governing bodies.

To me, these days Dublin is more reliant on its atmosphere drawn from the people; yes, apart from its disappearing architecture, it's mainly people. When the old Hibernian Hotel was still standing, as an expatriate I made my first visit to the city. Will I ever forget the old porter taking my bags and saying, 'Follow me, Mr Milligan, I'll be right behind you'? I'd come over for the Ireland–South Africa rugby match. There was an anti-apartheid demo outside the hotel; when they discovered I was going to the match, they barred the way. But, and this could only happen in Ireland, they said through the loudhailer if I would 'confess' I was going to the match and condemn apartheid, they would let me through. This I did for five minutes, after which I was allowed to go.

It didn't end there – John Howard, a friend of mine and rugby fanatic, was supposed to meet me at Landsdown Road. I waited and waited – after ten minutes, the pull of the game was too much and I went in. Apparently his flight was delayed and when he arrived half an hour late at the game he wished he'd got a piano because that's where he'd left his rugby ticket. Fortunately there was a lady tout outside the grounds.

'Have you got any tickets left?' asked John.

'That I have,' said the woman.

'How much?' said John desperately.

'It'll cost you one hundred pounds,' said the female tout.

John, now even more desperate, said, 'My God, for that money I could have the most beautiful woman in Dublin.'

The female tout chuckled and said, 'Maybe so, but she wouldn't give you forty minutes each way with a band playing in the interval.'

It's people, Dublin is people.

Another Dublin tale. I was going to see *Juno and the Paycock* and I told the porter at the Hibernian Hotel I wouldn't be back till gone half past eleven.

'Tank you for telling me,' said the porter.

I hadn't finished. I continued, 'Yes, half-past eleven.'

'I've got dat,' he intervened.

'So,' I continued, 'could I have a late supper in my room? I'd like …'

'No trouble at all, what would you like?' he said.

I managed to get in 'A prawn salad' before he spoke again.

'Dat'll be fine,' he said.

'And a bottle of Blue Nun,' I managed to say.

'Blue Nun it'll be,' he said.

That night, as I returned to my room, he was wheeling my supper in. The table was set for two, not prawn salad but Dover Soles and two bottles, not Blue Nun but Orvieto. I tried to point it out.

'Oh, I'm sorry, sir, I tort dere was two of you.'

I remonstrated with him. 'You can *see* there's only one of me.'

'Yes, sor,' he said, 'but I tort a good-lookin' man like you would ha' brought someting back.'

'I ordered prawns.'

'Oh, I'm sorry, sor – look, sir, to help you out I'm willing to eat dat second dinner for you.'

So we seated for dinner, he conversed with some knowledge on Shaw, Joyce and Synge, and in between he consumed most of the two bottles of wine. Finally, in the wee hours he departed, pushing the dinner trolley. He paused at the door and said, 'Can I be perfectly honest with you, sir?'

I nodded.

'Well, I'd ha' tort a man with your money could ha' afforded a better bloody dinner dan dis,' and was gone.

Dublin people – ah!

As I was walking down Grafton Street, it was a cold morning, everyone seemed to be walking fast, or was I walking slow? I could hear a harp, I followed the sound and came across an old lady wearing mittens playing a small Irish harp. I was totally moved at the sight, I was filled with compassion. I took out the only money I had, a ten-pound note, that I handed to her. She took it and on whiskey-soaked breath she said in a personal whisper, 'I'm here every Thursday.' Dublin people!

Yes, Dublin to me is people, not just people like London or Paris, these Dublin people are easy talkers, always a sense of drama. Take the case of me at Dublin airport. I was returning from an Ireland–All Blacks rugby match. Because of snow, the flight was delayed – that's the announcement Aer Lingus made, though there wasn't a sign of snow, that's how it goes. 'No,' said the girl at the ticket desk, 'there is no snow, it's only because there *might* be.'

Ah Dublin! Dublin!

The Bible ... According to Spike Milligan: 1993

CHAPTER VII

A ND IT CAME TO PASS, Moses spoke unto the children of Israel. It was the fortieth year of their time in the wilderness. And Moses said, 'Remember when the Lord spake unto us, "Behold, I have set the land before thee, go in and possess the land." And you went forth and possessed the land, taking down the "For Sale" signs as you did.'

Moses said, 'The Lord hath multiplied you as the stars of heaven, go now and multiply.'

'Multiply? Again?' said the children of Israel. 'You must be mad, half of us are at the bottom of the council housing list.'

And Moses said, 'How can I myself alone bear your cumbrance, and your burden, and your strife?'

'Get a secretary,' they said.

Moses beat his breast and said, 'My life.' He spoke on: 'Remember when we went through that great and terrible wilderness?'

The Israelites said, 'Yes, we would never have booked our holidays there had we known.'

2. 'Remember how in the wilderness the Lord bore thee, as a man doth bear a son?' And Moses recalled he and his wife couldn't bear their son. 'And ye are come to the land of the Amorites and the Lord God doth give it to you.'

'But', cried the children of Israel, 'it was only leasehold.'

'And you were fearful of taking the land of the Amorites and cried out, "Lord, the Amorites are taller and bigger than us," and the Lord replied, "That is because they are on cod liver oil and malt and Sanatogen." And the Lord went before us and looketh for new land for the children of Israel PLC to settle. And the Lord said, "Ye are to pass through the coast of the children of Esau. Meddle not with them." And the Lord spake unto me, "Ye shall buy meat of them for money." '

'Oi vay money,' cried the Israelites. 'Hadn't we suffered enough?'

And Moses said, 'And the Lord spake, "Ye shall also buy water of them for money." '

'Oh,' cried the Israelites, 'money for water! We can make money for nothing.'

And in time Moses said, 'Rise ye up.'

It took a while to get them all up.

Moses continued, 'And the Lord said unto me, "Now, pass over the River Arnon, I give unto you the king of the Amorites, and his land: begin to possess it. This day I put the dread of thee and the fear of thee amongst all nations."

' "Lord," I said unto him, "you are doing a great PR job."

'The Lord said, "Thou shall pass through the land of the Heshbon." '

'Any properties going?' said the children of Israel.

'In that land you will buy meat for money.'

In a flash all the male Israelites formed a circle round their money crying, 'Nobody eats tonight.'

The Lord was wrath: verily, he was pissed off with the Israelites.

The Lord charged the children to possess the land of the Sihon, then Gillead, then Ammon, then Tabhok.

'Be careful, Lord,' said the children of Israel, 'we're becoming a monopoly!'

3. And it came to pass, Moses called all Israel again and said, 'You will put up no graven images nor the likeness of male or female nor any beast or any winged fowl nor anything that creepeth on the ground or any fish in the waters.'

And the children of Israel said, 'Can't we put up the wedding photographs?'

Moses spoke: 'Behold, the Lord, ye have heard the Lord speak to you from the midst of the fire.'

'But', said the Israelites, 'it's so hot we couldn't get near enough to hear what He was saying.'

The Lord called out, 'Get into your tents.'

4. They went into their tents and said, 'Now what?'

God said, 'I will speak unto thee all the commandments.'

'But Lord,' said the Israelites, 'we already know that, we've got them down on two stone tablets.'

'Hear me,' said the Lord, 'you will walk in the ways of the Lord, you will not turn left or turn right.'

'How are we going to turn round corners?' said the Israelites.

God said unto Moses, 'Thou shall teach the children, and they shall be as frontlets between thy eyes.'

'Quick,' said Moses to the people, 'look up what frontlets are because whatever they are I'm going to get it right between the eyes.'

The Lord said, 'Thou shall say unto thy son, we were Pharaoh's bondmen and I brought you out with a mighty hand.'

5. Moses gritted his teeth. 'But had we known this from the youngest to the oldest?'

'Yes,' said the Lord, 'it was by way of a repeat, and thou will smite the Hittites, the Girgashites, the Amorites, the Canaanites, I shall deliver them unto you.'

Surely that morning, six vans were delivered with the tribes and so the Israelites smote them and they were hard-pressed. 'Lord, I fear we are losing; do some of your tricks, please.'

6. And the Lord sent angels with fiery swords, and the enemies withdrew and surrendered. 'I am the Lord that freed you from Egypt.'

'Another repeat,' said Moses.

7. The Lord said, 'Thou shall not eat of them that chew the cud or them that divide the cloven hoof.'

'Lord,' said Moses, 'that only leaves rabbits.'

8. 'Then thou shalt turn it into money, hold thy money in thy hand, go unto a place which the Lord thy God shall choose, the mattress.' The Lord said, 'But of all clean fowl ye may eat – but of that that dieth of itself: thou shall give it to the stranger at the gate that he will eat it and snuff it.' The Lord said, 'Remember, I am the God that tookest thee from Egypt.'

And Moses said, 'Lord, they're fed up hearing it.'

The Lord appeared in a raincloud and was drenched. 'Thou shall surely smite the inhabitants of the city, destroying it utterly and thou shall gather all the spoil and stuff thy mattresses.'

Moses, 'Sayeth, Lord, don't you think you are overdoing it? Wait until you get the bill for damages.'

The Lord said, 'Does thou trust me? I got you out of Egypt, remember.'

'Remember it? You never stop,' said Moses.

'Beware false prophets, thou must kill him, thou must be the first hand that shall stone him.'

'Lord,' said Moses, 'the town is full of stoned prophets and the dustmen won't take them away.'

'Fear not, they shall come to pass,' said the Lord.

'You're right, Lord, these dustmen go right past.'

The Lord spoke. 'The holy things thou hast thou shall take unto a place the Lord will choose, Milton Keynes.' And He said thy children will write the names of the chosen on the gateposts and they wrote Duran Duran, Elton John, Prince, Eric Clapton, Dick Strangle.

9A. From in the Jordan the Lord spoke; there were bubbles everywhere. 'Ye are the children, ye shall not cut yourselves, nor make any baldness between your eyes for the dead.'

And the children of Israel spoke: 'What's He talking about?'

'You are a crowd of ignoramuses,' said the angel of the Lord. 'The Lord wills you to have plenty and turn it into money and put it in a safe place.'

'The mattress,' cried out the Israelites.

'And the poor man thou will help sufficient for his need in that which he wanteth, a Porsche. And thou shalt roast and eat in a place the Lord has chosen. Blooms. Also, thou shalt make an aul, and thrust it through his ear unto the door, and he shall be thy servant for ever.'

'Lord,' said the people, 'we don't want a servant hanging up by his ear on a door.'

The Lord said, 'At the end of seven years thou shall make a release.'

So Moses released his accountant because he was bloody awful.

9B. 'Hear me,' sayeth the Lord, 'thou shall not respect persons, neither take a gift: for a gift doth blind the eyes.'

The children of Israel said, 'Ye make it hard to give people presents.'

The Lord said, 'If there be found among you, men and women that had done wickedness in the sight of the Lord, they shall be cursed.'

'What happens to those you don't see?' said the Israelites.

'They will be remanded into custody,' said the Lord. 'And,' said the Lord, 'he that will not hearken to the Lord he shall die.'

'How?' sayeth the Israelites.

And the Lord said, 'You just have to wait.' After a lie-down the Lord continued: 'The time will come when I will set a king over thee.'

'What about a queen?' said the Israelites.

10. The Lord said, 'The priests of the tribe shall eat the offering of the Lord made by fire grilled lightly with a side salad with prunes and custard.' And the Lord spoke of the king. 'Yea, when he comes, he shall not multiply horses to himself, nor cause the people to return to Egypt, to the end that he should multiply horses.'

'What are you talking about?' said the Israelites.

'Neither', went on the Lord, 'shall the king multiply his wives.'

'He must rest between each,' said the Israelites, 'that way he can see to the lot.'

11. The Lord said the priests shall eat the offering of the Lord made by fire, in this case sausage and mash, and there will be his inheritance, which are the fish knives and the parrot. Otherwise he will own nothing like the names at Lloyds.

'Amen,' said the Israelites.

'To the priest,' said the Lord, 'thou shall give to the priest an ox or a sheep, but only the best cuts, the first of thy corn, thy best wine, thine best oil, the first fleece of thy best sheep.'

And the children of Israel said, 'Lord, we'll have bugger-all left.'

The Lord was wrath. 'Do you want to go to arbitration?'

There beath no comeback as the Israelites were sore afraid and their solicitor was on holiday.

The Lord said, 'Behold, the priest shall also eat food that cometh from the sale of his patrimony, which is a two-bedroom flat, £8,000 ono.'

A low moan ariseth from the priest; he prostrateth himself at the altar and said, '£8,000 it's a giveaway.'

12. The Lord said, 'There shall not be found among you any one that maketh his son or daughter pass through the fire.'

'Lord,' said the Israelites, 'we could make anyone pass through the fire; it goes up the chimney.'

The Lord said, 'There shall be no wizards, witches, TV show host, an enchanter or a necromancer; these are abominations the Lord God will drive them out – they are all on the 9.20 to Glasgow.'

13. 'Thou shalt be perfect with the Lord thy God.'

'We are perfect with you, Lord,' said the children of Israel; 'it's the bloody neighbours.'

The Lord said, 'I will give unto thee a prophet.'

'We could do with a profit,' said the Israelites.

He bade them divide the land and submit plans to the Borough Council to build three cities; one city will be for wrongdoers, like a man who maketh a living pulling short measure beer. He can flee to a city called Birmingham where he will never be found. Two more cities they built: King's Cross. And the Lord spoke of the law. 'A life for a life, eye for an eye, tooth for a tooth, a piano for a piano, a deepfreeze for a deepfreeze, and a foot for a foot. Innocent blood must not be spilt; use a Band Aid. And thou shall not remove thy neighbour's landmark.'

'But it's the Sheraton,' said a voice.

'When thou goest to battle be not afraid, for the Lord is there to fight for you.'

And the Israelites said, 'Good, we'll stand and watch.'

'And any men in ye battle line, that hath betrothed a wife and not yet taken her, let him return to his house, lest he die in battle, and another man take her.'

And lo, the army of Israel disappeareth.

14. After extra time the Israelites beat the Canaanites and the Lord said, 'Thy beaten enemy will serve thee.'

'Twenty beers and three whiskies,' said the Israelites.

'Ye shall battle and destroy the Amorites, Perizzites, Hittites,

Tottenham Hotspur, Arsenal, the Hivites and the Parasites.' The case was adjourned 'till after lunch. The Lord spake [spoke? speak?] 'When thou besiege a city, thou shalt not destroy the trees, for thou must eat of them.'

The Israelites gave a low moan. 'We have to eat trees, Lord?'

'Only trees that be not meat, thou shalt cut down.'

'What for?' said the Israelites.

'Bulwarks,' said the Lord.

'And bulwarks to you,' said the Israelites.

15. Of wars, the Lord spake from a deck chair. 'If seest among battle captives a beautiful woman thou desirest, take her home and shave her head.'

'Lord, that's kinky,' said the Israelites. 'More daddy.'

'Next,' said the Lord, 'pare her nails.'

'What about the black stockings and suspender belt?' cried the Israelites.

The Lord loseth heart, and was cast down. 'If', said the Lord, 'thou lose interest in her, let her go where she will; thou will not sell her for money, but charge by the hour, that or place her with the Alfred Marks Bureau. If a man have two wives, one beloved, and one hated.'

'Keep the ones with the big boobs,' said an Israelite voice.

16. 'Now', said the Lord from 300a Bargery Road, Catford, 'if a wife bear a son and he is stubborn and rebellious and will not obey – kill him.'

'Lord,' said the Israelites, 'is there no alternative?'

'Yes, there's always a recording contract. I am the Lord thy God, and a bit of a goer. If a man commit murder, hang him on a tree.'

'There are no trees in the desert, Lord,' said the Israelites.

'Then hang him on the wall.'

'Amen,' said the Israelites.

The Lord appeared in a pillar of cloud and couldn't see a thing: 'If thy brother's sheep go astray, bring them back to thy brother; the rate for finding sheep is three shekels an hour. The same applieth to thine brother's ass; thou must not be cruel and kick his ass. Thou shalt not plough with an ox and ass together because they go sideways ... Thou shalt not wear a garment of divers sorts, as of woollen and leather together.'

'This will kill the trade,' said the Israelites.

17. The Lord appeared in a new ball of fire with better insulation and said, 'If a man taketh a wife, and go in unto her, and hate her ...'

'Hard bloody luck,' said the Israelites.

The Lord said, 'If a man find a damsel that is a virgin and lay with her; he shall give her father a hundred silver shekels.'

'It's too much,' said a voice. 'We've seen her.'

'I am the Lord God who took you out of Egypt, etc., etc.'

'It's the commercial,' said the Israelites.

The Lord said, 'He that is wounded in the stones; or hath his privy member cut off, shall not enter the congregation.'

'It's his own fault,' said the Israelites; 'he kept a Rottweiler.'

18. 'If a man among you is not clean by reason of that which chanceth him in the middle of the night, then open all the windows and be rid of it. When evening come, let him goeth out the camp and wash his parts; when the sun is down, let him return to the camp with a room next to the WC.'

And they praised the Lord in his wisdom.

The Lord appeareth in a further pillar of cloud fitted with double glazing. 'Thou shalt have a place also without the camp, whither thou shall go abroad; it is called timeshare. And thou shalt have a paddle*, that when thou ease thyself abroad, thou shalt dig therewith, and shalt turn back and cover that which has come from thee. And let there be Andrex ... Thou shalt not bring the hire of a whore, or the price of a dog, into the house of the Lord.'

'Don't worry,' said the Israelites, 'we won't use your house.'

19. 'Tsu, tsu,' said the Lord, 'when thou shalt vow a vow unto the Lord, thou shalt not slack to pay it, and thou dost pay; it must be cash. When a man taketh a wife, and has found uncleanness in her, like the dishes, let him write her a bill of divorcement and send her out to post it, then change the locks on the doors. If she become another man's wife ...'

'Sell him her clothes,' said the Israelites.

The Lord appeared in a Mark II fiery bush with asbestos shields: 'When a man taketh a new wife, he shall not go to war, neither shall he do any business but stay at home and cheer his wife.'

'Who'll look after the shop?' said the Israelites.

20. The Lord spoke. 'If a man stealeth from one of the children of Israel and maketh merchandise, he shall die unless he pay it all back with interest.'

'We'd rather die,' sayeth the children of Israel.

The Lord spoke, 'Take heed in the plague of leprosy, for if thine legs fall off surely thou has it. Now remember what the Lord thy God did unto Miriam after ye left Egypt.'

The children of Israel couldn't remember what God had done to Miriam, but many of the children of Israel doth gossip.

'If a man be poor, thou shalt not sleep with his pledge, but keep the ticket in the office. Remember the poor of the parish.'

'We are the poor of the parish,' said the children of Israel.

21. The Lord returned in a new pillar of cloud fitted with de-misters. 'If thou cuttest down the harvest put some aside for the stranger, the fatherless and the widow. If thou beatest thine olive trees, put some aside for the stranger, the fatherless and the widow. When thou gatherest grapes, put some aside for the stranger, the fatherless and the widow.'

The stranger, the fatherless and the widow then went on to open a thriving grocery shop.

The Lord spake, 'If a man like not to take his dead brother's wife, then shall his brother's wife go with him to the elders, loose his shoe from his foot and spit in his face, and for ever more his shall be called in Israel "the house of the man that hath his shoe loosed". [Big Deal.] When men strive together, the wife draweth near to her husband, putteth forth her hand and take him by the secrets.'

22. 'We come to weights and measures,' said the Lord, and a great hush fell over the children of Israel, many of whom kept shops. The Lord said, 'Thou shalt not have in thy bag divers weights, great and small.'

A shudder went though the children of Israel.

'Thou shalt have perfect measures and just weights.'

A great groan came from the children of Israel.

The Lord heard and said, 'Did I not bring you to the land of milk and honey?'

They said, 'Yes, Lord, but the milk goes off very quickly.'

The Lord was wrath, the Israelites were funnier than him. 'Remember what Amalek did unto thee when ye came forth from Egypt?'

No, the children of Israel couldn't remember, which was a pity because neither could God.

23. 'Now,' said the Lord, 'take the first fruits of the earth.'

'They're prunes, Lord,' said the Israelites.

'Take them unto the priest and he shall eat of them.'

And they took the prunes and the priest eateth them, and soon he got them badly.

'Remember,' said the Lord, 'I brought you out of the wilderness with outstretched arms and signs "This way to the milk and honey".' Then the Lord disappeared and was gone.

24. And the Israelites said, 'Look down on us, O Lord, and bless thy people that liveth in the land of milk and honey but what we want is oil.'

And Moses said, 'Hello, I'm back. This day thou art become the people of the Lord.'

'Do we have to sign anything?' said the children of Israel.

Moses said, 'Thou shall stand upon Mount Gerizim and curse the Canaanites.'

So the Israelites stood there and shouted, 'You Canaanites are a lot of bastards.'

Moses said, 'The law says cursed be the man who make a graven image in a secret place like Golders Green post office.'

25. 'Cursed be he who setteth fire to his mother or father. Cursed be he who removeth his neighbour's landmark, like Canary Wharf. Cursed be he who maketh the blind to wander out of his way, or under a bus.

Cursed be he who lieth with his father's wife; because [wait for it] he uncovereth his father's skirt. Cursed be he who lieth with his mother-in-law.'

'Give him a medal,' said the Israelites.

Moses gave a smile – the only one in the whole Bible. 'Children,' he said, 'blessed shalt thou be in the city, blessed be thou in the field.'

'The city is better, there's more business,' said the Israelites.

'Blessed', said Moses, 'shalt thou be when thou comes in, blessed shall thou be when thou goest out.'

'What about when you're only halfway in and halfway out?' said the Israelites.

Moses turned a deaf ear and a rheumatic elbow. 'The Lord shall cause thine enemies that rise up against you to be smitten before your face.'

'We don't need any of that,' said the Israelites.

26. Moses went on: 'The Lord said thou shall lend unto many nations, but thou must not borrow.'

A groan of despair came from the children of Israel. 'The mortgage, what about the mortgage?' they wailed.

Moses said, 'The Lord shall make thee the head, and not the tail; thou shall be above only, and not be beneath.'

There was a pause and a voice said, 'He's pissed.'

Moses said, 'If you hearken not to the Lord, He will smite thee with a consumption, a fever, an inflammation, burning in the loins and mildew.'

'Who's going to argue?' said the Israelites.

27. Moses hadn't finished the threats. 'The Lord will cause thine enemy to punish thee. Thou will flee seven ways before them, mostly "B" roads. The Lord will smite thee with, and I have the list here: with the botch of Egypt, haemorrhoids, the scab and the itch. He will smite thee on the knees and in the legs with a sore botch that cannot be healed.'

'Thank God we're all on BUPA,' said the Israelites.

Moses said, 'The Lord will smite thee with madness.'

'Tell Him not to worry, we've got enough,' said the Israelites.

Moses went on: 'The Lord will smite thee with blindness; thou shall grope at midday.'

This frightened not the Israelites as they gropeth at all times.

The Lord said: 'Time will come when these things will come to you, the blessing and the curse.'

'Make up your mind, God,' said the Israelites. 'One day we're all sinners being cursed, the next day we're the chosen children of God; half of us are under a psychiatrist.'

28. The Lord heard them not as his pillar of cloud was sound-proofed.

Moses came and spake unto all Israel. 'I am an hundred and twenty years old this day.'

'Happy birthday to you,' sang the crowd.

Moses said, 'I can no more go out or come in.'

'Then where are you?' said the Israelites.

Moses said, 'The Lord said I shall not go over the Jordan.'

Cries of Shame! and You need a holiday.

29. Moses said, 'The Lord shall go across the Jordan to the promised land and do all travel arrangements with Thomsons.'

And Moses said unto Joshua, 'Go thou to Jordan and prepare the land that the Israelites may possess it. Take a solicitor.'

And the Lord said unto Moses, 'Behold, the days approach when thou must die.'

'I know, Lord,' said Moses, 'that's why I sleep in a coffin.'

30. And the Lord appeared in the tabernacle in a pillar of cloud, and the pillar of cloud stood over the tabernacle causing condensation, rust, mildew and verdigris. And the Lord said unto Moses, 'Thou sleep with thy fathers.'

'Lord,' said Moses, 'there's only room for one in the coffin.'

31. In time the Lord would take His children unto the land of milk, honey and cholesterol. When Moses had finished the law book, he offered it to Michael Joseph, who published it under the pen name of Jeffrey Archer. And he placed publishers' copies on the ark of the

covenant at a knockdown price of £7.50. And he spoke to the Levites who carry the ark. 'I know thy rebellion and stiff neck; believe me, it's better than piles.' Here he inserteth a suppository. 'Call all the elders of the tribe that I may speak words in their ears or any other orifice that works.'

32. 'Remember the days of old, consider the years of old generations, ask thy father and he will show you rheumatism. Jacob is the Lord's inheritance. He found him in a desert, a real yobbo, in the waste of a howling dead land, East Ham, he crieth out " 'ere we go, 'ere we go, 'ere we go", but the Lord quietened him with six packs of Fosters, and He instructeth him in the ways of the Lord.'

Moses paused to take a Novmison and said, 'As an eagle stirreth up her nest over her young, spreadeth her wings, taketh her young and bear them on her wings.' [Wrong. There is no record of an eagle carrying her chicks on her wings.]

Moses groaned, 'Don't quote me,' he said, 'I'm under contract to Penguin.' He continued in the death-is-apparent position. 'The Lord took Jacob and made him ride the highest places on earth, where he nearly died through lack of oxygen, he made him suck honey [wait for it] out of the rock, and oil out of the flinty rod.'

What he needed was a rig.

33. The Lord said, 'Fire is kindled in mine anger and set on fire, the foundations of the mountains. They shall be burnt with hunger, devoured with burning heat, all will be destruction. I will send the teeth of beasts upon them, the sword without, the terror within, all will die the young man, the virgin, the man with grey hairs.'

'Same time tomorrow, Lord?' sayeth Moses.

The children of Israel were wrath. This Lord, one day He's okay, next day He's going to set fire to the world, was He on something?

The Lord started early the next day at 6.30. 'To me belongeth vengeance.'

'He's off again,' said the Israelites.

'Silence,' said the Lord.

34. 'Thine religion is thy rock – that rock shall be all the hours of the day.'

'Lord,' said the baffled Israelites, 'does that mean rock around the clock?'

The Lord in his pillar of cloud smote His chest as He knew not what the children of Israel meant, relations were strained, they were put in a muslin bag and squeezed.

The Lord said, 'I lift up my hand to heaven and say I love forever-more.'

Genealogists say there is no evidence of a man holding up his hand to heaven has ever lived for ever, the oldest was ninety-three and came from Slough. Moses said, 'Beware of all that is false.'

'Does that go for teeth?' said the Israelites.

Moses said, 'The Lord came from Sinai and He came with ten thousand saints, though a poll only showed three hundred; the rest were workers for Datsun on a day out.'

35. From the Lord's right hand went a fiery law.

The Israelites were glad they had fitted smoke detectors. And of Levi, the Lord said, 'Let thy Thummim and Urim be. I'll say that again, Thummim and Urim be thy holy one. Thou shalt put incense before thee and put the whole burnt sacrifice on thine altar. Let Reuben live and not die.'

'Why me?' said Reuben. [Who he?]

The Lord worked in mysterious ways and these were some of them.

Moses said, 'To the Lord belongeth vengeance [again?], thy foot will slide in due time – because there's a lot of it about.'

36. A Levi sayeth unto his father, 'I have not seen him.'

'Seen who?' sayeth his father.

'I don't know,' said Levi, 'all I know, whoever it is I have not seen him.' Neither did he acknowledge his brethren, nor knew his own children. The doctors diagnosed amnesia. 'Bless the Lord and his substance, which I think is Polyfilla, smite the loins of them against thee, which usually cripples 'em, praise the Lord. His glory is like the firsting of his bullocks. He shall push the people together to the ends of the earth.'

'They'll fall off,' said the Israelites.

Moses said, 'And of Benjamin, the Lord shall cover him all day, and he shall dwell between his shoulders.'

So Benjamin got between his shoulders and lived.

37. 'For the righteousness, they shall suck an abundance of the sea, and treasures hid in the sand, like lug worms.' Of God he said: 'He dwelleth like a lion, and teareth the arm with the crown of his head.'

'He must be deformed,' said the Israelites.

And of Dan, he said, 'He's a lion's whelp: he shall leap from Mount Bashan.'

'The fall will kill him,' said the children of Israel.

Moses still went on: 'Of Naphtali: possess thou the west and the south, thus avoiding the awful Northern Line.'

38. And of Asher: 'Let him be acceptable to his brethren, let him dip his foot in oil, using 3 in One.'

'That's no good,' cried the children of Israel, 'we need a rig!'

Moses said, 'Children of Israel, thy shoes will be iron and brass.'

The children of Israel beat their chests and shouted, 'It's time you retired.'

Moses didn't retire, instead he said, 'Israel shall dwell in a land of corn and wine.'

'What happened to the milk and honey?' said the Israelites.

'It's crop rotation,' said Moses.

39. And Moses went up the mountain and the Lord showed him all the land of Gilead, unto Dan, all Naphtali, all Catford and Lewisham. 'This is the land which I swore unto Abraham.'

'It's enough to make anyone swear,' said Moses; then he died.

He was a hundred and twenty when he died. His eye was not dim, nor his natural force abated, but the drink finally got him. He was buried in the land of Moab, leaving many unpaid bills and maintenance orders.

Lady Chatterley's Lover According to Spike Milligan: 1994

The second volume in the 'According to' series.

Four

After her affair with Paddy, other men meant nothing to her, Tom Loon meant nothing to her nor did Dick Squats, Len Lighthower, nor Lord Louis Mountbatten nor Eric Grins, not even Houdini! No, she was married to Clifford, she would stand by him, something he couldn't do for her. She wanted a good deal from life but this poor cuckolded cripple couldn't give it to her, he had tried but it gave him a nose-bleed, She had insured his legs in the event of him walking again. She thought of Paddy and knew that their affair was at an end, she knew he couldn't keep anything up (Eh?). The world was full of possibilities. There was lots of fish in the sea but no chips. The vast masses of fish were mackerel or herring, so reasoned Constance, if you're not mackerel or herring, you're not likely to find good fish in the sea. Mackerel was an excellent fish and a fine swimmer, it was splendid eating, people eating it looked splendid, they were best grilled with basil, it was best to catch them already cooked, if you caught chips with them even better. So reasoned Constance.

Clifford was making strides* into fame, even money. He had his wheelchair resprayed, centrally heated and fitted with a periscope. People came to see him: Dick Squats, Len Lighthower, Lord Louis Mountbatten and Eric Grins. He saw them all through his periscope.

Constance always had somebody at Wragby. There were a few regular men, Brigadier Tommy Dukes who was a regular man, there was Charles May who had constantly been a regular man, there was Hammond who was ever so regular a man, all intellectuals and philosophers, they believed it was 'all in the mind,' no one asks how long someone was going to be in the WC, it wasn't interesting to anyone but the person in the WC. 'The sex problem,' said Hammond, tall and thin,

---

* Lawrence's unfortunate choice of word for a cripple. Ed.

with a wife and two children, and who reeked of Horlicks: 'There's no point to it. We don't want to follow a man into the WC. So why should we want to follow a man into bed with a woman?'

'To have a look,' said Constance.

'No, no, no,' said Hammond angrily, it was way past his Horlicks' time.

'But', said May, who was a Catholic, wore his underpants back to front to avoid temptation, 'supposing another man started to make love to your wife, what would you do?'

'I should get between them,' said Hammond. 'I would tell the bounder to leave and give him a biff.'

'Wait a minute,' said Charles May. They all waited a minute, nothing much happened so he continued. 'Why shouldn't we be free to make love to any woman who inclines us that way?'

'Oh, be as promiscuous as rabbits,' said Hammond from the I-am-shocked position.

'Why not?' said May. 'What's wrong with rabbits?'

'Mixamatosis,' said Hammond, pursing his lips like a chicken's bum.

'But we're not rabbits,' intervened Clifford.

'I know that,' said May. 'Anyone can see we're not rabbits.' He had never seen a rabbit in a wheelchair, May reflected. 'If you want to go on you can say we're also not elephants,' said May.

Constance was standing with her back to the fire, warming it. 'Life is a juxtaposition of appetites, nutritional and sexual,' she said.

'Not it!' shouted May. 'I don't over-eat myself and I don't over-fuck myself.'

How, thought Constance, does he fuck himself, he must be an acrobat?

'Ah, Charles,' said Dukes, 'Sex is just another form of talk. We exchange emotions with women as we do ideas about the weather.'

'Are you suggesting', said May, 'that while we're fucking a woman we give her the weather report?'

'I think', said Dukes, 'if you have emotion or sympathy with a woman you should sleep with her.'

May laughed loud jettisoning little spit balls into the air and down to the carpet. Everybody watched as they floated down. The dirty bugger, thought Constance.

'Sleep with a woman,' repeated May. 'You must be mad, you don't get any sleep in bed with a woman, you're at it all the time.'

'I still say', said Dukes, 'the only decent thing is to go to bed with her.'

'It's not only bed,' said May, 'some persons go to the cupboard, some do it in the bath, some do it against brick walls and some do it in doorways.'

How wonderful thought Constance.

'I don't think there's anything wrong in Charles running after women,' said Dukes.

'I don't understand,' said Clifford. 'Why does he only chase women who are running? There are plenty of them standing still.'

'Without women life would be like being chained in a kennel like a monk,' said May.

'Monk in a kennel?' said Clifford. 'Surely you mean dog.'

May laughed loud; more spit flew out. 'What I meant to say was life would be like a dog chained in a monastery.'

'That's enough from May,' said Dukes. 'What about Hammond, you'll see he'll be a man of letters.'

Dukes was right, Hammond never stopped writing them.

'Then there's me,' said Dukes. 'I'm nothing. Just a squib.'

'I thought you were a brigadier,' said Hammond, the man of letters. 'How do I address you?'

'It's Brigadier T. Dukes, HQ Waterloo Barracks Aldershot Hampshire,' said Dukes. Turning to Clifford he said, 'Well, Clifford, what do you think of this sex thing?' Clifford and his wheelchair blushed. Embarrassed he picked up the telephone. 'Hello, who's that?' he said.

'Darling,' said Constance. 'It hasn't rung.'

'I know,' said embarrassed Clifford. 'I didn't want to wait until the last moment.' Then, regarding sex, he said, 'Myself I am *hors de combat.*[*] You see mine was shot off on the Somme, I got the DSO.'

---

[*] War horse.

'DSO?' queried Dukes.

'Yes,' said Clifford. 'Dick Shot Off.'

Clifford, in high emotion, spun his wheelchair around and fell out. Using block and tackle they restored him to his wheelchair. He spoke, 'Love between man and woman is a great thing.'

Constance's heart beat as she recalled Paddy's great thing. Silence fell. Fortunately it landed outside. The men smoked while Constance steamed. She had been at so many of these evenings, the men talk, talk, but they didn't seem to get anywhere, not even Lewisham. None of them spoke well of her Paddy. They called him by terrible names! Mongrel *arriviste*! Uneducated bounder! Charlton Athletic! 22 Gabriel Street! The Kaiser! Spotted Dick and custard! Constance thought of Paddy and wondered what he was doing. He was doing Madge Gibson in the doorway of 17 Peabody Buildings.

Dukes was saying he had no real talent. 'I'm merely a fellow skulking in the Army.'

'Are you skulking in the Army at the moment?' said Clifford.

'No,' said Dukes looking ashamed. 'No, you have to be in uniform to do it.'

Constance broke the silence. 'Oh, come on, Dukes, please do a little skulk for us.'

Dukes did a little skulk.

'Was that it?' said May.

'Yes,' said Dukes.

'I couldn't tell the difference,' said May disappointedly.

'That's because I wasn't in uniform, it doesn't show otherwise.'

'Wait,' said Constance, 'I noticed it, when you laid face down on the carpet and did swimming strokes I thought that *must* be a skulk.'

Dukes smiled. 'I'm glad you noticed,' he said, puffing his pipe and piping his puff.

Hammond was saying, behind our backs we all spoke badly of each other, 'Else we bust apart.' Constance prayed they wouldn't bust apart in here, she'd have to clean it up.

'Fathomless spite,' said Hammond striking a 'I'm going to say something brilliant' pose. 'Look at Socrates, in Plato, and his bunch around him!'

So they all looked at Socrates, in Plato, and his bunch around him. 'Now what?' said May.

'Socrates', continued Hammond, now standing on a chair, 'found sheer joy in pulling somebody else to bits!'

'That must be very difficult,' said May. 'I wouldn't know where to start pulling. Do you know where he did?'

'Athens,' said Hammond. 'I would prefer Buddha, quietly sitting under a bo-tree.'

'What a bore he must have been, what a pointless exercise in fertility if we all sat under bo-trees,' said May. 'In any case there aren't enough bo-trees to go around.'

'How do you know?' said Hammond. Agitatedly he thrust his hands into his trouser pockets, splitting the seam of one and releasing all his loose change down his trouser leg.

'I read it somewhere,' said May. 'I think it was Lewisham.'

'It doesn't *have* to be a bo-tree,' said Hammond, picking up his change. Twelve shillings had fallen on the carpet, seven pennies in his shoe and tuppence in his sock. 'And', he continued, 'there was Jesus peacefully preaching to his disciples.'

'Why wasn't *he* sitting under a bo-tree?' said May.

'Because', said Hammond now in a fury, 'they don't grow in Palestine!' Pausing for breath he went on: 'No, we are rooted in spite and envy. Ye shall know the tree by its fruit.'

'What's the fruit of the bo-tree?' persisted May.

'It has no fruit,' said Hammond.

'No bos?' chuckled May.

'I don't agree with you, Hammond,' said Clifford running his wheelchair forward.

'Ow, Christ!' yelled Dukes.

'What's wrong?' said Clifford.

'You've run over my bloody foot,' howled Dukes.

Clifford told Hammond, 'I don't think we are as spiteful as you say.'

'Oh, my bloody foot,' said Dukes, hopping round the room, out the door, along the passage, out into the garden, through a gate and across a ploughed field and back. 'Ah,' he said, 'there's nothing like a ploughed field to cure a crushed foot. By the by when I was away was there any mail for me?'

Hammond was in full flow. 'I infinitely prefer spite to the concocted sugaries.'

'I'm not allowed concocted sugaries,' said Dukes, 'I'm a diabetic.'

'Real knowledge', said Hammond, 'comes out of the whole corpus, out of your belly and your penis.'

'Well,' said May, 'I can't speak for others but I never had any real knowledge come out of my prick, though I've listened very closely.'

'Perhaps you've got a stupid prick,' said Hammond, laughing fit to burst. 'Oh dear, I could do with a drink,' he said. Constance took him to a tap.

'Hammond thinks we should lead a mental life,' said Clifford, who thought Hammond *was* mental.

Hammond continued. 'Life is like an apple tree.'

'Why is life like an apple tree?' said May.

'How should I know?' said Hammond, blowing his nose in a paper handkerchief and going through it. 'If', said Hammond cleaning up the mess, 'if you've got nothing in life but the mental life, you are a plucked apple.'

'Well then,' said Dukes, 'we're *all* plucked apples.'

'Yes,' said May. 'I'm a Granny Smith.'

'Get plucked,' said Dukes.

A new guest had joined the party, a Mr Berry. 'What do you all think of Bolshevism?' he said as everything led up to it.

Clifford asked among them all, then said, 'I've just asked and none of us ever think of Bolshevism, why?'

'Bolshevism', said May, 'is a hatred of things called bourgeois.'

'What *things* do you call bourgeois?' said Clifford, oiling his wheel-chair. 'Would you call a wooden leg bourgeois?'

'If it was on a sailor, no, but if the Queen had one, yes,' said Dukes, who sprang to attention when he mentioned the Queen. 'Here', he said, 'is a photograph of her.'

Clifford took the photograph. 'This isn't the Queen,' he said. 'This is a photograph of a horse.'

'Yes,' said Dukes. 'I haven't got one of the Queen.'

'I don't think the Queen with a wooden leg is bourgeois,' said Hammond. 'I'd say she was aristocracy.'

'Ah yes,' said May. '*She* is aristocracy but her wooden leg is bourgeois.'

'To be a Communist', said Hammond, 'you must submerge yourself in the greater thing.'

At the mention of the 'greater thing' Constance thought of Paddy and his.

'The only time I submerged myself was at Lewisham municipal baths, does that make me a Communist?' said May laughing.

'Russian Communism is nothing to be laughed at,' said Clifford.

'Oh, I'm sure they can't hear me from here,' said May.

'I can think of nothing worse than being a Bolshevik,' said Hammond.

'Yes, you could be Tom Loon, Dick Squats, Len Lighthower, Lord Mountbatten or Eric Grins, any of those,' said Clifford.

Mr Berry changed the direction of the argument to NorNorEast, roughly parallel with the London and North Eastern line to King's Cross where, in fact, at this moment the eleven-fifty train was arriving. By coincidence the engine-driver's name was Dick Squats.

'Do you believe in love?' Berry said.

'Oh,' said Dukes. 'You mean fellows fucking jazz girls with small-boy buttocks, like two collar-studs.'

There was a baffled silence, then Clifford said, 'What *are* you talking about?'

'I think', said Dukes, 'I'm talking about twelve words a minute, the world record is twenty-three held by Arthur Mince Junior, a Canadian haddock-stretcher.'

'Don't you believe in anything?' said Berry. 'I believe in a good heart and a chirpy penis.' A good penis roused his head and said, 'How do you do!'

'Renoir said he painted his pictures with his penis. I wish I could do something with mine,' concluded Dukes.

'Why not tie a brush to it and start painting?' said May.

That night Constance looked at her behind in the mirror. At no stretch of the imagination did it look like two collar-studs. What utter rubbish they had been talking, she would rather have talked to Dick Squats. Alas! He was on the footplate of the eleven-fifty to King's Cross.

Goodbye Soldier: 1986

Capri

Lovely! It's a sunny day, nice and warm with a cool breeze. I pack my suitcase, only taking the bare essentials – like me. I'm too excited to eat breakfast, so I have a cup of tea. I buzz the porter and ask him to get me a taxi. When it arrives, he buzzes me: *'Taxi pronto, signore!'* Toni is waiting in the foyer of her hotel; she is all beaming and giggles. She lights up when she sees me; she must know that I'm carrying what *was* 72,000 lire. Our taxi turns into numerous buzzing backstreets on the way to the Porto Grande. There, waiting for us, is our dream boat – Spirito del Mare.

At the quayside ticket office, I buy our two returns and we board. We go into the airy saloon bar: we are early, the saloon is empty save for the barman. Can we have two coffees? *'Si accomodino.'* We sit at a window overlooking the deck; we hear the engines start up. There are only a few passengers carrying bundles. All of them appear to be peasants who have come to Naples to shop or collect something. They are all much more sunburnt than the mainland Italians.

We hear the bell on the ship's telegraph; there are shouts as the hawsers are slipped and the donkey engine takes them in. Expertly we move away from the quay; Tony and I finish the coffee and go to the ship's rail. We turn slowly; clear of the harbour wall, we increase speed and the ship vibrates to the engines. There is that gorgeous sound of a ship slicing through warm waters. We leave the brown waters behind and soon are into the clear blue waters of the Bay of Naples. The city starts to recede, is gradually obscured by the heat haze. Capri lies about twenty-five kilometres ahead.

A few vest-clad crewmen are moving about the ship, all looking rough and unshaved. They shout their conversations even when face to face. I always thought it made you go blind; apparently, it makes you go deaf.

'What did you say Toni?'

'I feel sick.'

Oh, my God, she's allergic to sea travel. She runs to the ladies and is in and out of there for the whole trip. What bloody luck. I breathe a sigh of relief as we pull up to the Marina Grande. We disembark; with me carrying Toni's case and mine and Toni holding a handkerchief over her mouth. I ask a tourist guide for the nearest hotel; he points to one five minutes away.

'Albergo Grotta Azzurra, *signore.*'

'*Grazie, grazie.*'

We walk uphill to the hotel. Up a few steps in reception, a smiling old Italian greeted us. Are there any vacancies? *O, si, si, molto.* Would we like 'una camera matrimonia?' No no no, I say; we would like separate rooms with adjoining doors. '*Ah, si, si.*' We register in our own names, killing any breath of scandal. They are modest, old-fashioned, unpretentious rooms with a view of the sea. We didn't know it, were totally ignorant, that this was the 'poor' part of the island. Further up on the far side, was where it was all happening, which we would in time find out – only, too late.

Toni is still feeling queasy, so she'll have a lie-down. OK. I repair to my room, unpack my few belongings and read Mrs Gaskell's *Life of Charlotte Brontë.* Will I never finish? I'm taking longer to read it than she lived. From my window I can see down to the Marina Grande, which is primarily a fisherman's port. Little boats are beached on a laticlave of sand; painted on each prow is an eye to ward off evil. They all appear to be looking at me. At about four o'clock Toni comes into my room; she's feeling a lot better. What would she like to do? Why not a swim? OK, we change into our costumes and walk down to a small beach this side of the Marina. No one else is in the water. We have a good hour's swimming.

Then a little sunbathe. It's so peaceful; in the distance, we can hear the chatter of the fishermen's wives and their children. We decide that we will have dinner at our hotel and really start exploring the island tomorrow. Toni says she is feeling much better now; *I* am feeling much better now. We *both* feel so much better that we get back into bed, which is even better than better. We watch the twilight approach.

'I think I'll have a bath, Toni – wash all the salt water off.'

She laughs a little. What is it?

She says, 'I think you wash you self away.'

She's referring, I think, to my thinness.

I return to my room and turn the light on. It is a very low voltage bulb that just about illuminates the room. The same bulb in the bathroom. I have a lovely long hot bath in braille. I get out before I pull out the plug, just in case. All together, now:

SING: Your baby has gone down the plug'ole
       Your baby has gone down the plug
       The poor little mite
       Was so thin and so slight
       He should have been washed in a jug.

Toni and I are the only couple in the dining-room. The waiter says the season is '*passato*'. It's a fixed menu, under celluloid: potato soup, vermicelli, then fish and the wine of the island, Vino Capri Scala, Grotta Azzurra – a light white, very fruity. We eat in silence with three unemployed waiters and a waitress standing in attendance. 'Food very nice,' says Toni. When we've finished, we are bowed out of the room.

We decide to take the funicular up to the piazza. We wait as the little box car descends and climb in. It's a slow ascent to the top. The view is a night setting: in the distance, we can see the lights of Naples and the bay winking in the dark. It's a clear night, cool with a starry sky; the air is like velvet. We reach the top and usher out into the piazza. All is brightness with the shops around still open. We sit ourselves at a table outside the Caffè al Vermouth di Torino. A few American officers and their wives/birds are in evidence. It's two coffees and two Sambuccas, that daring drink that they set on fire. Our waiter speaks English.

'You here on holiday?' he said.

'Yes.'

'Ah, good time – not many people on the island.'

Milligan the human skeleton escaping from jellyfish, Capri
Toni swimming in sewage-ridden water, Capri

In the square, a few landaus with sorry-looking horses wait for customers. Around us, at other cafés, people are partaking of the night.
Among them are the élite of Capri, well-dressed, haughty, never looking left or right as though the rest of the world doesn't exist, and on
Capri, it doesn't. The waiter puts a match to our Sambuccas, a blue
flame appears. We watch it whisper on the surface as they burn the coffee beans. It's the first time Toni has had one. We blow out the flames,
wait for the glasses to cool; we clink them together.

'To us, Toni.'

'Yes,' she says and clinks again. 'To us', which she pronounces 'to
hus.' (I'd better explain that Toni spoke with a pronounced accent,
which I have straightened out for the benefit of the reader.)

She sips it rather like a food taster at the court of the Borgias.

'Ummm!' she says, closing her eyes. 'Very good. What they make it
with?'

I tell her it's Strega, a drink that can revive dead horses and cause
Brongles to rise earlier than normal. 'I no understand.'

'What a pity. I was hoping you'd tell me.'

She knows I'm out of my mind and it's showing.

We don't want to go to bed; the air is so invigorating. Let's have another two Sambuccas. Yes, why not? The night is young even if I'm not. Again the two flames burn in the night; shall *we* blow them out or call the fire brigade? Toni says, 'You mad, Terr-ee!' As an inspired guess that was pretty accurate. After the second Sambucca, Toni says she feels really fine and I say that I am really fine. So we go back to the hotel, get into bed and have a fine time, bearing in mind that my mother would say 'You are ruining your health.'

Wuthering Heights According to Spike Milligan: 1994

Chapter IV

Adjourned to my study weak as a kitten to enjoy a cheerful fire. Mrs Dean brought in my supper, as I ate, we talked.

'You have been here a considerable time, did you not say?'

'No, I did not say,' she said. 'I haven't said anything,' she said. By putting an arm lock on her she admitted to having worked here eighteen years.

'I came when the mistress was married to wait on her. After she died, I didn't see the point of waiting any longer. The master kept me on for groping duties. By the way, you look as weak as a kitten.'

'Indeed.'

There ensued a pause. I took advantage of this by doing some knees bend. She was not a gossip, I feared, unless about her own affairs (among which was a Chinaman). I had no interest. I asked her why Heathcliff had let Thrushcross Grange.

'Had let it, what?' she said.

'Rented it,' I ejaculated.

'He let it for money,' she said.

'He had a son?'

'Yes.'

'Is he dead?'

'I think so, they buried him.'

'And Mrs Heathcliff is his widow?'*

'Yes, she is my late master's daughter. Catherine Linton was her maiden name.'

'What? Catherine Linton!!!' I ejaculated in a shower of spittle that showered Mrs Dean. She had to sponge her glasses before she could see again. While she did, I did some press-ups to keep me fit. 'Who is Hareton Earnshaw?' I said.

* Even I am baffled. Ed.

'That bastard is the late Mrs Linton's nephew.'

'Is that who the bastard is?' I inquired.

'Yes, he is the last of the Earnshaws. Isn't that good?' she said, clapping her hands together. 'When you were a guest at Wuthering Heights, how was Cathy?'

'Mrs Heathcliff? She looked very well, handsome, not very happy and a pain in the arse. She likes reading books by the fireside, she's all scorched down one side.'

'What about her master, Heathcliff? He's so mean, if he were a ghost he'd be too mean to give you a fright,' she said.

'He must have had some ups and downs in his life,' I said.

'Yes,' she agreed. 'He used to be a lift attendant.'

Excited by this information, I asked for more. 'Very well,' she said, folding her arms and putting them on her knitting basket. 'I used to be at Wuthering Heights.'

'So, you used to be at Wuthering Heights.'

'I used to play with the children, and I used to run errands too,' she said.

'So,' I said, 'you used to run errands too?'

'Yes, they never let me walk.'

'So, they never let you walk,' I said.

'Look!' she said, shaking me by the throat. 'For Christ's sake, will you stop interrupting.' For a while I lay on the floor doing sit-ups.

'One fine summer morning', she continued, 'Mr Earnshaw, the old master, came down dressed for a journey. He wore a tram driver's uniform. "You going by tram?" we said. "No," he said, "I'm going by uniform." He turned to Hindley and Cathy. "Now, I'm going to Liverpool. What shall I bring you?" Hindley named a fiddle, he named it Dick. Cathy chose a whip, for strict discipline. The lunatic set off to walk sixty miles there, and sixty back. We waved him goodbye, some waved him goodbye for ever. He was gone three days, then one midnight he returned. He threw himself at a chair and missed.

'He opened his great coat, holding a bundle in his arms. We crowded round to see a dark, ragged black-haired child. "Aye up!" said Mrs

Earnshaw. "Aye," said Mr Earnshaw. The child was talking in a language we could not understand. "It's Pakistani." The master tried to explain. The children refused to have the child in bed with them or even in the room. They called him Heathcliff. Bit by bit, they got used to him. First a bit of his leg, a bit of his arm, bit of his teeth and so on, he got on very well with Cathy, and said one day they would open up a corner shop in Leeds. To Cathy it was magic!

'Hindley hated him and frequently rendered the boy senseless with an iron bar. Then Heathcliff went ill with measle, just one measle. I stayed by his bed all night, every hour giving him spoonfuls of curry. Despite this, he recovered. By now we all doted on him, he was covered with dote marks. Hindley hated him, he had seen him naked in the bath, and was jealous of his porportions.

'Then Mrs Earnshaw died, worn out with making curry for Heathcliff. Cathy and her brother love practical jokes like practising setting fire to me. Mr Earnshaw sought a couple of horses, a lover of horse flesh, he looked forward to eating one. Heathcliff took one and Hindley the other. But Heathcliff's horse went lame in the teeth that kept falling out. "You must exchange the horses," said Heathcliff. Hindley gave Heathcliff his horse. "You better hurry up and ride it, because Mr Earnshaw is having it for dinner." '

Goodbye Soldier: 1986

So, dear reader, we come to my two blank days. However, on 23 September my diary continues. 'Lazy day, went to Parco Botanico. Lunch in park. Carriage drive back home. Madame Butterfly in evening, awful singing. Toni tells me organised by black marketeers, claque in evidence.'

Yes, *Madam Butterfly* was at the Rome Royal Opera House. Toni had two free tickets that her mother had given to her by a customer at the CIT travel agency. What a treat to look forward to! But it was a night of suppressed hysterical laughter. The whole opera was financed and cast by black marketeers. I couldn't believe it. When first I saw Madam Butterfly, she was *huge*, with a heaving bosom. I thought, out of this frame will come a most powerful voice. When she opened her mouth to sing, you could hardly hear anything. To accentuate the short-coming, she overacted, throwing her arms in the air, clasping her hands together, falling on her knees with a groan, running across the stage with loud, thudding feet – all to thunderous applause from an obvious claque. Then we wait for Lieutenant Pinkerton: my God, he's half her size! He can't be more than five foot five inches and so thin that when he stood behind her, he vanished. He has a piercing tenor voice, high up in the nose, with a tremendous wobbly *vibrato* that fluctuates above and below the real note. He is obviously wearing lifts in his shoes that make him bend forward from the ankles as though walking in the teeth of a gale. If that isn't all bad enough, he is wearing what must be the worst toupee I've seen. It appears to be nailed down, the front coming too far forward on the forehead with a slight curl all round where it joins his hair.

Trying to laugh silently, I'm almost doubled up in pain. All around me are Mafia-like creatures – one wrong move and I'll be knifed. So be it, no comedy could exceed this. We notice that when Pinkerton tries for a high note, he shoots up on his toes, putting him at an even more alarming angle. When he and she embrace, she envelops him com-pletely, his little red face appearing above her massive arms as though he's been decapitated. I'm carried on the tide of enthusiasm. When the claque jump up applauding, so do I. '*Bravo, encore*,' I shout. It was a night I can never forget.

At the little restaurant after the show, I keep breaking into fits of laughter as I recall it all. Toni is split down the middle, both halves being equal to the whole. She's ashamed that something so bad should go on at the Royal Opera House. '*Disgrazia*,' she says, but continues to laugh through it.

I remember that, as we sat outside eating, for no reason it started to rain. We retreat inside while a waiter rescues our food. The waiter is amusing; he apologises for the rain and says even though some has settled on the food, there'll be no extra charge.

Seated inside, Toni suddenly says to me, 'You know, in two day you leave me.'

My mood changed, was it that soon? I was so impervious to days that each one came as a shock. Why wasn't time timeless?

'Toni,' I said, 'I'll come back as soon as I can and I'll write as much as I can.'

That's followed by us just looking at each other in silence.

'I miss you very much, Terr-ee.'

She looks so small and helpless; I *feel* so small and helpless.

'I tell you what, we have some champagne, yes?'

She pauses reflectively. 'OK,' she says.

The restaurant hasn't any champagne. '*Tedeschi hanno bevuto tutto*,' says the waiter. Would we like Asti Spumante? Yes, when in Rome.

When midnight strikes in some campanile, we toast each other. We'd done it so often before, but this time it's a little more meaningful – our sand is running out. In the taxi back, I sit with my arm around her, her head on my shoulder (sounds like a transplant). I hum her favourite tune, 'La Valzer di Candele' ... We tiptoe into the apartment and I instinctively wait for my mother's voice, 'Where have you been at this time of night.' No, it's Signora Fontana asking is that Toni. Yes, so goodnight.

This day is suit-fitting day. When we arrive at the tailor's, a man is leaving wearing a terrible suit that appears to have been made by a blind man. No, no, no, says the little tailor, he didn't make that. It's only his father-in-law visiting to collect the alimony. My suit is all ready on a hanger. Will I step into the cubicle and change? The suit is a great success; I can't wait to get outside for a photograph.

Oh, yes, this is a Robert Taylor suit. Quick! I must be seen walking about the town. What's the best street? Ah, yes, driver, the Via Veneto and step on it. When we arrive it's midday and the morning promenade is coming to an end. Nevertheless Toni and I and the suit walk up and down, then down and up. Toni and I and the suit sit at a restaurant and Toni and I and my suit have an ice cream. All Rome must be talking about me. My suit is now smoking a cigarette. Toni is totally bemused: is this a man or a little boy she's going out with, or is it a suit? If only they could see me in Brockley now, standing outside the Rialto Cinema waiting for Lily Dunford. My picture would be in the *Kent Messenger*.

By mid-afternoon I think Rome has seen enough of the suit, so we return to the apartment. Gioia opens the door to my suit, *she doesn't seem to notice it*!!!! She'll *have* to be killed. I have a good reason to take my suit off: Gioia has to go out shopping. It's the last chance of Toni and I being alone. I draw Miss Toni's attention to this by making her take her clothes off and getting into bed, where we foreclose on the world. There *is* a Father Christmas. He was early this year. However, though it was divine making love to her, it lost a bit by Toni breathlessly telling me all the time to 'hurry up' as Gioia was due back. I did my best, finishing in under twenty-three minutes – beating Gioia by five and my own record by ten. With Gioia fiddling at the door with the keys, I rush madly back to my room, just slamming the door on my bare bum in time. Worn out by pressurised love-making, I have a siesta. It's a warm afternoon but nice and cool in the room. I can hear Gioia clinking and clanking in the kitchen …

I awake in the evening to the sounds of Signora Fontana and Lily talking. As this is my last evening here, they want me to have dinner '*a casa*'. They know my love of pasta and have prepared Spaghetti

Napolitan. Toni wants her mother to see 'the suit', so I put it on and do an 'entrance' into the sitting-room. Oh, yes, her mother thinks it's very smart. But should the flies be undone? Oh, dear. Today is Signora Fontana's wedding anniversary. She shows me a photo album: That's her as a young woman on holiday with her mother and father in Savona. Did I know her mother was French? No? Well, I did now. I see grinning photos, from her mother-in-law grinning in Ravenna to her husband grinning outside his soap factory in Abyssinia in 1936. It was possibly one of the best records of grinning I had seen.

We dine to a mixed conversation about the world: things aren't getting any better. I agree, I know my thing isn't getting any better. Shoes are very expensive, '*Troppo caro*,' says Signora Fontana. Has she thought of bare feet? They must be economical. The communist leader Togliatti is a very dangerous man. 'He want revolution in Italy,' says Toni. So a ragbag of conversation. Gradually, I'm left out of it altogether as they all jabber heatedly in Italian. As the conversation swung from Toni at one end and her mother at the other, I must have looked like a spectator at a tennis match. I call out the score: 'Fifteen, love … thirty, fifteen …' They ignore me, but it's fun.

Dinner over, they listen to the news in Italian on the radio as I sip a glass of white wine. After the news comes Italy's premier dance band led by Angelini. Lily wants to know if I can 'jitter bugger'. Try me. We move back the chairs a little and Lily and I 'cut a rug'. She's very good, I am not. Toni and mother watch on with amusement. Gioia looks on in amazement. The phone rings, Lily hurls herself at it: it's *him*! She is running her finger up and down the wall. The evening ends with us playing snap. How delightfully simple it was, the simplest of all was me …

Comes the morning of my final departure. I put on my CSE uniform for the journey, then comes amnesia, folks. I remember that I made the return journey by military lorry, a three-tonner returning empty to a depot in Salerno – but as to why and how I managed to get a lift on it, I can't remember. I've racked my brains, I've even racked my body and legs, but to no avail. Anyhow. There I was, saying goodbye to the Fontanas: they all cry, even Gioia, the maid. So with one suitcase and a much-reduced bankroll, I depart.

I depart to amnesia because where I picked up the lorry is lost for ever. However, I remember the journey back. The driver was a north-countryman, he hardly said a bloody word all through the journey. I sat there in silence with Rome falling farther and farther behind. It was a hot, dusty day and I dozed frequently in the cab. When we reach the Garigliano plain, I can see Colle Dimiano where I was wounded. It all seemed so unreal now, but I think I left part of myself up there forever; after the incident, I was never the same.

Suddenly, as we near Naples, the creep driver seems to speak. 'Do you know what time is?'

'Yes,' I say. Period. I'd make the bugger suffer.

He pauses and repeats, 'Do you know what time is?'

'Yes.'

'Oh, what is it then?'

Finally, I tell him. He nods his head in acknowledgement, his vocabulary expended. He drops me at the bottom of the Via Roma. I delighted in saying goodbye. 'Tatar, you little bundle of fun,' I said.

I'm in the welter of the Neapolitan rush hour and garlic. I manage to get a taxi back to the hotel. The old fragile porter grabs my bag; he'll take it to my room. He strains and staggers to the lift. I have to wait for him, I have to help him into the lift where he stands gasping for breath. He must be training for a coronary. On my floor, he staggers behind me. I offer to carry it. '*No, no signore, tutto a posto*', he'll just have a little rest in the corridor. I go ahead and wait in my room – poor old bugger, he's doing it in anticipation of a tip or death, whichever comes first. I give him two hundred lire – it's a good tip. '*Mille grats, signor*,' he says in Neapolitan dialect and shuffles out the room. I put through a phone call to Toni. After a delay it comes through.

'Hello Toni.'

'Terr-ee,' she gasps, 'my Terr-ee, you go all right Napoli?'

'Yes, I go all right in Napoli.'

' 'ow lovlee 'ear your voice, *mio tesoro*. I miss you much already. Why you go away?'

'What are you doing?'

'Just now we have dinner. Tell me you love me.'

'I love you.'

A little more of that type of chat and we finish. Yes, I promise I'll phone tomorrow. No, I won't go out getting drunk with Mulgrew. No, I won't go near other girls. Now, where is that man Hall. I buzz his room.

' 'oos that?'

'Me, Spike. Are there any gigs going? I'm at a loose end till the boat sails.'

No, no gigs tonight. There's one tomorrow. Do I mind playing in a sergeants' mess? Well as long as it isn't too big a mess.

'Wot you doing tonight?'

'I'm not doing anything tonight.'

'Well, good luck with it,' he says.

I meet him in the dining-hall for dinner. Has he seen Mulgrew or Bornheim lately? Yes, he's done a couple of gigs with them. What about the *Dominion Monarch* and the sailing date? That's all fixed, I have to collect my ticket from Major Ridgeway. So the end is in sight: it's goodbye Italy and hello Deptford.

The remaining days were very very boring. So I won't bore the reader. I do a couple of band gigs on guitar with Hall, Bornheim and Mulgrew at military establishments. I collect my boat ticket and passport and I buy a few trinkets for my mother and father. Most days I spend in my room reading books from the hotel library. The very last one was the story of San Michele by Axel Munthe, a most moving story about Capri.

The night before I sail, Jimmy Molloy checks into the hotel. He's booked on the same ship as me. He wants to have a night out; he knows a good officers' nightclub on the seafront. OK, I'll come with him and wear the suit. It's the Club Marina, 'Officers Only'. We show our CSE passes. Down a corridor to a large room with a central dance floor, where a good Italian band are playing the music of our time. There are hostesses at the bar: no, Jimmy, I'm not interested. Well, he is. He goes over and chats to one and brings her back to our table. Ah, good, wait till she sees my suit. She is pretty stunning, small, petite, saturnine-dark with a pair of giant olive eyes.

'This is Francesca,' says Molloy.

'Piacera,' I say.

She throws me a dazzling white-toothed smile. More than that, as the evening progresses I realise that she fancies me and my suit. 'I fink I've picked a loser here,' chuckled Molloy. Do I want to take her over? No no no, Jimmy, I am promised to another. He gives me a disbelieving look. 'Come on, a bit on the side won't hurt.' I told him I had no bits on my side, all my bits were at the front, so I'd be the wrong fit for her. However it's nice flirting with her.

The lights go down: a spotlight on the stage illuminates an Italian MC in a white jacket. 'Laddies and Gintilmin, nower oura starer of thee cabareter, Gina Escoldi.' He points left, the band strikes up and a ballerina on points pirouettes on to the floor and sings 'a hubba hubba hubba' with red-hot accompaniment. She has a coarse croaky voice, loaded with sex – all the while standing on points. It was a head-on collision between jazz and ballet, but very successful. She goes down big with what is in the majority, an American officer audience.

At the end of the evening Molloy says, 'You takin this bird or not.' I decline, cursing the fact that I have a conscience. 'One day,' he laughs, 'you'll regret this decision!' What did he mean 'one day', I was regretting it *now*. While he offs with her, I off to the hotel and bed. While I lay there, my mind was going through the long years away from home. Had I really been in action in North Africa? Had I really taken part in the Tunis Victory Parade? Did I land at Salerno? It all seemed unreal, like a distant dream ending up in the most distant dream of all – Toni and me on Capri. Would the sun ever shine like that again?

On departure morning I awake and, first thing, put in a call to Toni.

We say our final goodbyes – tears on the phone from Rome. At breakfast, I meet Jimmy Molloy. 'That bird last night, what a con. When we get to 'er place, she just kisses me goodnight then pisses off. I think it was all your bloody fault, Milligan.' Smugly, I say, yes, it undoubtedly was.

Our ship sails at midday. We have to start boarding at 10.30. We take a taxi to the quay where the *Dominion Monarch* awaits. We both have first class passages – I'm nominated a cabin on the port side. A young English steward carries my bag and calls me sir. It's a fine, single-berth cabin with a porthole for looking out – or, if you hang on the outside, for looking in. 'If there's anything you want, sir, just ring the service button.' I locate the Purser's Office where a grim-faced staff change my lire into sterling, which looks much less. Up on the promenade deck I find Molloy and I get him to take my photo.

The ship is alive with bustle, with sailors shouting yo ho ho and pouring hot tar down the hatches. At midday the gangplank is removed, the ship gives a long mournful blast on the hooter and a tug starts to manoeuvre us out to sea. Molloy and I stand at the rail. Slowly, the great ship puts on speed, the Italian mainland recedes into the distance, finally lost in a haze. It's over: it's goodbye Italy, goodbye Toni and goodbye soldier.

5
Milligan Preserved

Peace Work: 1991

Seventh and final volume of the war memoirs. I was sorry to see these memoirs come to an end.

Restarting the Trio

What to do? First I had to contact Bill Hall the violinist from our trio – 6 Legard Road, Highbury. After a spaghetti of buses and trams, through grey, grotty, postwar streets, I was knocking on the door of a Victorian terraced home, had I gone in a circle? It looked like 3 Leathwell. A dying female circa 1880 opened the door, 'Oo?' she said. 'Spike Milligan.' What did I want? I didn't want anything, I wanted to see Bill Hall, her son, 'Ee's out gettin' some fags.' Could I come in and wait or rape her? Grumbling, she let me into the kitchen of 6 Legard Road, with identical laundry overhead.

Seated in an identical blue moquette armchair was Bill Hall's father Albert. 'Oh yes, Spike Millington, Bill told us you might be cummin', didn't 'ee Vera?'

The living dead Vera said, 'Yer, but I dinn knowed wot 'ee looked like, 'ee could 'ave been anybody; I done like lettin' stranglers in.'

'She means strangers,' said Albert.

A dog has appeared, an old English mongrel with a huge nose. 'It swooled up when the cat bit 'im – here, Rex, Rex, good dog.' Good dog Rex, good dog, ignored him and started to sniff my balls. It happens not only in working-class families, I was at a black tie dinner with Lady Nethersole – among the guests were Kenneth Tynan, Sir Bernard Miles, Field Marshal Montgomery – post-dinner a poodle was released under the table and sniffed all our balls.

The front door slamming announced the return of Bill Hall. 'Oh, 'ello,' he said with a smile, his lips parted, a cigarette stuck to the bottom. We shook hands, 'When you get back?'

I gave him chapter and verse, spicing it up with Molloy's extra-marital bunk-ups – Bill frowns, looks at dying mother and puts his fingers to his lips. 'Shush! me muther,' he whispers; 'me muther is in the back kitchen making a "nice cuppa tea", I don't want her to hear about Molloy's bunk-ups, it's bad enough 'er 'earing about mine.' Hall and I are making arrangements to get our postwar career started. We have to get an agent. 'Fosters,' says Bill; 'Fosters are the biggest.' I like big agents, they're easier to see. Bill has Johnny Mulgrew's address, 13 Linden Gardens, Notting Hill Gate. Park 3535, thank God a phone!!! We'll leave all messages there.

We have an appointment with Leslie MacDonnell, one of the agents at Fosters' agency in Piccadilly; fancy, *me* in Piccadilly! I remember before the war simple-minded me thought of Piccadilly in the same distant terms as Moscow. Piccadilly, oh no, that was where special people went, the toffs, you had to dress up to go there – have money – I recalled my father did a speciality song and dance:

> Picc-a-dilly – London West
> That's the place – that I like best
> There's the place to drive you silly
> Willy-Nilly dear old Picc-a-dilly.

But the army, the war and Toni Pontani had changed me, now I would go anywhere with or without money, mostly without.

Work

Hall and Mulgrew met me in Lyons Corner House, Coventry Street, at eleven. We sat around, the Nippies flitting between tables, 'Pot of tea for three, please Miss.' A palm court trio are playing a medley of tunes from Ivor Novello's *Perchance to Dream*, which was showing at Wyndham's Theatre. ' 'E can write tunes can't 'e,' said Mulgrew with witty smile.

'Never mind,' said Hall, 'if we are as popular in England as we were in Italy, mate – we might be in the dibs.' As a prophecy it was a disaster. All this time Harry Secombe was appearing at the Windmill in a nude review; he was the one with clothes on, though had he been offered more …

Being there gave us ingression to the stage door in Archer Street –
'Yes?' said the Stage Door Keeper. 'I've come to see Mr Harry
Secombe.' I thought the Mister bit made me sound respectable, whereas
all I wanted to see was birds' tits. Harry took me to the 'green room',
where all the girls were in dressing gowns; yes, yes, yes, yes, he liked
it here, yes, yes, yes, all the girls, yes, yes, yes, was he allowed to stand
in the wings, yes, yes, yes, yes, he had to get on the stage, was he going
blind, yes, yes, yes. He gets me a free seat; doing comedy at 11 a.m. can't
be easy. I watch with popping eyes, and aroused loins, as naked
women, NAKED WOMEN, a tableau, 'Spring In Arcadia'; the nudes
stay stock still as the waiting onanists vibrate our row of seats, the only
moving entertainment on stage is *premier danseur* Peter Glover, who is
leaping everywhere to the Spectre de la Rose. Curtain.

Enter one who a while back was a Lance Bombardier in a hole in
North Africa, he comes on like a dynamo carrying a table and shaving
kit – 'Everybody's got to shave,' he says. He is hypnotically funny – the
energy could light a city, in eight explosive minutes he's finished, a few
wankers laugh, and they've got five more shows. Between shows, Harry
and I visited Poppa Allens, a first-floor 'club' on Windmill Street, others
from the Windmill were Jimmy Edwards, Frank Muir, Michael Bentine.
'Have a drink, Spike,' said Harry, over the moon at being in the West
End. He was on £20 a week, and I wasn't.

It was Harry who gave us an introduction to the nightclub circuit.
The first one was the Florida in Carnaby Street; it was six phone-
boxes square, the 'house band' was the Ike Isaacs Trio, unbelievable
Ike was at school with me in Rangoon, they took one corner, the
bouncer Mike Noonan the next, the rest were customers. We
appeared in a serving hatch. It was our first appearance in England,
and by God we tore 'em up folks, oh yes, here was an unusual comedy
act, literally in rags but playing like the Hot Club de France. We were
soon inundated with work, we did the circuit: the Blue Lagoon,
Panama, ending up in Edmundo Ros' Coconut Grove, featuring his
and Syd Phillips' bands. We were kept on for an extra week.

Publicity postcard drawn by Bill Hall

Rawicz and Landau came regularly to see us, so did Eugene Goosens and Eileen Joyce.

Syd Phillips took us on one side, he couldn't manage two, and said, 'Now listen, I'm going to make a lot of money out of you boys.' Another disastrous prophecy. Syd was Jewish, how did he go wrong? What did we do in the day? To start, I was living with my parents, who weren't at home when I had returned from the war, and the surprise was extended. They had been staying with 'Aunt Nance in Sittingbourne, whose husband is a builder you know,' so when they got back from Aunt Nance in Sittingbourne, whose husband was a builder you know, I was out. I left a note saying I was 'back from Italy and was now in Catford' visiting Aunty Kath, whose husband was an insurance agent you know. So during the first days I was back, I tried to revive

1939. I had to see Lily, Beryl, Ivy and anybody but! Lily Dunford had been unfaithful to me, she'd married!!!! So had Beryl Southby and Ivy Chandler, yes beautiful me – me with my five times a night, had they all forgotten the one and threepenny seats at the Rialto, Crofton Park? Those dinners of egg, chips, tomatoes, bread and butter and pot of tea for two in Reg's Café – opposite Brockley Cemetery? *And* I used to change my hair oil every three-hundred miles. Very well, they'd regret it – in gloom over the loss of Lily I wrote this bizarre letter of farewell, which I never posted:

Dear Lily,

Remember this – one day in years to come, you will cry – cry for the fool that you were and are – cry for me, Lily – remember that – No one will ever love like me – You will come back to me one day. Love has many children – one is called HATE – you will smile when I say 'I hate you – want to kill you – see you with your face blue and black and the eyes I love to see – sightless.' I mean that – all that. To finish this – I will make you hate me – hate me till your mind is full of poison – hate me till it hurts –

And I will still love you.

Goodbye, Lily.

God, what a monster! No wonder she didn't marry me. Ex-soldier kills ex-girlfriend, paints her face black and blue then does her in. When I read the letter after forty years, it made me wonder what kind of person I used to be. Well, for a start, I liked to choke and blind people. I could have been another Neville Heath; help!! When I eventually booked a room at 13 Linden Gardens, I discovered the previous occupant had been the murderer Neville Heath himself, I mean, who else could he be? ' 'E was a real gentleman, 'oo would 'ave thought it of 'im?' said Blanche the lady cleaner who 'did the place'. Dear Blanche, about forty-five, with a face that could have modelled Palaeolithic man – she was still a virgin. 'I still got it – an' no one's 'aving it,' mainly because no one wanted it.

I wasn't earning, so I had to budget, to-ing and fro-ing from 3

Leathwell to London was boring and expensive so I moved to 13 Linden. Aren't we strange. Two years away from home, come home, leave. It was one room with sit-up bath, top floor at back, it was £1.15.0 a week with breakfast, usually a kipper. If you stand in Notting Hill High Street next to Lloyds Bank, look up, you can see the window of my bedroom.

Margo, the landlady, was a short, plump, prettyish, mid-forties, dark, feline, very rouged with dark red lipstick. She reminded me of Theda Bara, in that she was dead. Margo spoke so slowly, people dozed off in her presence. She lived in the basement in Stygian gloom with the smell of cats and Mansion polish, a widow, but there came into her life a humpty-backed lodger, Mr Len Lengths, an insurance broker who 'worked from home'. He was about five feet six inches, an inch taller than Margo, he had a face like Charles Laughton's and Boris Karloff's superimposed on his, he wore pebbledash glasses which magnified his pop eyes, giving him the countenance of a man being garrotted, yet Margo was attracted to him. She had him down for supper and while there he had her down for screwing.

'What does he see in her?' I said.

Mulgrew, who is evil, says, 'His hump turns her on.'

'Hump, my arse,' said Hall, 'I bet he's got a huge chopper, lengths by name, lengths by nature.' How did Hall deduce this?

'Listen mate – admit the number of good-looking wimmin with ugly blokes, well, it's a big prick, wimmin will stand anything as long as the bloke's chopper is big.' All these theories seem to clash with medical evidence, but neither Margo nor Lengths had heard of them. All we knew was he wasn't paying rent.

Yes, what did we do in the day? One time at the Windmill canteen, Harry introduced me to 'Jimmy Grafton who owns a pub'; he was to figure in my life in those immediate postwar years. He had served as an officer in the infantry and was at Arnhem. He was now serving behind the bar; he had, somehow or other, become a scriptwriter to Derek Roy, a would-be comic appearing on *Variety Bandbox*, so Jimmy had an 'in' into broadcasting.

Michael Bentine introduced Harry to Jimmy, as Harry recalls, 'Mike told me of this pub in Strutton Ground where I got a drink after hours, and somehow Jimmy became my manager and scriptwriter.' He started back to front by me telling him what bloody awful scripts Derek Roy had, and Jimmy said, 'Well I write them'. A strange start to a forty-year relationship.

Hackney Empire

'I've got a week for you at the Hackney Empire,' the words fell from the mellifluous lips of Leslie MacDonnell, our agent, sitting behind his desk at Piccadilly House, Piccadilly Circus.

We were overjoyed, I could see our name in lights. MacDonnell then added, 'I've arranged for Val Parnell to see you on the Monday performance.'

Val Parnell!!!! This was something. If Parnell was coming to see us, MacDonnell must have thought pretty highly of us; for giving us this break, Bill Hall proffered his thanks, 'Ta,' he said.

I burst out laughing. 'Bill,' I said, 'Ta? Ta? Excuse him, MacDonnell, Bill is a man of few words and that was one of them.' I then thanked MacDonnell more formally, 'Like this, Bill,' I said. I knelt in the grovelling position, my head on MacDonnell's shoe, 'Oh a thousand thanks, oh great wise one.'

MacDonnell was highly amused. 'Is he always like this?' he said.

'Only when the money's right,' said Mulgrew, pulling me away. 'There, there boy,' he said, patting me on the head and feeding me pretend sugar lumps. So to the big time.

'Oh, we'll be there* son,' said my dad when I told him. My parents, especially my father, were very proud, he having been a stage performer. 'I never knew you had it in you,' he said. I told him I myself had never had it in me, but I had had it in other people, the opposite sex, well that's where they were at the time.

* At home

By now, Spike was getting bored with the 'According to' series, so decided to 'jazz it up a bit'. He started each chapter with a poem.

Part One

EARLY HOME

There once was a horse called Black Beauty
He was well bred and always did his duty
He came from very good stock
He had a lovely body with a huge cock
His mother was lovely with a wonderful tail
Which dragged behind her like the Holy Grail
His father died, a handsome dude
And he ended up as dog food
Black Beauty would lead a long life
A mixture of Peace, Tranquillity and Strife.

13 THE DEVIL'S TRADE MARK

One day, John and I saw hence
A boy forcing a horse to jump a fence
He was giving the horse a thrashing
John wanted me to go and give him a bashing
Just then the horse threw him off her back
And he hit the ground with a thwack
He tried to grasp the horse's reins
But my master came and blew out his brains.

One day, John and I had been out on some business of our master's – we were buying shares in Woolworths – and we were returning gently, flat broke, on a long straight road. It must have been a Roman road. At some distance, we saw a boy try to leap a pony over a gate. The pony would not take the leap, so the boy jumped it for him to show him the way. Then the boy tried again, and hit the pony with a whip, but he only turned off on one side, scratching the boy's leg. He whipped him again, the pony turned, and scratched his other leg. Then the boy got off and gave the pony a hard thrashing. When we reached the spot, the pony put his head down, threw up his heels, and hurled the boy neatly into a hedge of nettles and, with the rein dangling from his head, he set off at a full gallop.

'Oh! oh! oh!' cried the boy, as he struggled about among the nettles, 'I say, do come and help me out.'

Then my Master rode up, dismounted, picked up his blunderbuss, and blew the boy's brains out.

'Thank ye,' said John. 'I think you are in quite the right place, and maybe a little scratching will teach him not to leap the pony over a gate that is too high for him.'

The farmer was hurrying out into the road, and his wife was standing at the gate looking frightened.

'Have you seen my boy?' said Mr Bushby as we came up. 'He went out an hour ago on my black pony.'

'Oh yes, he fell off,' said the master, 'and to put him out of his misery, I blew his brains out.'

'What do you mean?' asked the farmer.

'Well, sir, I saw your son whipping and kicking the pony, so I took careful aim and blew his brains out. It seemed to calm him, and your son is now sleeping in my garden.'

The mother began to cry, 'Oh! I must go and see my boy.'

'You will have to dig six feet down,' said John, 'that's where he is.'

We went on home, John chuckling all the way. He told James about it who laughed and said, 'Serve him right. I knew that boy at school: he took great airs on himself because he was a farmer's son; he used to swagger about and bully the little boys; of course, we elder ones would not have any of that nonsense and let him know that, in the school and playground, farmers' sons and labourers' sons were all alike, so we beat the shit out of him. I found him at a large window catching flies and pulling off their wings, so I am glad you blew his brains out.'

John said, 'There is no religion without love, and people may talk as much as they like about their religion, but if it does not teach them to be good and kind to man and beast, it is all a sham – all a sham, James, and it won't stand when things come to be turned inside out and put down for what they are.'

I personally have never had my things turned inside out, so I didn't know what he meant.

Fleas, Knees and Hidden Elephants: 1994

Hidden Elephant

Splitty splitty splat!
What was that?
Splitty splitty splat!
Was it a rat?
Can a rat go splitty splitty splat?
No! Then can a cat?
No! Cats only go miaow
Don't ask me how
Can a cow go splitty splitty splat?
No cows go moo
That's what they do
Splitty splitty splat!
Heavens! It's somewhere in my flat!
Got it! It's an elephant under my hat!

Terence Blatt

Terence Blatt
Wore bells on his hat
To keep the wolves at bay
With a gun by his side
He went for a ride
In his one horse open sleigh
A wolf pursued him
As snow began to fall
It ate him up bells and all
Oh dear Terence what terrible luck
The wolf of course didn't give a fig.

The Dancer

He danced with a monkey
He danced with a cat
And he danced with a man
In a big black hat
He danced with a Muslim
He danced with a Jew
And he danced with a Chinaman
Six foot two
Then he took all his clothes off
And he danced all day
That's when they came
And took him away.

The Hills Are Alive

Climb every mountain
Ford every stream
Follow every rainbow
Till you find you're knackered.

My Nanny

I had a Nanny six foot three
She nearly was the death of me
Through roaring traffic she'd push
my pram
Down my throat my food she'd ram
It made her ecstatically happy
To never ever change my nappy
So it shouldn't surprise you a bit
That I grew up a bit of a shit.

Peace Work: 1991

Back to Rome

Now off to the lasagne-caked shores of Italy. More props, suitcases, good suit to meet Toni, portable mattress and hormone tablets. Let's get the journey to Paris over, eh? And the Brenner Pass, eh? The Simplon, eh? And into a sunlit Roma Centro Ferrovia, eh? We have to go to digs with wartime friends Signora Ciampaglia and two ballerina daughters, Marisa and Marcella, on the Via XXI Aprile. We hardly knew them during the war, but we and our money were very welcome. I am keen to see Toni; that will be 'arranged' says Marisa. But first we must get a taxi to the Teatro Belle Arte. It's where all the latest acts are given a break. A charming miniature opera house. Backstage we meet Ivaldi's rep, a fat Egyptian, Arzanofata, a sixty-year-old agent who's seen it all except his own. Top of the bill is Byron Cutler, a gay Negro dancer from the Katherine Dunham Troupe, beautifully made, very sensitive, with BO. Very fine pit orchestra who are amused at our tatty 'Tiger Rag' play-out music. The conductor smiled, 'Is that eet, sir?' I assured him it was. Byron Cutler's dancing is exquisite.

On our bill is a girl singer, god save us from goddesses, she is *beautiful*, a saturnine Medusa without the snakes, eyes the size of lifeboats, coal-black magma intensity; her skin is like Carrara marble and her voice like ice and fire. '*Monastaire de Santa Ciarra*,' she sings. If she'd taken her clothes off, I'd have eaten them. It's a very, very good first night; Toni is with Marcella, but there's something wrong. There's a distance between us – is it the orchestra? We go for dinner afterwards, but Toni is avoiding me; all very jolly, mind you, but it's not on. It's painful, but only from the waist down. She looks so petite and stunning.

The Three Nights. We are a big success. We are invited to a jazz club to play but no Toni. Plenty of excitement at the jazz club, wine, a few partisans about, signs, *Partito Comunista* – Good God! a police raid all in the wagons – Perhaps Toni knew something!! We show our

Left Johnny Mulgrew with Marcella amid the ruins of Rome, taken by the ruins of Milligan. *Right* Johnny and me indicating each other under the Arch of Constantine, Rome

British passports and are released, but are warned the club is a Communist recruiting depot.

Rome *was* a beautiful city; there was space, no bottom-pinchers no crowded pavements, the traffic was light, Tourists o Rangers 2. Johnny, Marcella, Toni and I just strolled in the spring sunshine through the ruins of ancient Rome. Toni teases Mulgrew, whom she calls Ginetto, about his drinking and smoking. She is a class above us. I've no idea what's below. Marcella too is good family, quietly dressed, polite; they are both aware of their Roman heritage – and me of my Deptford one. Worlds apart, was that what Toni was realising? I acted polite but crazy, jumping up beside Roman statues, jumping on podiums, a bit of Mussolini impressions. 'Stop it, Terry – *pericoloso cosi.*' We had tea in the Villa Borghese, then the show.

Oh, that girl singer, Mitti Mille, the voice, where did she go? Where did Byron Cutler go? Where did I go?

There's a girl at the digs, a friend Pia. Very pretty, very mischievous, red light. One night, after the show, the girls do Mulgrew and me up as tarts – we went on the streets to see what happened. What happened is the *Carabinieri* ran us in, we had to get the Assistant British Ambassador to fix that we were not gay. It was a bloody-minded *Carabiniere* that ran us in in the first place – I think he fancied us and was stricken in the nethers when he found we were men. Fun while it lasted. Johnny has the girls in hysterics; as pasta was being rolled, he made incredible willies out of them. How can you be jealous of pasta? I was amazed at the variation of willies he had in his repertoire. I think the ladies were disappointed when it had to be made into spaghetti.

Johnny and Marcella by the Pool of the Vestal Virgins, who were at lunch

Toni is difficult to see. She has many appointments. Pia fancies me. One afternoon I'm in my bedroom in the flat, she sleeks in, locks the door behind her, and without a word, strips off. My God, she's got a beautiful body, so when in Rome … On the last night I take Toni to dinner, but she is very distant; is there another man? Well, I know now there wasn't – not even me. Since those days she has told me I seemed too unbalanced, too quixotic, and my life had no centre. I had no regular job, and she thought I would be influenced by the lifestyle of Billiard Johnny, who both drank and smoked too much. You can see by her letter she isolated me from them as a personality.

' 'Ow you gettin' on with 'er?' said Wretch Hall.

I told him, 'Not too well.'

' 'Ave you given it to 'er yet?'

No, I had not 'given it' to her.

He's met a bird and, 'She's lovely – she does it slowly.'

Not too slow, Bill, in that condition you can catch cold – no, people who screw slowly should wear thermal underwear and woollen contraceptives – yes, contraceptives should be used on every conceivable occasion. Wow. So that last dinner with Toni.

'I don't understand you, Terry,' she said.

'What don't you understand?'

'You life – you so uncertain – you understand?'

'No, what about my life?'

'For me it is very difficult, no *stabilità* –'

'No *stabilità* – no stability.'

'Yes, in one year where you are?'

'I don't know, I don't know.'

'You see, I don't think this life very good for you.'

'But I have to make a living, Toni.'

'I know, Terry, but I think some better for you.'

'What?'

'I don't know,' she shrugged. 'I don't know.'

There followed a long traffic-filled silence. My hand was on the table, she reached out and put her hand on mine. 'I love you, Toni.'

She laughed, and it hurt. 'You love me? I don't think so, you love me in good time like Capri, but now I here in Rome, you go away Milan, then where, you go home, no. I think not you love me.'

She was wrong, I did love, it's just that the setting was wrong. I needed a steady job and money enough to marry – buy a house – I wasn't in that league, and it was breaking us up. Money, Fuck Money. Yet she didn't want money, she wanted me but to the beat of a different drum. So I saw her back to her flat at 53 Via Apeninni – and said a sort of goodbye – then back to my flat.

The Ciampaglia family are all waiting for any gossip. Am I going to marry Toni – is she pregnant: my God they're like harpies, Pia among them but simmering with jealousy. Johnny has been home some time and is rightly pissed with Marisa on his lap teasing him. She doesn't know she's sitting on his volatile packed lunch, which if aroused would hurl her to the floor. Senora Ciampaglia had once been the 'girl' friend of Reg O'List. She asks about him. I say he was married now but still sang. She says she's very sorry. He had lived with her, she had cooked and washed for him, he had promised to come back. I said there was time – he was in good condition and could still sing the world's worst version of 'Begin the Beguine'. Ah yes, she remembers him singing, the worst possible memory 'I Recordo'. How could she forget, how could anybody forget List's version of 'Begin the Beguine'. It stayed in the mind like the memory of a terrible accident, which it was. I went to my room to pack for the journey on the morrow, but wait for Pia. This time she does exactly the same act – door locked, strip off then screwing. She wants to know what that perfume is. I say it's Toni's (days before aftershave). '*Cattivo, te molto Cattivo.*' I'm bad, very bad, but now she seems to be screwing in revenge against Toni – she's beating me on the chest, crying and orgasming and in that order. I lie back and think of England.

Ten o'clock. Rome Station – crowded with people, Toni is not coming, but Pia is there, done up like a dream with black woollen stockings to the knee and cork-soled shoes. She throws her arms around me crying.

' 'Ow Christ, 'oo's this one?' says Hall.

'We're just good friends,' I said.

'What's she howling for?'

'She has a headache and it's me.'

Pia clings to me even as the train moves away. She walks along the platform, a tearful handkerchief in one hand, waving with the other. Isn't life cruel.

'Did you give it 'er?' said Hall, who is interested in such things.

'No, I didn't give it her – she gave it to me.'

' 'Ot stuff, eh?' he said.

Yes, she was very hot stuff. We all are stuck in the corridor as the train is packed. One of us takes turns to guard the luggage, while two of us make for the buffet car. Hall and I manage to get a table. 'The smell of bleedin' garlic,' says Wretch. 'Do they carry it in their bleedin' pockets?'

A lady waitress the size of Mount Everest takes our order – '*Due caffè e latte.*' We dunk the pastry into the coffee.

' 'Ow do you think we did at the Belle Arte then?'

'Well, we did best on the bill with Byron Cutler a close second.'

' 'Ee was a brown-hatter, wasn't he?'

'Actually, he was a black one.'

' 'Ave ter watch yer arse with Negros like 'im around.'

'I'd found him very civilised and an excellent piano player.'

'Wot's 'ee doin' over 'ere – I mean there must be more work in America – wonder why he left the Katherine Dunham dancers?'

'Same as us – work – adventure.'

'I wonder what's waitin' for us in Milan. This wog, what's 'is name, Arzanofata?'

'Yes, I wonder if you can trust him. I remember the bleedin' A-rabs in the war – a twistin' lot of bastards.'

'I think Arzanofata is a bit more civilised.'

'I don't know, one minute they're scrubbing camels' arses in the desert, the next they're theatrical agents – I bet he's got desert sores on his legs.'

We must have a look when we see him. Hall relieves Mulgrew.

'He took long enough,' moaned Mulgrew. 'Yes, Johnny, he was talking about sores on Arzanofata's legs.'

'Who's Arzanofata?'

'He's the Egyptian rep. for Ivaldi in Milan.'

'Oh, that bloke.'

'We were discussing the sores on his legs.'

'What, am I hearing proper?'

'Yes.'

'What about the sores on his legs?'

The waitress comes, '*Uno caffè e latte, per favore.*'

'Bill said he wouldn't be surprised if he's got sores on his legs.'

'Oh – so – he's got sores on his legs – so I've got pimples on me bum – but I don't go round discussing them.'

'No, it's just we were talking about his reliability as an agent.'

'What have the sores on his legs got to do with it?'

'Nothing, it was all a joke – forget it.'

Long pause, looking at the landscape.

'I need new strings for my bass.'

'Oh, they'll sell them in Milan.'

'They ought to, that's where the Milan Opera House is.'

'Oh, I've just remembered – I forgot to pay Mrs Ciampaglia the rent.'

'You can post it.'

'Yes, so I can; damn.'

The journey is uneventful, save for us being clambered over in the corridor. I hate perambulating travellers, those idiots who, once aboard a train, walk the corridors till they get to their destination, putting miles on their journey.

Hound of the Baskervilles According to Spike Milligan: 1998

This was a leatherbound special limited edition to mark Spike's eightieth birthday. It was agreed that there would not be a paperback edition.

Chapter I. Mr Sherlock Holmes

Sherlock Holmes usually arrived brilliantly very late in the morning; his record for lateness was not coming down until the next morning. As we sat eating breakfast at 3 a.m., I stood upon the hearthrug and picked up the stick which our visitor had left behind the night before. It was a fine, thick piece of wood with a bulbous head known as a brain smasher. Just under the head was a broad silver band inscribed 'To James Mortimer, MRCS, from his friends of the CCH', with the date '1884'. It was just such a stick as murderers or old family practitioners used to carry – dignified, solid, and bloody heavy.

'Well, Watson, what would you make of it?'

'Firewood,' I said.

Holmes was sitting with his back to me and I had given him no signs of my occupation.

'Now what is your occupation, Watson?'

'I am a Coastal Spotter.'

'And what is that?'

'Well, I'm a Coastal Spotter. You go to the coast, you spot things and you report them to the Coast Guard.'

'And do you spot anything unusual?'

'Yes, I saw a man starving on a raft.'

'And what did the Coast Guard do?'

'They shot him.'

'Isn't that murder, Watson?'

'Not on the high seas,' said I. 'Spotting in Japanese is Yamaguchi. I did Yamaguchi for two years. I spotted a pirate ship and the Coast Guard sank it by gunfire. As the pirates swam ashore, the Japanese police drowned them by putting rocks in their clothes.'

'It seems, Watson, that the Coast Guard is hellbent on eliminating the human race.'

'Well, there do seem a lot of them.'

'Tell me, Watson, what do you make of our visitor's stick, since we have been so unfortunate as to miss him?'

'I think,' said I, analysing the implement as best I could using the methods of Holmes, 'that Mortimer is a successful elderly medical man, well esteemed – since those who know him gave him this stick as a mark of their appreciation.'

'Good!' said Holmes. 'Excellent! Ten out of ten!'

'Now this stick would seem to be the property of an elderly man,' I added.

'You know, Watson, you are a genius and have a remarkable power of stimulation. I must confess, my dear fellow, that I am very much in your debt.'

'Well, I would be grateful if you would start paying it off.'

He lit a cigarette, which flared up and set fire to his shirt front, which I doused with a soda siphon.

The doorbell had gone.

'Do come in,' cried Holmes.

The appearance of our visitor was a surprise to me since I had expected a typical country practitioner. He was a very tall, thin man, with a toothless dog by his side.

'Good morning,' said Holmes.

As he entered his eyes fell upon the stick in Holmes's hand, and he ran towards it with an exclamation of joy.

'Whooee! Whooee!' he said. 'I am so very glad,' said he. 'I was not sure whether I had left it here or in the Shipping Office. I would not lose that stick for the world.'

'Ah, a presentation, I see,' said Holmes.

'Yes, sir. From one or two friends at Charing Cross Hospital on the occasion of my marriage.'

'Pardon me, do I understand you received a walking stick as a wedding present?'

THE COMPULSIVE SPIKE MILLIGAN

'Yes.'

'I am sorry but, if you will pardon me, what a crappy present. I got a toast rack.'

'Ah yes,' said Mortimer, 'but you can't take a toast rack for a walk.'

'Nonsense! I take my toast rack for a walk in the country. I took it to the Himalayas and made toast on K2 at twenty-two thousand feet and it worked perfectly.'

'I presume that it is Mr Sherlock Holmes whom I am addressing and not –'

'No, that is my friend Dr Watson. I am here near the window.'

'Good heavens!' said Mortimer. 'You're not going to jump out, are you?'

'Not yet. It depends on you.'

'Oh, I am glad to see you, sir. I have heard your name mentioned in connection with that of your friend. You interest me very much. I hardly expected so dolichocephalic a skull or such well-marked supraorbital development. Would you have any objections to my running my finger along your parietal fissure?'

'Look here, man,' said Holmes. 'You leave my parietal fissure alone! It's bad enough to have one.'

'My dear Holmes, as you wish, but a cast of your skull, until the original is available, would be an ornament to any anthropological museum. It is not my intention to be fulsome, but I must confess that I covet your skull.'

'No! No! Don't covet my bloody skull! It's bad enough just having one!' Sherlock Holmes waved at the visitor. 'Have a chair.'

'No, I'll stand.'

'All right, then bloody well stand on the chair.'

'You are an enthusiast in your line of thought, I perceive, sir, as I am in mine,' said Mortimer.

Holmes was silent, but his little darting glances showed me the interest which he took in our curious companion.

'I presume,' said Mortimer, 'that your little darting glances show an interest in me.'

'I presume,' said Holmes, 'it was not merely for the purpose of examining my skull that you have done me the honour to call here?'

'No, sir, but I am happy to have the opportunity of doing that as well, Mr Holmes, because I recognise myself that I am an impractical man who cannot tie my shoelaces nor roll a cigarette and because I am suddenly confronted with a most extraordinary problem, and recognising, as I do, that you are the second highest expert in Europe –'

'What, sir! May I enquire who has the honour to be the first?' said Holmes, his face white with anger.

'To the man of precisely scientific mind the work of Monsieur Bertillon must always appeal strongly.'

'All right, then, you had better consult him, and bugger off! And that will be ten guineas!'

'It is acknowledged that you stand alone.'

'At the moment I have insufficient funds to stand a loan,' said Holmes quickly. 'My fee is ten guineas an hour with a down payment of one hundred guineas.'

At the mention of a fee Dr Mortimer fainted and was revived only by pouring a bucket of water over him and extracting the money from his pocket.

A Mad Medley of Milligan: 1999

This was the last comic verse book that Spike wrote.

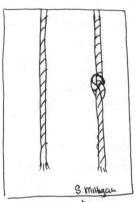

Jam

I'm warning you Uncle Sam
Beware beware of jam
It's always there at breakfast and tea
That's how it gets in you see
There is no escape from Jam
It will find you wherever you am
There's that moment of dread
When you find Jam on your bread
No matter where you are
Dam, dam, dam, dam
Jam.

Something

I saw a piece of something
What it was I cannot say
You see that piece of something
Was going the other way
Suddenly that piece of something
Turned round and back again
I just couldn't see it
Because of the rain
Just then that piece of something
Shot up in the air
As far as I know that something
Is possibly still up there

I CAN READ HER LIKE A BOOK $\frac{6}{10}$

S. Milligan

Joan of Arc

Joan of Arc
Got up in the dark
And put her foot in the Po
Oh bugger she said
Connecting with the bed
Dislocating her big toe
How can I lead France
When I lead such a dance?
Her tears were beginning to flow
To hell with le Brits
They're all a lot of shits
So now we'll give 'em a go
So she led the French Army
Half of whom were barmy
Then a terrible blow
How was she to know
The Brits beat the frogs
Who got stuck in the bogs
Joan's end was dire
The Brits set her on fire

Harrods Sale

Oh wonderful Harrods, gracing the street
Pushing shoving steaming feet
Sales-mad loonies care not a jot
Spending everything they've got
Look a hammock that looks nice
I've no garden but it's half-price
Buy! Buy! Corsets, carpets, a hat
And bye-bye money
That's the end of that
Carry on suckers spend the lot
Help Al Fayed buy his yacht

Paddy

My name is Paddy O'Hare
And sometimes I'm not there
Sometime when I feel right
I'll be on the Isle of Wight
If I'm not there I'll be
On the Isle of Innisfree
If I'm not there
I'll be elsewhere
I might also be
In the lovely vale of Tralee
I spend some time in Spain
And then move on again
I keep on moving you see
The police are after me

The Nation's Favourite Children's Poems: 2001

Spike was asked to write the foreword to this delightful book. It was his last writing assignment to be published.

I have been asked by the BBC to write a foreword for *The Nation's Favourite Children's Poems* book. I can't believe and never would have thought, all those years ago (I've just realised it's nearly 50 years ago), when I was telling my children bedtime stories and making up rhymes such as 'On the Ning Nang Nong' to make them laugh, that I would be writing a foreword for all these wonderful children's poems.

This book is for children whatever their age. I myself would draw the line at 97 years of age. If they survive over that they must be on something that the NHS is dispensing like longevity tablets, which are a mixture of monkey glands and diddledums. I can't take any credit for any of this; believe me, I have tried to get them at every bank in England but I have failed, so that's that then.

I myself dote on children and if you look closely you will find that most children are covered all over in dote marks. Don't worry: Persil will remove these dote marks and leave them smelling fresh – fresh dote marks. So please don't dote on children; it leaves them covered in marks – dote marks. I wish all you children a lovely life. I hope none of you in your lifetime gets leprosy.

Now please don't bother me anymore – I'm busy washing off dote marks. So goodbye and stinky poo to all of you.

6

Milligan Remembered

The Goon Show: 1954

5th Series, Show 3

---

*In the prologue to *Adolf Hitler, My Part in His Downfall*, Spike wrote: 'After *Puckoon*, I swore I would never write another novel. This is it ...'

Well, if Spike can change his mind, so can I.

I swore I wouldn't put a *Goon Show* in this book. This is it ...

It's one of my favourites. I simply couldn't disappoint his many *Goon Show* fans.

So there you are, Spike. You're dead, and here is a *Goon Show*. (Spike would have loved that.)

I've entitled this section 'Milligan Remembered'.

That says it all.

The Dreaded Batter Pudding Hurler (or Bexhill-on-Sea)

The main characters

Mr Henry Crun	Peter Sellers
Miss Minnie Bannister	Spike Milligan
Ned Seagoon	Harry Secombe
Lance Brigadier Grytpype-Thynne	Peter Sellers
Sergeant Throat	Spike Milligan
Major Denis Bloodnok	Peter Sellers
Eccles	Spike Milligan
Odium	Spike Milligan
Moriarty	Spike Milligan
Willium	Peter Sellers
Bluebottle	Peter Sellers

The Ray Ellington Quartet
Max Geldray
Orchestra Conducted by Wally Stott
Announcer: Wallace Greenslade
Script by Spike Milligan
Production by Peter Eton

How young Ned Seagoon was called in by the terrorised gentlefolk of Bexhill to help track down the dreaded Batter Pudding Hurler. Striking when least expected, the 'Hurler' caused such havoc during the blackout of 1941 that troops, massed against the German invasion, were ordered to join the hunt. A trail of cold Batter Puddings eventually led Ned Seagoon to North Africa where, with the aid of Major Bloodnok, he finally cornered the traitor ...

BILL	This is the BBC Home Service.
F.X.	PENNY IN MUG.
BILL	Thank you. We now come to the radio show entirely dedicated to the downfall of John Snagge.
HARRY	He refers, of course, to the highly esteemed Goon Show.
GRAMS	SORROWFUL MARCH WITH WAILS.
HARRY	Stop! Time for laughs later – but now to business. Mr. Greenslade? Come over here.
F.X.	CHAINS.
BILL	Yes, Master?
HARRY	Tell the waiting world what we have for them.
BILL	My lords, ladies and other National Assistance holders – tonight the League of Burmese Trombonists presents a best-seller play entitled:

ORCHESTRA	TYMPANY ROLL. HELD UNDER:-
PETER	The Terror of Bexhill-on-Sea or ...
ORCHESTRA	THREE DRAMATIC CHORDS.
HARRY	The Dreaded Batter Pudding Hurler.
ORCHESTRA	CLIMAX. THEN DOWN NOW BEHIND:-

BILL	The English Channel 1941. Across the silent strip of green-grey water – in England – coastal towns were deserted, except for people. Despite the threat of invasion and the stringent blackout rules, elderly gentlefolk of Bexhill-on-Sea still took their evening constitutions.
F.X.	EBB TIDE ON A GRAVEL BEACH.
CRUN	Ohhh – it's quite windy on these cliffs.
MINNIE	What a nice summer evening – typical English.
CRUN	Mnk yes – the rain's lovely and warm – I think I'll take one of my sou' westers off – here, hold my elephant gun.
MINNIE	I don't know what you brought it for – you can't shoot elephants in England.
CRUN	Mnk? Why not?
MINNIE	They're out of season.
CRUN	Does this mean we'll have to have pelican for dinner again?
MINNIE	Yes, I'm afraid so.
CRUN	Then I'll risk it, I'll shoot an elephant out of season.
BOTH	(*Go off mumbling in distance*)
BILL	Listeners who are listening will, of course, realise that Minnie and Henry are talking rubbish – as erudite people will realise, there are no elephants in Sussex. They are only found in Kent North on a straight line drawn between two points thus making it the shortest distance.
F.X.	PENNY IN MUG.
BILL	Thank you.
CRUN	... well, if that's how it is I can't shoot any.
MINNIE	Come Henry, we'd better be getting home – I don't want to be caught on the beaches if there's an invasion.
CRUN	Neither do I – I'm wearing a dirty shirt and I – mnk – don't –
F.X.	CLANK OF IRON OVEN DOOR.
CRUN	...Minnie?
MINNIE	What what?

CRUN   Did you hear a gas oven door slam just then?

MINNIE   Don't be silly, Henry – who'd be walking around these cliffs
            with a gas oven?

CRUN   Lady Docker.

MINNIE   Yes, but apart from the obvious ones – who'd want to ...

F.X.   WHOOSE – SPLOSH – BATTER PUDDING HITTING MINNIE

MINNIE   Oooooooooooooooohohohohohohohohohohohohohohohoho
            hoho...

CRUN   No, I've never heard of him.

MINNIE   Help, Henery – I've been struck down from behind. Helpp.

CRUN   Mnk – oh dear dear. (*Calls*) Police – English Police – Law
            Guardians???

MINNIE   Not too loud, Henry, they'll hear you.

F.X.   POLICE WHISTLE.

SEAGOON   (*approaching*) Can I help you, sir?

CRUN   Are you a policeman?

SEAGOON   No, I'm a constable.

CRUN   What's the difference?

SEAGOON   They're spelt differently.

MINNIE   Ohhhhhhhh.

SEAGOON   Oh! What's happened to this dear old silver-bearded lady?

CRUN   She was struck down from behind.

SEAGOON   And not a moment too soon – congratulations, sir.

CRUN   I didn't do it.

SEAGOON   Coward – hand back your OBE. Now tell me who did this
            felonous deed. What's happened to her?

CRUN   It's too dark to see – strike a light.

SEAGOON   Not allowed in blackout.

MINNIE   Strike a dark light.

SEAGOON   No madam, we daren't – why, only twenty-eight miles
            across the Channel the Germans are watching this coast.

CRUN   Don't be a silly-pilly policeman – they can't see a little
            match being struck.

SEAGOON   Oh, alright.

F.X.	MATCH STRIKING – QUICK WHOOSH OF SHELL – SHELL EXPLODES.
SEAGOON	Any questions?
CRUN	Yes – where are my legs?
SEAGOON	Are you now aware of the danger from German long-range guns?
CRUN	Mnk ahh! I've got it – I have the answer – just by chance I happen to have on me a box of German matches.
SEAGOON	Wonderful – strike one – they won't fire at their own matches.
CRUN	Of course not – now …
F.X.	MATCH STRIKING AND FLARING – WHOOSH OF SHELL – SHELL BURST.
CRUN	… Curse … the British!!!
SEAGOON	We tried using a candle, but it wasn't very bright and we daren't light it – so we waited for dawn – and there, in the light of the morning sun, we saw what had struck Miss Bannister. It was – a Batter Pudding.
ORCHESTRA	DRAMATIC CHORD.
CRUN	It's still warm, Minnie.
MINNIE	Thank Heaven – I hate cold Batter Pudding.
CRUN	Come, Minnie, I'll take you home – give you a hot bath – rub you down with the anti-vapour rub – put a plaster on your back – give your feet a mustard bath, and then put you to bed.

SEAGOON   Do you know this woman?

CRUN   Devilish man – of course I do – this is Minnie Bannister, the world-famous poker player – give her a good poker and she'll play any tune you like.

SEAGOON   Well, get her off this cliff, it's dangerous. Meantime, I must report this to the Inspector. I'll call on you later – goodbye.

F.X.   (PAUSE) DISTANT SPLASH.

SEAGOON   As I swam ashore I dried myself to save time. That night I lay awake in my air-conditioned dustbin thinking – who on earth would want to strike another with a Batter Pudding? Obviously it wouldn't happen again, so I fell asleep.
Nothing much happened that night – except that I was struck with a Batter Pudding.

SPIKE   Mmmmm – it's all rather confusing, really.

BILL   In the months to come, thirty-eight Batter Puddings were hurled at Miss Bannister – a madman was at large – Scotland Yard were called in.

ORCHESTRA   LINK.

GRYTPYPE-THYNNE   (*Sanders throughout*) Inspector Seagoon – my name is Hercules Grytpype-Thynne, Special Investigation. This Batter Pudding Hurler –

SEAGOON   Yes?

GRYTPYPE-THYNNE   He's made a fool of the police.

SEAGOON   I disagree – we were fools long before he came along.

GRYTPYPE-THYNNE   You silly twisted boy. Nevertheless, he's got to be stopped – now, Seagoon –

SEAGOON   Yes yes yes yes yes yes?

GRYTPYPE-THYNNE   ... Please don't do that. Now, these Batter Puddings
          – they were obviously thrown by hand.

SEAGOON   Not necessarily – some people are pretty clever with their
          feet.

GRYTPYPE-THYNNE   For instance?

SEAGOON   Tom Cringingknutt.

GRYTPYPE-THYNNE   Who's he?

SEAGOON   He's a man who's pretty clever with his feet.

GRYTPYPE-THYNNE   What's his name?

SEAGOON   Jim Phlatcrok.

GRYTPYPE-THYNNE   Sergeant Throat?

THROAT   Sir?

GRYTPYPE-THYNNE   Make a note of that.

THROAT   Right. Anything else?

GRYTPYPE-THYNNE   Yes.

THROAT   Right.

GRYTPYPE-THYNNE   Good. Now Seagoon, these Batter Puddings – were
          they all identical?

SEAGOON   All except the last one. Inside it – we found this.

GRYTPYPE-THYNNE   Oh! An Army Boot! So the Dreaded Hurler is a
          military man. Any troops in the town?

SEAGOON   The fifty-sixth Heavy Underwater Artillery.

GRYTPYPE-THYNNE   Get there at once – arrest the first soldier you see
          wearing one boot.

SEAGOON   Ying tong iddle I po.

GRYTPYPE-THYNNE   Right – off you go.

ORCHESTRA   BLOODNOK SIGNATURE TUNE.

BLOODNOK   Bleiough – aeioughhh – bleioughhhh – how dare you come
          here to my H.Q. with such an –

SEAGOON   I tell you, Major Bloodnok, I must ask you to parade your
          men.

BLOODNOK   Why?

SEAGOON   I'm looking for a criminal.

BLOODNOK   You find your own – it took me years to get this lot.

SEAGOON   Ying tong iddle I po.

BLOODNOK   Very well then – Bugler Max Geldray? Sound fall in – the hard way.

MAX & ORCHESTRA   THEY WERE DOING THE MAMBO
(*Applause*)

ORCHESTRA & CAST   (*Murmurs of distrust*)

BLOODNOK   Silence, lads! I'm sorry I had to get you out of bed in the middle of the day – but I'll see you get extra pay for this.

ORCHESTRA & CAST   You flat 'eaded kipper – Gawn, drop dead – I'll claht yer flippin' head – Gorn, shimmer orf.

BLOODNOK   Ahhhhhhh, that's what I like – spirit. Now, Seagoon – which is the man?

SEAGOON   I walked among the ranks looking for the soldier with one boot but my luck was out: the entire regiment were bare-footed – all save the officers who wore reinforced concrete socks.

BLOODNOK   Look Seagoon, it's getting dark. You can't see in this light.

SEAGOON   I'll strike a match.

F.X.   MATCH ... WHOOSH OF SHELL EXPLOSION.

SEAGOON   Curse, I forgot about the Germans.

ECCLES   We want our beddy byes.

SEAGOON   Who are you?

ECCLES   Lance Private Eccles, but most people call me by my nick-name.

SEAGOON   What's that?

ECCLES   Hahum. Nick.

SEAGOON   I inspected the man closely – he was the nearest thing I'd seen to a human being, without actually being one.

BLOODNOK   Surely you don't suspect this man – why, we were together in the same company during that terrible disaster.

SEAGOON   What company was that?

BLOODNOK   Desert Song 1933.

SEAGOON   Were you both in the D'Oyly Carte?

BLOODNOK	Right in the D'Oyly Carte.
SEAGOON	I don't wish to know that, but wait!! At last – by the light of a passing glue factory – I saw that Eccles was only wearing – one boot!
ECCLES	Well, I only got one boot.
SEAGOON	I know – but why are you wearing it on your head?
ECCLES	Why? It fits, dat's why – what a silly question – why – why –
SEAGOON	Let me see that boot. (*Sotto*) Mmmm, size nineteen ... (*Aloud*) What size head have you got?
ECCLES	Size nineteen.
SEAGOON	Curse – the man's defence was perfect – Major Bloodnok?
BLOODNOK	How dare you call me Major Bloodnok.
SEAGOON	That's your name.
BLOODNOK	In that case – I forgive you.
SEAGOON	Where's this man's other boot?
BLOODNOK	Stolen.
SEAGOON	Who by?
BLOODNOK	A thief.
SEAGOON	You sure it wasn't a pickpocket?
BLOODNOK	Positive – Eccles never keeps his boots in his pocket.
SEAGOON	Damn. They all had a watertight alibi – but just to make sure I left it in a fish tank overnight. Next morning my breast pocket 'phone rang.
F.X.	RING.
SEAGOON	Hello?
CRUN	Mr. Seagoon – Minnie's been hit with another Batter Pudding.

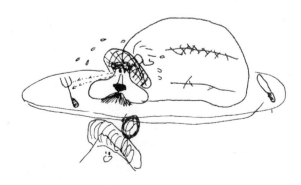

SEAGOON	Well, that's nothing new.
CRUN	It was – this one was stone cold.
SEAGOON	Cold???
CRUN	Yes – he must be losing interest in her.
SEAGOON	It proves also that the phantom Batter Pudding Hurler has had his gas-pipe cut off! Taxi!
F.X.	BAGPIPES. RUNNING DOWN.
SPIKE	Yes?
SEAGOON	The Bexhill Gas Works, and step on it.
SPIKE	Yes.
F.X.	BAGPIPES. FADE OFF.
BILL	Listeners may be puzzled by a taxi sounding like bagpipes. The truth is – it is all part of the BBC new economy campaign. They have discovered that it is cheaper to travel by bagpipes – not only are they more musical but they come in a wide variety of colours. See your local Bagpipe Offices and ask for particulars – you won't be disappointed.
SPIKE	It's all rather confusing, really …
PETER	Meantime, Neddie Seagoon had arrived at the Bexhill Gas and Coke Works.

SEAGOON	Phewwwwwww blimeyyyyy – anyone about?
ODIUM	Yererererere.
SEAGOON	Good.
ODIUM	Yerrer.

SEAGOON	I'd like a list of people who haven't paid their gas bills.
ODIUM	Yererererere –
SEAGOON	Oh, thank you. Now here's a good list – I'll try this number.
F.X.	DIALLING.
SEAGOON	Think we've got him this time – hello?
PETER	(*Winston Churchill – distort*) Ten Downing Street here.
SEAGOON	(*gulp*) I'm sorry.
F.X.	CLICK.
SEAGOON	No, it *couldn't* be him – who would he want to throw a Batter Pudding at?
F.X.	QUICK 'PHONE RING.
SEAGOON	Hello? Police here.
SPIKE	This is Mr Attlee – someone's just thrown a Batter Pudding at me.
ORCHESTRA	TYMPANY ROLL HELD UNDER NEXT SPEECH:–
SEAGOON	Months went by – still no sign of the Dreaded Hurler. Finally I walked the streets of Bexhill at night disguised as a human man – then suddenly!!
ORCHESTRA	FLARING CHORD.
SEAGOON	Nothing happened. But it happened suddenly. Disappointed, I lit my pipe.
F.X.	MATCH. WHOOSH OF SHELL. EXPLOSION OF SHELL.
SEAGOON	Curse those Germans.
MORIARTY	Pardon me, my friend.
SEAGOON	I turned to see the speaker – he was a tall man wearing sensible feet and a head to match. He was dressed in the full white outfit of a Savoy chef – around his waist were tied several thousand cooking instruments – behind him he pulled a portable gas stove from which issued forth the smell of Batter Pudding.
MORIARTY	Could I borrow a match? You see, my gas has gone out and my Batter Pudding was just browning.
SEAGOON	Certainly. Here – no – keep the whole box – I have another match at home.

MORIARTY	So rich. Well, thank you, m'sieu – you have saved my Batter Pudding from getting cold. There's nothing worse than being struck down with a cold Batter Pudding.
SEAGOON	Oh yes.
MORIARTY	Good night.
SEAGOON	I watched the strange man as he pulled his gas stove away into the darkness. But I couldn't waste time watching him – my job was to find the Dreaded Batter Pudding Hurler.
BILL	Those listeners who think that Seagoon is not cut out to be a detective – please write to him care of Rowton House.
SEAGOON	On December 25th the Hurler changed his tactics – that day Miss Bannister was struck with a Christmas Pudding. Naturally, I searched the workhouse.
WILLIUM	No sir – we ain't had no Christmas puddin' here, have we mate?
SPIKE	No.
WILLIUM	We ain't had none for three years, have we mate?
SPIKE	No – it's all rather annoying, really.
CRUN	(*approaching*) Ahh Mr Sniklecrum …
MINNIE	Ahhhhhh.
SEAGOON	Mr Crun, Miss Bannister, what are you doing here?
CRUN	Mnk, Minnie had a letter this morning.
MINNIE	I had a letter.
CRUN	Mn gnup … I'll tell him, Minnie.
MINNIE	Thank you, Henry.
CRUN	Mnk – yes, she had a –
MINNIE	Yess, you tell him.
CRUN	Alright, I'll tell …
MINNIE	… Yes …
CRUN	She had a lett …
SEAGOON	Yes, I know she had a letter – what about it?
CRUN	It proves that the Batter Pudding Hurler is abroad.
SEAGOON	What? Why? How?
CRUN	It was post-marked Africa – and inside was a portion of

Batter Puddin'.

MINNIE Yes – he hasn't forgotten me.

SEAGOON So he's in Africa – now we've got him cornered. I must leave at once. Bluebottle!

BLUEBOTTLE I heard you call, my Capatain – I heard my Captain call – waits for audience applause – not a sausage – puts on I don't care expression as done by Aneurin Bevan at Blackpool Conservative Rally.

SEAGOON Bluebottle – you and I are going to Africa.

BLUEBOTTLE Good – can we take sandwiches?

SEAGOON Only for food – any questions?

BLUEBOTTLE No.

SEAGOON I can't answer that – can you?

BLUEBOTTLE No.

SEAGOON Ignorant swine. Got that down, Sergeant Throat?

THROAT Yes.

SEAGOON Good.

THROAT Yes.

SEAGOON Right, we catch the very next troop convoy to Algiers. And who better to drive us out of the country than Ray Ellington and his Quartet?

QUARTET 'OL' MAN RIVER'.

(*Applause*)

ORCHESTRA 'VICTORY AT SEA' THEME.

PETER   And now ...

F.X.   WASH OF WAVES ON SHIP'S PROW.

BILL   Seagoon and Bluebottle travelled by sea. To avoid detection
             by enemy U-boats they spoke German throughout the
             voyage, heavily disguised as Spaniards.

PETER   As an added precaution they travelled on separate decks
             and wore separate shoes on different occasions.

SEAGOON   The ship was disguised as a train – to make the train sea-
             worthy it was done up to look like a boat and painted to
             appear like a tram.

SPIKE   ... All rather confusing, really.

SEAGOON   Also on board were Major Bloodnok and his regiment.
             When we were ten miles from Algiers we heard a dreaded
             cry.

ECCLES   (off) Mine ahead – dreadful sea-mine ahead.

BLOODNOK   (approach) What's happening here – why are all these men
             cowering down on deck, the cowards?

SEAGOON   There's a mine ahead.

BLOODNOK   Mi –

F.X.   HURRIED FOOTSTEPS AWAY AND THEN SPLASH.

SEAGOON   Funny – he wasn't dressed for swimming.

ECCLES   Hey, dere's no need to worry about the mine.

BLUEBOTTLE   Yes, I must worry – I don't want to be deaded – I'm wearing
             my best sports shirt. (Hurriedly puts on cardboard tin hat.)

ECCLES   Don't worry – dat mine, it can't hurt us – it's one of ours.

F.X.   EXPLOSION.

SEAGOON   Eccles, is the ship sinking?

ECCLES   It's no good, the ship won't fit in the lifeboat.

ECCLES	Only below the sea.
SEAGOON	We must try and save the ship – help me get it into the lifeboat.
ECCLES	O.K. ...Upppppppppp.
BOTH	(*Grunts and groans*)
ECCLES	It's no good, the ship won't fit in the lifeboat.
SEAGOON	What a ghastly oversight by the designer. Never mind, it leaves room for one more in the boat.
BLOODNOK	I'm willing to fill that vacancy.
SEAGOON	How did you get back on board?
BLOODNOK	I was molested by a lobster with a disgusting mind.
SEAGOON	Right, Bloodnok, do your duty.
BLOODNOK	(*calls*) Women and children first.
SEAGOON	Bloodnok, take that dummy out of your mouth.
ECCLES	Hey, don't leave me behind.
BLOODNOK	And why not?
ECCLES	... Give me time and I'll think of a reason.
BLOODNOK	Right, wait here until Apple Blossom Time – meantime, Seagoon, lower away.
F.X.	WINCHES GOING.
ECCLES	Hey – if you make room for me, I'll pay ten pounds.
F.X.	SPLASH.
SEAGOON	(*off*) You swine Bloodnok –
BLOODNOK	Business is business – get in, Eccles.
ECCLES	Ta.
SEAGOON	(*off*) Look, I'll pay *twenty* pounds for a place in the boat.
F.X.	SPLASH.
BLOODNOK	(*off*) Aeiough, you double-crosser, Eccles.

ECCLES   Get in, Captain Seagoon.

HARRY   Ahhh, thank you Eccles – myyy friend.

BLOODNOK   (off) Thirty pounds for a place.

F.X.   SPLASH.

ECCLES   (*off*) *You ain't* my friend.

BLOODNOK   Ahhh, good old Seagoon, you've saved me.

SEAGOON   My pal.

ECCLES   (*off*) Fifty pounds for a place in the boat.

F.X.   TWO DISTANT SPLASHES.

SPIKE   Alert listeners will have heard two splashes – this means
                that both Bloodnok *and* Seagoon have been hurled in the
                water – *who* could have done this?

BLUEBOTTLE   Ha heuheuheuheuheuhuh – I dood it I doo – I hid behind a
                tin of dry biscuits and then I grabbed their tootsies and
                upppp into the water – ha heheu huehhhhh –

ECCLES   Bluebottle, you saved my life.

BLUEBOTTLE   O ha well, we all make mistakes! I like this game – what
                school do you go to?

ECCLES   Reform. (*Both fading off*)

SEAGOON   Tricked by the brilliant planning of Bluebottle and Eccles,
                Bloodnok and I floundered in the cruel sea.

F.X.   SEA.

BLOODNOK   Fortunately we found a passing lifeboat and dragged our-
                selves aboard.

SEAGOON   We had no oars but luckily we found two outboard motors
                and we rowed with them.

BLOODNOK   Brilliant.

SEAGOON   For thirty days we drifted to and fro – then hunger came
                upon us.

BLOODNOK   Aeioughhhhhhhh – if I don't eat soon I'll die and if I die I
                won't eat soon. Wait – (*snifffff*) can I smell cooking or do
                my ears deceive me?

SEAGOON   He was right – he has smelly ears – something was
                cooking – there in the other end of the lifeboat was – a gas
                stove! Could this be the end of our search?

BLOODNOK	I'll knock on the oven door.
F.X.	KNOCKING ON OVEN DOOR.
MORIARTY	(*off*) Just a minute, I'm in the bath … (*Pause*)
F.X.	COMING DOWN IRON STAIRS. MORIARTY SINGING. OVEN DOOR OPENS.
MORIARTY	Good morning – I'm sorry – *you*!!!
SEAGOON	Yes – remember Bexhill – I lent you the matches.
MORIARTY	You don't want them back?
SEAGOON	Don't move – I arrest you as the Dreaded Batter Pudding Hurler. Hands up, you devil – don't move – this finger is loaded.
MORIARTY	If you kill me I promise you'll never take me alive.
BLOODNOK	Wait – how can we prove it?
SEAGOON	That Batter Pudding in the corner of the stove is all the evidence we need. We've got him.
ORCHESTRA	CRASHING TRIUMPHANT THEME.
F.X.	QUIET SEA. LAPPING OF WAVES.
BILL	But it wasn't easy – forty days they drifted in an open boat.
FIDDLE	'HEARTS AND FLOWERS'.
BLOODNOK	Oooaeioughhh, I tell you Seagoon – let's eat the Batter Pudding or we'll starve!!
SEAGOON	No, d'yer hear me – no! That's the only evidence we've got – though I must admit this hunger does give one an appetite.
BLOODNOK	We must eat it or die.
SEAGOON	Never!!!
BLOODNOK	We must.
BOTH	(*Fade off*)
BILL	And that, we fear, is the end of our story except, of course, for the end – we invite listeners to submit what they think should be the classic ending. Should Seagoon eat the Batter Pudding and live or leave it and in the cause of justice – die? Meantime, for those of you cretins who would like a happy ending – here it is.
GRAMS	SWEET BACKGROUND MUSIC, VERY, VERY SOFT.

HARRY	Darling – darling, will you marry me?
BLOODNOK	Of course I will – darling.
BILL	Thank you – good night.
ORCHESTRA	SIGNATURE TUNE: UP AND DOWN FOR:-
BILL	That was The Goon Show – a recorded programme featuring Peter Sellers, Harry Secombe and Spike Milligan with the Ray Ellington Quartet and Max Geldray. The Orchestra was conducted by Wally Stott. Script by Spike Milligan. Announcer: Wallace Greenslade. The programme produced by Peter Eton.
ORCHESTRA	SIGNATURE TUNE UP TO END.
	(*Applause*)
MAX & ORCHESTRA	'CRAZY RHYTHM' PLAYOUT.

Unpublished Poem: 1987

Spike sent me a batch of poems to read and give him an opinion. This one I particularly liked. I thought I would let him have the last word. He always did.

How many good-byes?
When I was born
My mother took me from hospital
The nurses said good-bye
That was my first one.
I was too young to hear it
One day I will die.
Some one will say goodbye
And I still won't hear it

Monkenhurst
Ap. 28. '87
0100 hrs

Goodbye Spike